QUEERING FREEDOM

QUEERING
FREEDOM

Shannon Winnubst

INDIANA UNIVERSITY PRESS
BLOOMINGTON AND INDIANAPOLIS

This book is a publication of

Indiana University Press
601 North Morton Street
Bloomington, IN 47404-3797 USA

http://iupress.indiana.edu

Telephone orders 800-842-6796
Fax orders 812-855-7931
Orders by e-mail iuporder@indiana.edu

The paper used in this publication meets the
minimum requirements of American National
Standard for Information Sciences—Permanence of
Paper for Printed Library Materials, ANSI
Z39.48-1984.

Manufactured in the United States of America

Library of Congress Cataloging-in-Publication Data
Winnubst, Shannon.
  Queering freedom / Shannon Winnubst.
    p. cm.
  Includes bibliographical references and index.
  ISBN 0-253-34707-6 (cloth : alk. paper)—
ISBN 0-253-21830-6 (pbk. : alk. paper)
    1. Liberty.   2. Boundaries—Social aspects.
3. Differentiation (Sociology)   4. Dominance
(Psychology)   5. Power (Social sciences)   I. Title.
  HM1266.W56   2006
    305'.01—dc22
2005023415

1 2 3 4 5   11 10 09 08 07 06

For Jenny

CONTENTS

Acknowledgments

Like most work in feminist theory, this book was written with and through many voices. While many of these are buried in the multiple pasts of my various educations, I would like to acknowledge the following for their ongoing support of me and my work, in many different ways: Anne Bowery, Jennifer Byrne, Helen Cordes, Jesse and Zoe Cordes Selbin, Carlos Cruz, Ruth Davis, Jan Dawson, Joseph Flay, Peter Gottschalk, Mark Hersh, Phil Hopkins, Craig Irvine, Kathleen Juhl, Mary Beth Mader, Thom McClendon, Helene Meyers, Sue Rivers, Shireen Roshanravan, Jimmy Smith, Cynthia Willett, Mark Winnubst, and Ton and Pat Winnubst. I am also grateful to the many students who have provoked, sustained, indulged, and sometimes endured our seminars together over the years. At Indiana University Press, I thank Dee Mortensen for her belief in this project through its various stages and Shoshanna Green for strengthening my prose. Finally, I have been fortunate enough to cultivate intellectual friendships that sustain me with immense generosity in what is otherwise solitary work. For their direct impact on the ideas and arguments of this book, I am particularly grateful to Michael Bray for his rare combination of incisive, speculative, and playful dialogue, not to mention his humor; to Amy Wendling and the gift of having her acumen, aesthetics, magnanimity, and laughter in the backyard while writing this book (some of the best examples are hers); to bell hooks for pushing me to find the courage and voice to write this book; to Eric Selbin for his unwavering generosity of both intellect and spirit that has buoyed me and my work for years; to Kimmy Dee Winnubst for the courage to be outrageously queer in all parts of her life, and for being one of the great blessings in my life; to the boyz, those companions who have always queered my world with play and pleasures; and to Jennifer Suchland for endless conversations, rhythms, explorations, and patience that never fail to stun me: stars above.

Acknowledgments

An earlier version of chapter 2 was published in *Philosophy and Social Criticism* 30(1): 25–50 (New York: SAGE Publications). A portion of chapter 5 was published under the title "Make Yourself Useful!" in *Etiquette: Reflections on Contemporary Comportment*, ed. Brian Seitz and Ron Scapp (Albany: State University of New York Press, 2006).

QUEERING FREEDOM

INTRODUCTION

The Seduction of Freedom

Changing from the perspectives of *restrictive* economy to those of *general* economy actually accomplishes a Copernican transformation: a reversal of thinking—and of ethics.

Woe to those who, to the very end, insist on regulating the movement that exceeds them with the narrow mind of the mechanic who changes a tire.

—GEORGES BATAILLE,
The Accursed Share,
volume 1

The founding of nation-states across the eighteenth and nineteenth centuries in Europe, the Americas, and South and East Asia corresponded to a heightened rhetoric of freedom. The concept of the nation grounded its moral authority in the fundamental claim to liberation— from autocratic regimes, from clerical hierarchies, from nature's savagery. Offering unmatched stability, the nation-state guaranteed greater freedom for the lives of its citizens and promised greater freedom to those who should aspire toward civility. Consequently, as the nation-state gradually consolidated itself into the most effective vehicle of power, that wide sweep of bodies who were not directly enfranchised by its socio-economic might became the primary targets of this rhetoric of seduction, taken up through the voices of imperialism and colonialism. If bodies and regions not yet 'civilized' could become deeply invested in the benevolent powers of the nation-state, the complicated politics of freedom could gain its necessary foothold in the globalized politics of domination.

In the early twenty-first century of the modern western calendar, the struggles and violence of much of the world can still be read through this narrative. While the work of imperialism and colonialism, the twin politics of nationalism's promises to freedom, has been forced underground, these slippery dynamics of domination have assumed the guise of liberation. The United States, for example, speaks under the banners of "democracy" and "liberation" as it legitimates its invasions of other nations and then initiates the bizarre process of 'nation-building' in the conquered lands, once again enacting the colonialist narrative of bringing civilization to savage, virgin, or empty soil. The designation of what constitutes a legitimate or illegitimate nation still rests in the imperialist hands of the eighteenth and nineteenth centuries, even if that power has largely migrated across the Atlantic Ocean. And the politics and rhetoric of freedom have wholly displaced the politics and rhetoric of imperialism, granting them newfound vigor through the very erasure enacted in the displacement. Who, after all, dares to argue against freedom?

The language of freedom thereby continues to frame one of the fundamental discursive sites of modern western cultures. It functions as the ethical value and space that no one can disavow: our political fealties seem to fall away in the face of freedom. We can dispute the nuances of its various meanings or disagree over the best ways to enact, ensure, protect, and cultivate it, but no one can articulate a politics or ethics without an appeal to this sacred value of modernity. Joining us together in the lasting project of modernizing humanity, these unassailable appeals to freedom place us all in the same discursive field and, ultimately, flatten any differences between political convictions. In the end, we are all freedom fighters.

While the languages of nationalism and imperialism are not the explicit subjects of this text, freedom is one of its constant refrains, even if lurking often in the background. In this way, this remains a modern text with very modern problematics—and, as I will develop across these pages, it thereby also remains a white text with very white problematics. Writing out of the theoretical frameworks of Georges Bataille and Michel Foucault, I am attempting to excavate the political and philosophical assumptions of our shared historical present of late modernity—namely, a historical present increasingly obsessed by the politics and rhetorics of freedom and its attendant modes of expression, the categories of identity. Attempting to think through the expression of freedom in the specific identity categories of our historical present (race, gender, religion, class, and sexuality) has led me to a very particular play of erotic politics: when we desire freedom, we may be seduced by systems of domination.

To excavate the contours of both domination and resistance in the shared discursive fields of freedom and whiteness, I bring together Bataille's efforts to think in general economies and Foucault's efforts to think from one's historical present. That is, I have attempted to think generally from and about our historical present.

A Practice in General Economics

In his three-volume work on political economy, *The Accursed Share*, Bataille describes and performs a kind of thinking that emerges out of "general economies." This involves a radical reorientation from the epistemological and political projects of modernity, where clarity and precision are the hallmarks of insight, argumentation, and good thinking. He frames his own project of political economy as the study of the movement "of excess energy, translated into the effervescence of life" (1988–91, 1:10), a project that involves "the movement of energy on the earth—from geophysics to political economy, by way of sociology, history, and biology . . . [with essential connections to] art, literature, poetry" (1988–91, 1:10). It is about everything, and thus risks being about nothing: the growth and stagnation of duckweed on a pond tells us more about the general economy than the sale of wheat (1988–91, 1:32–33). It threatens to become the Hegelian nightmare where all cows are black: all things are connected, and thus it appears that nothing is distinguished.

In writing in this way, Bataille realizes the impossibility of his own project, particularly in the historical present of late western modernity, where temporal and spatial norms demand the constant forward march of sequential, distinct units of meaning. How to undertake a project that issues from the utter excess of expenditure, joy, and luxury in a world that demands the unquestioned reduction of all values to the needs of utility, reason, and labor? How to write of "propositions according to which it is not necessity but its contrary, 'luxury,' that presents living matter and mankind with their fundamental problems" (1988–91, 1:12)?

Bataille asks us to think with him in these general ways, where questions of economics may land us in unexpected meditations on the sun rituals of Aztecs (as in his volume 1) and questions of freedom may land us in unexpected meditations on the temporality of ironing shirts (as in my chapter 5). This thinking cannot shape itself "if it [does] not consider the totality of small occurrences, wrongly supposed to be insignificant" (1988–91, 1:13). Attempting to think in these general economies when turning to systems of domination may require us to consider dynamics not usually deemed relevant to discussions of domination and resistance. For example, we may have to consider how the enclosure of private property into the conceptual unit of individual rights in the seventeenth century affects how we live and how we perpetuate a racist world of white domination (chapter 1). Or how the psychoanalytic theory of ego development leads us into temporalities of domination (chapter 2). Or how the Aristotelian concept of space leads us into concepts of desire that frame contemporary conflicts over marriage as a political and religious institution (chapters 3 and 4). In closing our thinking to such kinds of interconnective dynamics, the dominant form of modern rationality totalizes our sense of the world: instrumental reason subordinates all other kinds of knowing to its final mandates, reducing our worlds and lives to calculations of utility. It is this severance from a more general perspective, one that approaches the circulation of energy beyond the closed frame of immediate utility, that Bataille calls on us to resist.

Bringing Foucault to bear, I add some urgency to Bataille's calls: it is through this severance from a more general perspective that systems of domination perpetuate themselves in the very fabric of our experiences and lives. In *The Archaeology of Knowledge* (1972), Foucault writes of thinking from the historical present, that space which orients thinking toward its own historico-cultural conditioning and the blind spots which circulate within it to keep systems of power intact.[1] We must not mistake this for the Kantian schema of transcendental conditions of pure reason with history tacked on. Nor is it the Hegelian schema of Reason assuming historical shape: to think from the historical present is not to think of how the universal structures of reason express themselves in historical formations. To think from the historical present is to attempt at every stage, position, and moment of thinking to turn back upon that thinking and sort out its particular contours: why appeal to the concept of rights when theorizing about freedom? Or why theorize freedom at all? Why assume the clearly demarcated individual as the basic unit of ethical thinking? How are we subtly demanding some future and useful solution to the questions that we pose in our very posing of them?

These are the kinds of questions and connections I explore in this text. They spring from a more general question, one that brings Bataille and Foucault together: is our thinking in late modernity historically conditioned to function only within (allegedly) closed economies, and if so, does this render us helpless in any effort to resist structures of domination? For example, thinking from the historical present in the U.S., where violence and politics are deeply racialized, we are called upon to think about the contours and dynamics of race and racism. Race functions as a fundamental category through which we conceive of our identities and racism is the system through which this category operates. Accordingly, when we ask the question of racism in the U.S., we most often turn to questions of history (slavery, Jim Crow, the Civil Rights Movement), psychology (superiority, narcissism, the buzzword of 'privilege'), or politics (social movements, the construction of whiteness as a strategy of solidarity across class boundaries, the subtle dynamics of exclusion). But, heeding Bataille's warnings about closed economies, we must probe the blind spots of these very approaches. What if race and racism, along with other systems of domination, are not reducible to these closed economies of history, psychology, and politics? What if we need to reorient ourselves toward a different kind of thinking, one that can excavate the closed economies of domination through the normativity of their spatio-temporal frameworks?

Bataille gives us a concrete example of the difference that thinking generally enacts on our political and philosophical sensibilities. Writing of his own project, he explains,

> When it is necessary to change an automobile tire, open an abscess or plow a vineyard, it is easy to manage a quite limited operation. The elements on which the action is brought to bear are not completely isolated from the rest of the world, but it is possible to act on them as if they were: one can complete the operation without once needing to consider the whole, of which the tire, the abscess or the vineyard is nevertheless an integral part. . . . [T]hings are different when we consider a substantial economic activity such as the production of automobiles in the United States, or, *a fortiori*, when it is a question of economic activity in general. . . . [B]ut the economy taken as a whole is usually studied as if it were a matter of an isolatable system of operation. (1988–91, 1:19)

This is the domination and violence of our historical present, late modernity: to reduce our lives so completely to the order of instrumental reason that we cannot conceive of any political or philosophical problem without reducing it to that narrow conception of reason. This renders us captive to presuppositions which assume that solutions to problems must follow the same temporal register as the posing of the problem itself—i.e., that they must appear immediately effective and useful if we are to recognize them as solutions at all. But what if these are only truncated, shortsighted views? What if a vital resistance to politics of domination comes through freeing ourselves from these closed economies of late modernity and their clearly demarcated, controlled, mastered, and useful ends? What if a vital resistance to politics of domination requires a temporal register other than that of immediate and clear efficacy?

As Bataille tells us sympathetically, "It is not easy to realize one's own ends if one must, in trying to do so, carry out a movement that surpasses them" (1988–91, 1:21). His orientation toward general economies asks us to think differently from the habituated patterns of our historical present. In his language, this historical present is "characterized by the fact that judgments concerning the *general* situation proceed from a *particular* point of view" (1988–91, 1:39). This particularity can be outlined, described, pinned down, and its blind spots excavated: I attempt to do so in this text. But to think generally from and about the historical present may lead us into different questions and different orientations: it has led me to query systems of domination through the registers of temporality and spatiality, while framing them through the identity categories (race, gender, sexuality, class, religion) that are their most explicit historical tools. For example, how does the temporality of a persistent future orientation ground systems of racism, sexism, and heterosexism? What assumptions about the ontology of space allow for the biological conception of race that grounds racism, or of sex that grounds sexism and heterosexism?

Bataille warns us that, if we do not learn to think in this counter-cultural register of general economy, we will always be subordinated to the violent and even catastrophic expressions of the excess, abundant energy of the planet, such as war and imperialist domination. We do have a choice in this matter. But that choice is not one which will derive from calculating our interest, analyzing the specific problem, or charting the solution: it will not derive from the domains of instrumental reason and its persistent mandate of utility. It may, rather, involve recuperating senses of freedom lost to us in late modernity, where nation-states promise freedom as the facile liberation from subservience and mastery as the domination of nature and culture. To think generally may lead toward sensing freedom as "a dangerous breaking-loose . . . a will to assume those risks without which there is no freedom" (1988–91, 1:38). It is toward recuperating these more general senses of freedom, which Bataille signifies as "sovereign" and I signify as "queer" in this historical period of late modernity and phallicized whiteness, that this text moves.

A Foucaultian Archaeology, Of Sorts

I always think of Foucault's *The Order of Things* as beginning with his brilliant readings of Velázquez's *Las Meninas*. But in fact, in the good Foucaultian fashion of troubling and confusing origins, it begins before that: the preface begins with Borges. Foucault writes at length of the nervous and slightly anxious laughter that erupts upon reading Borges's recounting of 'a certain Chinese encyclopedia.'[2] He describes it as a disruptive and even violent, if playful, laughter, one that "shattered all the familiar landmarks of my thought—of *our* thought, the thought that bears the stamp of our age and our geography" (1970, xv). Piling text upon text, Foucault suggests that *The Order of Things* emerged as a response to Borges's account of this Chinese text. But how are we to read such a simple claim to an origin by this thinker of 'anti-origins,' this archaeologist and genealogist, this figure who seems always incapable of *beginning*?

Foucault depicts Borges's text almost entirely in the register of space—the space that it opens and the many familiar spaces of our thought that it resists or even undercuts. Citing this strange 'Chinese encyclopedia,' Borges's text offers a taxonomy of animals: "(a) belonging to the Emperor, (b) embalmed, (c) tame, (d) sucking pigs, (e) sirens, (f) fabulous, (g) stray dogs, (h) included in the present classification, (i) frenzied, (j) innumerable, (k) drawn with a very fine camelhair brush, (l) *et cetera*, (m) having just broken the water pitcher, (n) that from a long way off look like flies" (Foucault 1970, xv). Foucault's response is direct and explicit: the fable demonstrates, through the exotic charm of another system of thought, "the limitation of our own, the stark impossibility of thinking *that*" (1970, xv). It is not the fantastic, or even its contrast with the real, that our system of thought cannot think. It is the simple and elegant power of the alphabetical series.

The sequential listing links "each of those categories to all the others" (1970, xxvi), leaving an uncomfortable, slim, even impossible "narrowness" separating the phantasms of the imagination from the materiality of the real. It is this danger of losing all separation between these realms that threatens our thinking, and from which our thinking reels back in terror. There is not sufficient space between these categories. The clear demarcation has slipped away, eroded to the point that the binary system of 'fantasy/real' no longer has sufficient purchase to capture the error at work here. These categories must be *delimited* if we are to grasp their qualitatively different ontological work in the world. And that demand is scoffed at here. There is a grave category error here. And this is impossible to think.

Foucault casts this slippage in terms that anchor my text: it is the impossibility of containment, a slippage in what I have termed 'the logic of the limit.' As he spatializes the phenomenon, he writes, "Where else could [these categories] be juxtaposed except in the non-place of language? Yet, though language can spread them before us, it can do so only in an unthinkable space" (1970, xvi–xvii). This space is unthinkable because, as Foucault diagnoses across all of his texts, our thought—the thought of late western modernity, the thought of phallicized whiteness that champions a very particular concept of freedom—is inextricably entangled with the logic of the limit. And Borges's list (for we do finally read it as Borges's, and not China's, in our own ordering of the text as fable) presents us with a thought that is not bound to this logic, that does not operate in the space of thinking that demands a stable relation of container to contained between categories. A long passage from Foucault captures the impossibility concisely:

> The central category of animals 'included in the present classification,' with its explicit reference to paradoxes we are familiar with, is indication enough that we shall never succeed in defining a stable relation of contained to container between each of these categories and that which includes them all; if all the animals divided up here can be placed without exception in one of the divisions of this list, then aren't all the other divisions to be found in that one division too? And then again, in what space would that single, inclusive division have *its* existence? Absurdity destroys the *and* of the enumeration by making impossible the *in* where the things enumerated would be divided up. (1970, xvii)

This is the space of thinking that our thought cannot enter. Our thought demands that we think *in* some space, a space that grants us the possibility of ordering the world. And Borges's text "does away with [this] *site*, the mute ground upon which it is possible for entities to be juxtaposed" (1970, xvii).

In breaking open the arbitrary power of listing, Borges jars thinking into the space in which order is demanded and not yet fulfilled. Foucault describes this space as "a domain which, even though its role is mainly an intermediary one, is nonetheless fundamental" (1970, xx). It is the space in which thinking realizes the arbitrariness of the cultural codes into which it is habituated, and simultaneously cannot expunge the need for order itself. It is a difficult space to pin down or analyze. Hovering between the ordering codes of the culture and scientific or philosophical reflections upon order itself, it is the space of recognition that order, albeit arbitrary and historical, *exists.* Order is that without which thinking cannot think. It exists. And Borges's text, in ushering us into this unnerving, vertiginous space, spars with the possibility of a world in which it might not. He removes "the table upon which, since the beginning of time, language has intersected space" (1970, xvii).

Foucault continues to develop this space as a space that is more threatening than a mere disorder of the incongruous. It is the space of differing differences—of heterotopias and the heteroclite, where "things are 'laid,' 'placed,' 'arranged' in sites so very different from one another that it is impossible to find a place of residence for them, to define a *common locus* beneath them all" (1970, xvii–xviii). These spaces "destroy syntax in advance" and "stop words in their tracks" (1970, xviii). More generally, these figures of heterotopias and the heteroclite open thinking onto that space in which thinking is faced with the very task of *making order*. Returning to this discussion of Foucault in chapter 4, I signify these spaces as "queer"—spaces where meaning is not preordained as a useful or recognizable *telos,* and the possibilities of other sorts of meaning, often those lost in the past, are still viable. Such spaces jar us from the ruts of our historical habits, inviting us into differing and vertiginous senses of freedom that cannot be contained by the historical present of phallicized whiteness. It is toward such spaces that the following discussions attempt to move.

Reading Whiteness as Phallicized

The project of critically examining whiteness will, in our lifetimes, always be a dangerous one. Ruth Frankenberg's general diagnosis of the shifting borders of "whiteness" and the differing perceptions of racial order from place to place seems correct. Depending on where you find yourself—in Manhattan or Lincoln, Nebraska; in Seattle or Oklahoma City or a small rural community in Alabama; or in the more global settings of Buenos Aires, Frankfurt, Baghdad, Hong Kong, Moscow, or Lima—a differing discourse of "whiteness" is at work. While these discourses most often work to render whiteness invisible, allowing it to circulate as the unmarked master signifier, we also live in a time when whiteness perceives itself to be in some "trouble"—a time when the category of whiteness appears to itself to be becoming unstable, internally and externally.[3] The dominant culture of whiteness sometimes, but not always, perceives itself to be under attack.

The risks of studying and critically examining whiteness are thus high, running the gamut from playing into cultural discourses of white supremacy, to uncritically fixing white superiority, to reinscribing whiteness at the center of concern and focus. We must remain suspicious of discussions of whiteness, lest those discussions reinscribe the very same dominant set of cultural signifiers and practices that they aim to displace.[4] As Frankenberg, Naomi Zack (1997), Chris Cuomo and Kim Hall (1999), and many others have articulated, the danger is that an interrogation of whiteness might serve to recenter and even reinvigorate, rather than decenter, the dominant signifier.[5]

So, what do I mean when I read late modern western cultures and their normative concepts of freedom as cultures of phallicized whiteness? I have developed the short-hand of "phallicized whiteness" to signify how the interlocking epistemological and political systems of domination function within late modern western cultures, particularly in their proclamations of freedom. Emerging out of feminists' and other anti-racist theorists' sustained theoretical engagement with systems of domination over the last forty years, this shorthand of "phallicized whiteness" draws on the feminist development of the psychoanalytic category of morphology and Lacan's fundamental insights about how power works always to veil itself. It consequently emerges, also, out of the fraught histories of feminist and anti-racist movements in the U.S. that helped to bring theorists to this category of morphology.

▼ ▼ ▼

In ways that do and do not mirror the knots involved in the sex/gender distinction in feminist theory, anti-racist theorists must grapple with the role of the body in racist cultural symbolics such as the one we inhabit in the contemporary U.S.[6] The temptation to employ the conceptual schema of sex/gender—or of biology/culture, the larger categorical framework on which the sex/gender distinction turns—for questions of racial difference may be strong. It seems to appeal to several, even oppositional, political desires. For example, the biology/culture distinction appeals to a desire to maintain racial difference as biological, while ascribing racism to the cultural readings of that biology, thereby grounding an anti-racist politics of resistance. But, in more convoluted ways, the biology/culture framework also allows for an essentializing of culture that is nonetheless racializing, thereby grounding emergent strands of ultranationalism that parade under the banner of "ethnicity." As Paul Gilroy has shown, the allegiances to "raciological thinking" (2000) may enmesh groups on either side of the domination/oppression fault line in deep fealties to concepts of race, whether located in biological or cultural instantiations.[7] Either side of the dichotomy, biology or culture, is easily susceptible to essentialism: the move from race to ethnicity, a move that can be framed along the lines of the sex/gender distinction, does not ensure a move to liberatory, anti-racist politics or epistemologies.

Moreover, as the dominant narrative now circulates, the political history of the sex/gender distinction is particularly troublesome for anti-racist theorizing. Emerging as a political tool to combat the subordination of sexism to racism in the anti-racist movements of the Civil Rights Movement, it was pitted against racism from the beginning.[8] While scholars have complicated this simplistic narrative from a variety of angles, the sex/gender distinction has nonetheless always been implicated in perpetuating a perverse competition between sexism and racism.[9] It institutionalized a strict separation of gender from race, which turns on the prior separation of biology from culture. In so doing, the sex/gender distinction became a pawn in larger social dynamics that effectively raced gender and gendered race: the anti-sexist movement became a 'white problem' and the anti-racist movement became a 'male problem,' a dynamic that still haunts feminist and anti-racist theorizing and politics.

The sex/gender distinction thus emerged as a way to deflect attention away from racism; and this prioritizing of sexism over racism, predicated on an oppositional logic, continues to haunt its workings.[10] Following its expression in the late '80s and early '90s in the essentialism/constructionism debates, we can find its latest incarnation in the academic discipline of philosophy and the separation of 'critical race theory' from 'feminist theory.' We seem to be still working out the heritage of the politics and theories of the '60s, when race and the battles of anti-racism developed as and remained a manly pursuit, and the category of gender emerged as the terrain of white women and the problem of whites. Race is masculine; gender is white; and the hegemonic white patriarchy must be laughing.

In arguing against the use of the sex/gender distinction to approach racial difference, I am not suggesting that feminist theory has nothing to offer anti-racist theory. To the contrary, feminists of color, Anglo-American, "French," and Australian feminists have, since the mid-'80s, problematized the fundamental category of embodiment. This work not only calls into question the body/culture division, but also pluralizes the categories of difference from an essentialized focus on gender alone. The demand to think simultaneously across, about, through, and with multiple differences has radically altered the modes of rationality and politics appropriate for such tasks, thereby also calling into question the conservative politics that the sex/gender distinction spawned under the name of classical liberalism. It is this broader work by feminists on the category of embodiment that has much to offer our approaches to racial difference, and our thinking about difference more generally.

Moving from simplistic approaches to the body as a self-evident physical given, feminists have developed a more complex sense of embodiment as a nexus of historical, social, psychic, and physiological forces. In her path-breaking texts of *Borderlands = La Frontera: The New Mestiza* (1987), for example, Gloria Anzaldúa powerfully mixes Spanish with English to show how bodies are written on, by, and through language: her mestiza consciousness is the expression of her mestiza body, history, language, politics, and desires. This is an example, even if not usually categorized in this way, of what Judith Butler describes as undertaking "a critical genealogy of [the] formation" of materiality (1993, 32). Whether using conceptual tools from the history of European philosophy or their own experiences in this racialized and sexualized world, feminists that we might group under the awkward and inadequate heading of 'post-structuralist' have complicated the meanings and possibilities of 'materiality' and 'embodiment' considerably.[11] Resignifying the scope, mode, and limit of rationality from its ahistorical, disembodied Enlightenment perch, these feminist theorist-activists teach us how to approach materiality as a historicized phenomenon. They teach us how to approach our bodies and our lived experiences as the effects of historical, economic, social, and discursive matrices.

This radical reorientation toward materiality as a historicized phenomenon, rather than a natural given, alters the ways we understand the abstractions of various epistemological categories. For example, not only does the category of biology no longer have an extra-discursive, non-historical referent, but neither do the contemporary categories of identity, such as sex, gender, race, class, sexuality, and nationality. As feminists attuned to a historicized materiality began to reconceive domination, the salient social categories of feminism expanded to include all of these categories. But rather than positing this "list of differences" as merely an accumulation of discrete categories, the shift toward a historicized materialism challenges the separation of these categories from one another. Reading these categories as the effects of material dynamics, feminists grasp how aspects of contemporary identity emerge out of intersecting and overlapping historical formations.

To take the example that troubles the sex/gender distinction most directly, Judith Butler's reworking of gender, sex, and sexuality in *Gender Trouble* renders none of these categories separable from one another; but neither are any of them separable from the simultaneous registers of 'materiality' and historical discourse. Butler's work traces out a Foucaultian *Herkunft* (genealogy as discursive descent[12]) in the specific registers of sexuality, sex, and gender, showing how historical discourses of heterosexual normativity affect our lived, material experiences of 'the body.'[13] Historical discourses of heterosexual normativity affect both the kinds of bodies we have (e.g., intersexed bodies are a medically and legally regulated category through the widespread practice of sex assignment at birth in the U.S.[14]) and the ways we experience such bodies (e.g., the kinds of pleasures scripted onto our bodies as viable and legitimate produce varying kinds of eroticized bodies and body parts and, subsequently, varying politics[15]). Moreover, historical discourses of heterosexual normativity have also affected, in a dialectical relation of mutual formation, the ways we read and experience racial and class signifiers across the bodies of individuals, institutions, and cultures.[16] As the work of bell hooks has shown for some time, the matrix of white supremacist, heterosexist, capitalist patriarchy yields race sexualized and sex racialized, leaving all of our bodies marked by the confusion of what we try to understand as 'desire' in such a setting.[17]

The theoretical category that captures this work of historicizing materiality most fully may be, ironically for the historical narrative to which I alluded above, one that the Belgian feminist Luce Irigaray has been developing for some time: the category of sexual difference.[18] This category differs considerably from the categories of sex and gender as they have been deployed in Anglo-American work. Sexual difference, as Tina Chanter has explained lucidly, articulates the nexus of the body and history, which is reducible to neither.[19] It turns largely on recuperating a concept of the body, and implicitly of nature, as historicized, rather than as static, fixed, or universally given. While Irigaray has continued to be read by many as prioritizing sexual difference over all other differences,[20] particularly racial difference, the conceptual model out of which sexual difference springs—i.e., the psychoanalytic model of morphology, which bridges the alleged distinction between biology and culture—has much to offer our analyses of racial difference.

The larger irony here thus may be my attempt, in chapter 2, to trouble the Lacanian model and turn psychoanalysis against itself. Precisely through employing the concept of morphology as a way to read whiteness, I will shore up the limitations and blind spots of Lacanian psychoanalysis around the dynamics of race. In reading whiteness through the concept of morphology and as phallicized, I will show how we can better use psychoanalysis through realizing its limits and, more generally, through realizing its complicit role in grounding our white supremacist phallocentric symbolic.

▼ ▼ ▼

So, is race biological or cultural? Or is it perhaps neither and both? As many have articulated quite clearly by now,[21] race has no biological or physiological corollary or referent: nineteenth-century scientific racism should be long dead. But to argue that race is then 'socially constructed,' a rejoinder that dominates much contemporary work in this field, also seems to beg a number of questions, as scholars from a wide range of philosophical and ideological orientations have argued.[22] (Not to mention the ways that this dichotomy between biology and social construction reinscribes the conceptual model at work in the sex/gender distinction.) To say that race is socially constructed is thus a shorthand that I find increasingly dangerous. It plays all too easily into conservative aims to flatten out the social field of power at work in racial distinctions, evacuating us all of agency or responsibility with the simple exclamation, "we are all socially constructed." As I have seen too often in classrooms, it shuts down rather than opens up conversation: to say that race is socially constructed must heed Joan Scott's warnings about the category of "experience" (1993) and be the beginning, rather than the conclusion, of a critical examination.

If we are to read race, and whiteness particularly, as both biological and cultural (and thus reducible to neither), the psychoanalytic concept of morphology opens ways to read the role of the body, as a nexus of cultural and biological signifiers, in the play of racial difference in racist symbolics. Irigaray understands morphology as the ways that concepts shape bodies and bodies shape concepts. Placing racial difference in this conceptual framework, I interrogate 'whiteness' as a historically emergent phenomenon in which the role of the body—and of embodiment more broadly—becomes a central site of power. Embodiment becomes this site of power not only as the surface on which the concepts of white supremacy are written, but also as a primary vehicle whose logic shapes those very concepts—and in this, whiteness functions as the phallus in the socio-psychic field.

When read as phallicized, the signifier 'whiteness' becomes both the structuring element and the effect of a set of cultural practices and discourses that historically confer disproportionate, and often abusive, power on some persons over and in excess of others. As the structuring element, 'whiteness' functions much as the phallus does in Lacan's diagnosis: it is the dominant or 'master' signifier around which all other signifiers and practices are oriented—it shapes the ways they do and do not interact, the blind spots they do and do not perpetuate, the entities, acts, and desires they do and do not proclaim meaningful and thereby valuable.[23] As an effect of these cultural practices and discourses, 'whiteness' is sedimented by repetition into a pattern that *appears* as solid, as 'natural,' posing as a prediscursive, ahistorical, ontological given.[24] If we read this master signifier as a historically enacted set of power relations, we see what Frankenberg diagnoses: the characteristics which constitute this 'whiteness' are always in flux. Its borders "have proved malleable over time" (1997b, 633), granting it the power to regulate social fields of symbols (epistemology) and power (politics) while always remaining invisible. Employing the psychoanalytic category of morphology here, I discern the role of embodiment in what Richard Dyer calls the "semiotic flexibility" (1997, 21) of whiteness.

Two necessary conditions allow 'whiteness' to emerge as the dominant, phallic signifier and, in turn, allow the set of cultural practices and discourses which it engenders to dominate our socio-political field:

1) *'Whiteness' naturalizes and universalizes its structural advantage through remaining unmarked and unnamed as a specific, historical set of cultural practices and discourses.*

Following the pattern of privileged subject positions, whiteness poses as the universal and naturalized 'order of things.' In mutually grounding gestures, it renders itself both invisible and ubiquitous. These dynamics then sediment one another: the more transparent and invisible whiteness becomes, the more normalized and omnipresent it becomes, and so on. In this dual functioning of self-erasure and self-empowerment, whiteness relies on the continued veiling of its ongoing, historical shifting of categories, actions, inclusions, and exclusions that is necessary to keep its power intact. It must not surface as a historical set of signifiers. In this specific manner, I am suggesting that whiteness functions as the phallus functions in the Villa of Mysteries of Pompeii: only through remaining veiled can it control the signifying field as the master signifier. To historicize whiteness and mark it socially, therefore, is a critical tool in delimiting and localizing this alleged universal and totalizing grasp.[25] To historicize whiteness is to unveil its functioning as the phallus and displace its power.

2) *'Whiteness' relies on a slippery play of embodiment/disembodiment that the dualism of biology/social construction perpetuates and the psychoanalytic category of morphology diagnoses.*

Following Stuart Hall, I argue that whiteness operates as a structural set of cultural practices and discourses that historically confer disproportionate and often abusive power not only on specific persons, but on specific bodies—i.e., that this advantage is granted on the basis of bodily characteristics,

DuBois's haunting "hair, skin and bone" (Hall 1996b). Regardless of how much we hear from contemporary science (e.g., the much acclaimed Human Genome Project) about how race is not biologically grounded, U.S. culture will nonetheless continue to make racial distinctions—consciously, unconsciously, overtly, covertly, politically, personally, medically, and legally—on the basis of how bodies appear. The very appeal to biological science to 'prove' the falsity of race already places race in the domain of the body. The body—and particularly the body as surface appearance—simply will not go away in the carving up of racial distinctions and categories. It remains the intensely cathected site of and vehicle for the historically specific and changing discourse of race.

Reading whiteness as phallicized thereby affords many opportunities: we can unravel how whiteness functions as a historical set of cultural practices and discourses that poses as ahistorical and attempts to function structurally; we can read racial and sexual difference as cathected through the same nexus of signifiers in this phallicized symbolic, thereby grasping how power is negotiated differently for raced and sexed bodies, and the myriad combinations thereof; we can read racism as working through a binary logic that expresses itself as anti-black racism; and, as a primary location of these dynamics, we can begin to map the ways that the body, particularly "the body as seen" in the register of visibility, functions as the site through which a racist and sexist symbolic operates, thus ushering us into the thorny relations between the visible and language—or, in Lacanian terminology, between the imaginary and the symbolic.[26]

If 'whiteness' is the dominant, phallic signifier in the present discourses of race and if those discourses of race are centered on bodily distinctions, despite scientific and philosophical arguments exposing the lack of biological corollaries, then we need to interrogate the roles of embodiment and disembodiment in these discursive deployments of whiteness. How does whiteness's deployment of cultural and discursive practices ensure a continued fascination with the body, while simultaneously marking out the space of 'the disembodied' or transcendent as the space of power? How does whiteness inhabit the body in such a way as to ensure that it transcends the body and becomes a 'subject,' while non-white bodies are fully reducible to the body and thus objects or abjected others?

The twin dynamics of universalism and disembodiment collude to produce systems of power that allow 'whiteness' to emerge as the dominant, phallic signifier and, in turn, engender a specific set of cultural practices and discourses in the socio-political field. To frame these interlocking systems of domination as a system of "phallicized whiteness" is to argue that we can trace contemporary systems of domination, and their various interconnections, through these hallmarks of whiteness—namely, universalism and disembodiment. In the following six chapters, I trace how this system of phallicized whiteness expresses itself doubly: (1) in the identity categories of class and religion (chapters 1 and 6), race (chapter 2), sexual difference (chapter 3), sexuality (chapters 3 and 4), and nationality (chapter 5); and (2) in normative concepts of space (chapters 1–3) and temporality (chapters 4–6). My hope is that, through becoming more conscious of how domination writes itself on our bodies, we may better resist its seduction of freedom.

Queering Freedom: A Genealogy of Identity and Difference

So, why queer freedom? As queer theory has demonstrated for some time, categories of identity narrow our field of vision, and subsequently our fields of resistance. They constrict our experiences into parameters that are too sharply delineated and differentiated from one another: none of us experiences this complex world as only a gender or a race or a class or a nationality or a sexuality, and so on. The infamous 'and so on' already renders any such listing of identities incomplete. And yet identity categories, and the identity politics that they spawn, claim completion: they claim to totalize our experience of ourselves and of the world.

To queer freedom is not to disavow the political work of calling out the power differentials buried in these identity categories: it is not to return us to the allegedly neutral space of 'the human.' To queer freedom is, on the contrary, to deepen our grasp of the historicity of these categories. The conflation of dominant subjectivities with the posture of neutrality that we find in our contemporary cultures of phallicized whiteness did not occur recently. It reaches back, at a minimum, to the emergence of classical liberalism in the seventeenth century and its valorization of particular kinds of labor, rationality, temporality—and thereby of particular bodies, particular identities. We need to return to those roots of classical liberalism and trace out its subtle valorization of these characteristics, if we are to historicize the categories of identity that have since become some of its best tools.[27]

This work of historicizing our categories of identity is, among other activities, the work of queering freedom. It will both give us a deeper sense of how these categories emerged and show how the categories themselves intersect and interact to perpetuate the systems of domination in which we now find ourselves living. I develop much of this through the logic of the limit, a kind of logic that binds classical liberalism to phallicized whiteness through the shared value of individualism—a cornerstone, in turn, of advanced capitalism. Individualism simultaneously demands two apparently contradictory moves: 1) that we transcend material differences and understand ourselves as "just human"; and 2) that we conceive of ourselves through the rigid categories of identity that lock us into raced, sexed, classed (and so on) individuals. Individualism demands both identity and difference: the first of these perpetuates the Myth of Sameness, while the second reduces our subjectivities to the delimited categories of difference.

But these categories of difference are ultimately that which must be transcended—erased—if we are to ascend into the treasured neutrality of humanity. And, even more perniciously, these categories of difference only lock us into politics of alleged resistance, wherein difference is pitted against difference (e.g., the old story of race *or* gender), while the one who transcends such differences altogether walks away unscathed. In Hegelian parlance, difference is always only mediated by identity here. The logic of the limit shows how these concepts of identity and difference are ultimately two sides of the same coin—namely, the currency of phallicized whiteness. It also rings a loud cautionary note about the viability of any politics of resistance that grounds itself in identity.

The logic of the limit thereby helps to excavate how classical liberalism presents a hollow concept of freedom. In classical liberalism, freedom holds itself out as the transgression of boundaries and liberation from constraint. For example, we might think that we will liberate ourselves from domination if we engage in transgressive behaviors that violate our designated race, sex, gender, class, nationality, or religion. But the logic of the limit shows, as Bataille and Foucault among others also see, that such notions of freedom as the transgression of boundaries or liberation from constraint only enmesh us further in the very systems of domination we seek to resist. To queer freedom we must learn not only to resist the limited notions of difference enacted in categories of identity, but to resist differently altogether.

Yet, despite all this talk about identity and difference, 'queer' has a distinct ring of identification and identity. Let's not fool ourselves: being queer is about sexuality. So, what role does the specific identity category of sexuality play in queering freedom?

If we trace the roots of present identity categories to some of their historical emergences, the conflation of race and gender (and, less explicitly, class and religion) occurs through the dynamic of sexuality. Nineteenth-century laws against miscegenation, the one-drop rule, and practices of lynching all expose how sexuality serves as the nexus through which male and white domination are enacted in the psycho-social field. Moreover, given the historical and epistemological tension between whiteness and heterosexuality that I will demonstrate, sexuality is the Achilles' heel of phallicized whiteness's domination of the social field. The field of sexuality is thereby the most effective site in our historical present of late modernity for intervention into fixed concepts of subjectivity and freedom. But we cannot reduce such an insight to a claim about identity.

The projects of gay/lesbian liberation have been flawed in their conceptions of resistant politics as yet another kind of identity politics. The emergence of 'the homosexual identity' and its identity politics is ultimately just another clever tool of phallicized whiteness. To queer freedom we must therefore avoid this error of identification, while simultaneously embracing the field of sexuality as the most effective site of intervention into present systems of domination. In addition to its pivotal role in the politics of sexism and racism, what is it about sexuality that frames it as this specific site of intervention and resistance?

Another way of understanding the limitations of gay/lesbian liberation movements is through their reading of the gay/lesbian subject as a subject of desire. Desire enacts particular forms of spatiality and temporality that feed contemporary forms of domination. When we conceive of ourselves primarily as subjects of desire, we begin to understand ourselves as discrete bodies with desires that are essential to who we are. But as contained subjects, we lack that which we want. Consequently, we project ourselves outwardly both spatially and temporally: spatially, we conceive of other bodies as discrete entities that we must overcome, perhaps even master, to answer to our needs; temporally, we project ourselves into the future as the horizon on which we will find our satisfaction. A bound body that models itself on private property and a futural teleology that places desire in an infinite pursuit take hold as the normative spatiality and temporality in which meaning is forged.

If we can excavate the normative spatial and temporal registers through which our experiences are cathected in systems of domination, we locate radical ways to intervene—and to queer our lives. While sexuality will remain the historically privileged site for such interventions, this work of queering freedom places it in a more general economy of desires, pleasures, spaces, and times. It thereby opens onto resistances that we may signify as "queer" and yet that are not bound by or reducible to one's sexuality. Abandoning the spatial model of private property and turning toward temporalities of 'lost pasts,'[28] we may transform our lives from ones of anxiety endemic to desire, toward ones of joy that open onto freedom.

PART ONE

DEMARCATING THE SPACE OF
DOMINATION: THE POLITICS
OF FREEDOM

LIBERALISM'S NEUTRAL INDIVIDUAL

Delimiting Racial and Sexual Difference

1

Freedom ought to have some limits.
—attributed to
GEORGE W. BUSH;
a bumper sticker
seen in Tucson,
Arizona, March
2003

The Logic of the Limit in Two Registers: Enclosure and Prohibition

As the fences in my gentrifying, whitening neighborhood grow higher and higher, the political, economic, and personal functions of limits in cultures of phallicized whiteness become more and more clear. Limits constitute property and propriety. Demarcating a 'body' or 'subject' from the vagueness of backgrounds, conditions, cultures, or histories, they serve as the site of individuation. They circumvent an entity, orienting us toward the criterion of 'wholeness,' a primary demand of legibility in cultures of phallicized whiteness. Not unlike the rituals of urination contests among male dogs, limits mark out our territories. They ground our deep senses of ourselves as individuals, our narratives of ahistorical autonomous self-determination, and the many cultural forms of that self-determination.

In a slightly different mode, limits also function as internal and external constraints of possibility that frame personal, social, or even economic fields. We understand ourselves, for example, as limited internally by our social and cultural backgrounds or as constrained by our financial resources. Or, externally, limits also function as thresholds that stand at the outer limit of experiences and cannot be trespassed, exercising an external authoritative restraint that expresses itself as a prohibition. For example, nations (most nations, at least) are restrained and limited by international law; or, more locally, I may simply realize that, with age encroaching, my limit is three drinks. In all of these, limits function as that which one (a social attitude, a political entity, a person) cannot or must not go beyond. They indicate thresholds of experience, forming the contours of our desire and subjectivity, whether internally or externally imposed. When framed as prohibitions, they incite our desire: death and drugs, along with sex and love, are the most commonly explored 'limit experiences.'

Across all of these functions, a common operation is at work. From the function of limits as internal conditions of possibility or external boundaries of restraint to the demarcations of wholeness and individuation, limits constitute legibility. One belongs to one's cultural background, gaining identity and direction from its historical particularity; nations that disobey international law are "imperialist" or "rogue states," depending on their economic might; I am a hung-over sop, not an interesting person, the morning after an evening of more than three drinks; and, fundamentally to all of these, a true individual is he or she who can clearly stake his or her own identity—psychologically, politically, economically—in the chaotic world. It is this last phenomenon, the demarcating of the individual and all its permutations, that I want to explore and develop, rooting it particularly in the modern political projects of classical liberalism and their attendant concepts of freedom.

The logic of the limit thus expresses itself in two fundamental registers: as enclosure and as prohibition. These two registers are dialectically related. The demarcating of entities (persons, experiences, ideas, institutions) clearly and distinctly from other entities and from historico-cultural backgrounds enacts a mode of separation that leads us to frame desire as the careful negotiation—and prohibition—of boundaries. For example, we introduce ownership on the model of private property into the social field when we conceive of an entity as individuated on the basis of its enclosure and containment by clear boundaries. This model of ownership, grounded in a fundamental preference for labor that enacts a futural temporality, in turn initiates an economics of scarcity into the field of social relations. We demand that we must demarcate that which is properly "ours." Private property comes to dominate our senses of the world—of our selves, others, objects, and all possible relations therein. Each becomes a quantifiable unit. As the social field is reduced to modes of ownership, scarcity comes to dominate the kinds of relations that obtain therein. The fear of encroachment begins to override any desire to cross these clear and distinct boundaries. And the crossing of boundaries, whether between persons, classes, sexes, races, nations, or religions, becomes prohibited. Boundaries differentiate us; individuation becomes our most precious value; and the crossing of boundaries is forbidden, creating that tantalizing social realm of fetish and taboo.

The two registers of the logic of the limit, enclosure and prohibition, are thereby analytically distinct, but functionally intertwined. The resilience of phallicized whiteness and its domination of the social field in cultures of late modernity depend on these subtle, often unnoticed if not invisible, dynamics. Both enclosure and prohibition collude to ground the fundamental values of freedom and individualism, all bound by the model of private property and the fundamental value of labor that enacts a futural temporality, in cultures of phallicized whiteness.

Rights to Property: Rights as Property

We must continue to read our contemporary cultural symbolic as one that is still haunted by modernity—epistemologically, historically, and politically. The fundamental demarcation between body and culture that we have already seen at work in the sex/gender distinction operates not only epistemologically but also politically, in the modern project. In scripting politics in the language of rights, classical liberalism construes the individual as an atomistic unit who has, through its demarcation of its place in the world, exited the state of nature. The individual deserves and requires rights because it exists as a demarcated, separable unit unto itself; conversely, the individual also emerges as a product of the idea of rights.

We find these dynamics, and a particular grounding of them in a subtle evaluation of forms of labor through the temporalities and teleologies which they enact, performed in John Locke's classic *Second Treatise of Government*, a text that continues to read alternatively as the road map and rallying cry of contemporary U.S. capitalist-democratic culture. Many theorists have interrogated the classed, sexed, and raced assumptions and effects of liberalism's systematic claims to neutrality and universality.[1] In broad strokes, this work exposes how the alleged and self-proclaimed neutrality of liberalism's individualism is grounded in particular class, race, and gender politics that the project of liberalism, written in the register of ahistorical universality, must deny. Whether historicizing fundamental assumptions as the products of particular socio-economic European conditions or showing how the claims to neutrality function to hide the masculinist and white supremacist logic at the heart of liberalism, this varied work constructs a thorough critique of liberalism's claims to neutrality and, concomitantly, its claims to an ahistorically universal voice. I am, gratefully, taking that work as a point of departure here and hoping to push it yet further. Assuming that liberalism's claims to neutrality actually function to hide, disguise, and thereby perpetuate the power of particular subject positions, I want to diagnose how that neutrality functions to keep these structures of phallicized whiteness in power: how does neutrality function to perpetuate the power structures of phallicized whiteness and all its permutations—as white, as male, as propertied, as Protestant, and, eventually, as heterosexual?

My approach to Locke's text, therefore, is to read it as an exemplar of classical liberalism's insistence on the fundamental and natural neutrality of the individual. While wary of simply reading twentieth-century categories back into Locke's text, I approach it as a text that grounds fundamental assumptions and dynamics which continue to affect contemporary politics of oppression and domination in cultures of phallicized whiteness. Focusing on dynamics such as the rise of utility as the fundamental social, moral, and epistemological value, I do not pretend to offer a comprehensive reading of Locke's *oeuvre* here. My concern is, rather, to excavate the textual sites in which some of our fundamental values emerged: individualism, private property, labor guided by a clear intention and teleology, a futural temporality, and freedom as the ability to express one's power.[2] Framed as an abbreviated genealogy of concepts, much of the work in these early sections on Locke will not come to fruition until later chapters, where these concepts attain their full-blown expression as fundamental structures of phallicized whiteness.

I begin with one of the most recent examples of this work on liberalism and, more broadly, classical theories of social contract—Charles Mills's *The Racial Contract.* Following Carole Pateman's lead in her groundbreaking work *The Sexual Contract,* Mills focuses explicitly on the racialized effects of liberalism's alleged neutrality and universality. In his arguments concerning Locke, Mills locates the move from the state of nature to the state of civil society in that cornerstone of capitalist culture: the security of private prop-

erty. For Mills's project, this emphasis on property is what justifies the colonialist genocide of Native Americans:

> the mode of appropriation of Native Americans is no real mode of appropriation
> at all, yielding property rights that can be readily overridden (if they exist at
> all), and thereby rendering their territories normatively open for seizure once
> those who have long since *left* the state of nature (Europeans) encounter them.
> (1997, 67)

In their failure to use—or master or dominate—the land, Native Americans
suffer from a faulty mode of appropriation. They fail to constitute the land
as property and thereby fail to own it. And this failure confirms their inferior
moral and rational state: they have failed God's mandate to exercise rationality and reduce wild nature to human utility. All of these, the land that is
not owned and the evident moral and rational inferiority, seem to have been
ample justifications for genocide, insofar as Europeans could not recognize
any proper attributes of civilized human nature in these excessive Native
Americans.

The chain of argument allowing for such judgments is explicit in Locke's
texts: God gave man reason to labor upon wild nature, reduce it to his utility,
and thereby make it valuable to him as property, to which he has a right:
God–reason–labor–utility–property–rights. It is hardly a foreign argument,
enacted daily as it is across these Protestant lands of the United States. But
its authority must derive from cultural and historical repetitions, rather than
compelling connections between each of these links. Each juncture operates
on entire sets of assumptions; to investigate each of these far outstrips my
project here. More modestly, I want to focus on two fundamental conditions
that must be present for Locke's argument to work: the understanding of
one's body as one's property; and the complex dynamics between economics
of abundance and economics of scarcity that readily invoke the Christian
theology of fallenness as the human condition and, less clearly, rely on an
ambiguous evaluation of labor and money in the move into the state of
society. Central to each of these is the process of delimitation, the logic of
the limit.

▼ ▼ ▼

Property functions as the overriding metaphor and logic for Locke's
worldview. It grounds his understanding of human nature and all of its relations—to God, to one's self, to others, and to the world. Describing man

27

as he exists in the state of nature, Locke locates him first through his relation to his creator, God. In language that is freighted with larger meanings for his own project, he states in the *Second Treatise on Government* (Locke 1960),

> [m]en being all the Workmanship of one Omnipotent and infinitely wise Maker; All the Servants of one Sovereign Master, sent into the World by his order, and about his business, they are *his Property, whose Workmanship they are,* made to last during his, not one another's Pleasure. (section 6, my emphasis)

From this basic premise, that humans are the property of their creator God, we can unravel the conceptual building blocks and dynamics of Locke's social and political system: productive labor yields units of property that the laborer owns and over which he thereby exercises authority. Because man is made in the image of God, he too exercises proprietary rights over, first, his own body and, secondly, the products of that body's labor. This model of ownership constitutes one's relations not only to one's possessions and actions, but also to one's self: men in the state of nature exist in "a *State of perfect Freedom* to order their Actions, and dispose of their Possessions, and Persons as they think fit" (section 4). As we are owned by God because he created— or produced—us, so too do we own that which we produce in the world through our labor.

Property and labor are thereby fundamental to Locke's understanding of the human world and the political dilemmas that emerge within it. Human nature is destined both to labor and to produce property, and these are intertwined with one another. These activities are natural to humans. They subsequently form the bedrock assumptions of Locke's ontology of the human social world. He argues that we are driven to labor by our ontological lack, a lack that echoes the fallenness of Christian theology rather clearly: "God, when he gave the World in common to all Mankind, commanded Man also to labor, and the penury of his Condition required it of him" (section 32); or again, "God commanded, and his Wants forced, him to *labor*" (section 35).

This lack that drives us to labor stands in sharp contradiction to the abundance of (God's) state of nature. And it is in the clashing of these two dynamics, human's lack and nature's abundance, that the prohibition against waste emerges so strongly for Locke. The fundamental character of labor, for Locke, is that it renders nature useful; consequently, one must follow reason and not be led to overstep the very defining characteristic of that labor, utility. One must not labor upon—or enclose and subsequently own— more than one can use: "The same Law of Nature, that does by this means give us Property, does also *bound* that *Property* too . . . especially keeping within the *bounds,* set by reason of what might serve for his *use*" (section 31).

The logic of the limit thereby grounds Locke's sense of property multiply: we own that upon which we labor, as evidenced by our ability to enclose the cultivated land; and we only maintain our rights to such ownership through properly obeying the boundaries and enclosures of reason, which is bound in turn by the yoke of utility. Enclosure dominates Locke's conceptual world. It is what affords him his basic premise of self-ownership: "every Man has a *Property* in his own *Person.* This no Body has any Right to but himself" (section 27). The body is the temple of one's individuality, of one's clear and distinct separation from others and from nature, because it is an enclosed entity. This reading of the body already implies, and enacts, racialized and sexualized politics, while also introducing the logic of prohibition and transgression into the dynamic of desire. For Locke, it functions as the grounding assumption that cannot be otherwise: enclosure grants him a logic that allows him to connect a variety of phenomena.[3]

As he tells us early in this section on property, enclosure works in a circular and (literally) self-grounding fashion in this system of labor–utility–property–rights: man must enclose a piece of land before he can work on it, make it useful, and thereby have a right to it; and yet he only encloses it by working on it and making it useful. Enclosure is the decisive trait. It is only insofar as Locke reads the body as enclosed that he can frame the labor which issues from that body as an enclosing of the object upon which it labors. Because one's body is enclosed, one owns it as property; consequently, whatever issues from that body into the world marks the world by that body's characteristic—i.e., it encloses it and thereby owns it as property.[4] To labor is to extend the property that is one's body into the property of the world. To labor is to appropriate. Because Locke understands the body as enclosed and as one's property, he easily extends the logic of enclosure to understand labor and utility as also producing property. And this all functions through an expression of the logic of the limit: enclosure.

Both property and labor thereby exist in the state of nature. The mere gathering of acorns is sufficient for ownership: "And 'tis plain, if the first gathering made them not his, nothing else could. . . . That added something to them more than Nature, the common Mother of all, had done; and so they became his private right" (section 28). Consequently, "The Fruit, or Venison, which nourishes the wild *Indian,* who knows no Inclosure, and is still a Tenant in common," belongs to him, is his property—"i.e. a part of him"—because he gathered and hunted it (section 26). It would seem that Charles Mills's indictment of Locke as paving the way for the genocide of Native Americans may be misplaced. Mills's argument is that, grounded in a Lockean socio-political epistemology, the 'civilized' Europeans were incapable of recognizing that the Indians owned the land on which they lived because it did not display the evidence of utility's labor upon it—namely, it was not enclosed. How can Locke's theory of labor, property, and the state of nature simultaneously allow for the Native Americans' ownership of fruit and venison and the Europeans' confiscation of their lands?

To grasp these dynamics, and their racialized and classed effects in contemporary cultures of phallicized whiteness, I turn to two implicit notions of labor that Locke employs: labor that creates some new object in the world through intentional design and a futural mode of temporality; and labor that discharges its purpose virtually immediately in its own activity. These two kinds of labor initiate and function within two differing temporal modes. A simplistic example of the labor-by-design is the gathering of apples to bake a pie, an activity that requires both careful planning and a concept of the future in which that planning can and will come to fruition. The analogue for labor that fulfills itself through its very act would be the gathering of apples to eat them, two activities that complete themselves within such close temporal proximity that we can, from a general perspective, refer to them as happening simultaneously. In the first form of labor, the *telos* of the action is cast beyond and outside of the act of initial labor; in the second form of labor, the *telos* is achieved in the initial act of labor itself. As we cast these differing kinds of labor and the concept of a future into more complex examples (particularly into cultivating land, which was Locke's exemplar) we begin to see why it is that Locke argues we must—albeit willingly—leave the state of nature and enter the state of society.

For Locke, the impetus to move into the state of society comes from the threat of the state of war. This threat emerges from one central phenomenon: the insecurity of private property. Humans move into the state of society to secure the private property procured through their labor in the state of nature. While it is reasonable not to overstep the boundaries of reason itself and attempt to steal another's property, the state of nature does not offer any lasting protections against this constant threat of lapses into irrationality. Without any higher authority that all must obey, the state of nature only offers humans the retribution of killing the aggressor or appealing to heaven for further reparations. In order to forestall this violence over property, humans choose to leave the abundance of the state of nature and enter the security of the state of society. It is, from the beginning, a move that operates on a future temporality.

But none of this sufficiently answers the question of why these lapses in rationality occur: why, particularly in nature's abundance, would one wish to steal the property of another? Why is the state of nature constantly under threat of devolving into a state of war? Or, to foreshadow Bataille, why would humans introduce an economy of scarcity into the free life amidst an economy of abundance? It is here that Locke casts his longest shadows over politics of classical liberalism and cultures of advanced capitalism—or, to combine these with racialized and sexualized dynamics, cultures of phallicized whiteness.

First of all, Locke himself does not offer any satisfactory explanation for this critical transition. He offers a few general possibilities: irrationality apparently seduces some humans, so that they have "no other Rule, but that of Force and Violence, and so may be treated as Beasts of Prey" (section 16); or, more in tune with the Protestant work ethic to follow him, he indicts laziness, insisting that God gave nature's abundance "to the use of the Industrious and Rational, . . . not to the Fancy or Covetousness of the Quarrelsome and Contentious" (section 34). Locke writes of this transition from the state of nature into the state of society, as a way to avert the state of war, from the perspective of a *de facto* experience in human development. His discussion thereby focuses on the kinds of retribution that can be inflicted upon aggressors, not on what might initially lead a human to exercise irrational power over another. He does not offer any genetic account of the transition itself, only of what is gained through it.

C. B. MacPherson, in his classic commentary on possessive individualism and the emergent moralism of bourgeois accumulation in the early modern period, argues that this is a prime example of "Locke's unhistorical habit of mind" (1962, 229), a structure that centrally informs Locke's accounts of the states of nature, war, and society. MacPherson grounds his general reading of Locke in Locke's complete lack of historical self-reflexivity, or what we might term historicity in the twenty-first century: "contradictions and ambiguities in the theory can be explained . . . by Locke having read back into the nature of men and society certain preconceptions about the nature of seventeenth-century man and society which he generalized quite unhistorically" (1962, 197).[5] Regarding the specific question of the emergence of irrational men in the state of nature, MacPherson argues that Locke does not offer any explanation for the problem because he is reading a classed ontology of his own historical society back into the state of nature—namely, Locke assumes the bifurcation of individuals into propertied land owners and propertyless laborers, which translates into an ontology of two different *kinds* of rationality, as a transition that occurs in the state of nature, rather than as a shift that occurred specifically in seventeenth-century agricultural capitalism.[6] This simply leaves Locke with the conclusion that, as Mac-Pherson puts it, "there are, then, some natural criminals amongst the natural law-abiding people of the state of nature" (1962, 240).

Against the backdrop of MacPherson's historical argument, we can also locate the necessity for the move from the state of nature into the state of society in the two kinds of labor at work in Locke's text and the initiation of a future temporality enacted therein. Locke's preference for forms of labor which achieve their ends through complex designs that require a stable concept of the future over forms of labor that complete themselves in the singular act of labor functions not only as a historical preference (and thus a historicizing moment in this allegedly ahistorical text), but also as an instance of the totalizing reach of the logic of enclosure: once Locke grounds his understanding of labor and property through the logic of enclosure, a move that is conditioned by his own historical and socio-economic location, he will necessarily argue in favor of capitalist, individualist society over the state of nature. Furthermore, through this exploration of the two kinds of labor, we may also more deeply understand Charles Mills's indictments of Locke for justifying imperialist genocide.

In his long chapter on property, Locke appears to be trapped by several contradictory pairs of impulses: by a nostalgia for life in nature's abundance and the preference for cultivated over uncultivated land; by a nostalgia for exchange as the bartering of goods and the preference for designed, complex labor over immediate, simple labor; and by an awareness of the threat money poses to the reign of utility and the desire for durability in one's property. In language of increased rhetorical flourishes, which are all too tempting to read as an increased anxiety over his conclusions, Locke settles each of these dilemmas in favor of the latter options: civilized, propertied, capitalist society.

We see this most directly in his preferences for enclosed, cultivated land and complex forms of labor over their lesser counterparts. It is here that the economy of scarcity enters into nature's economy of abundance. Recall that the primary characteristic of property, for Locke, is its enclosure. Responding to his historical times and the aristocracy's moves to enclose private property from the common lands open to the use of peasants, Locke reads all instances of property through their status as enclosed—i.e., clear and distinct—objects. The ability to own a piece of property thereby manifests itself in the ability to set it apart and distinguish it from the world of nature's abundance that is common to all: it manifests itself in the ability to set boundaries around it. This move, one which is natural and inevitable for Locke, initiates a spatio-temporality that in turn introduces an economy of scarcity into nature's abundance.

Spatially, this setting of boundaries and limits around defined units of property introduces an order of finitude into what was understood to be an infinite, boundless abundance. It begins to set limits upon this infinite nature and, in step with its origins in an instrumental rationality bound by the yoke of utility, puts an order of quantification into play. We can hear this directly in Locke's language, as he deliberates carefully over what fractional increase in value cultivation introduces into uncultivated land: "of the *Products* of the Earth useful to the Life of Man, nine tenths are the *effects of labor* . . . nay, . . . in most of them ninety-nine hundredths are wholly to be put on the account of *labor*" (section 40). Lured by quantifiable units, Locke seems to feel increasingly compelled to justify the enclosure of nature's lands into finite owned units.

In this finite world of demarcated property, the potential of uncultivated land to be owned no longer holds itself out on an infinite, boundless horizon. It may all get 'used up,' an anxiety we hear in Locke's explicit refusal to worry over the increased population of the world; he insists, perhaps rather naively to our contemporary ears, "there is Land enough in the World to suffice double the Inhabitants" (section 36). As this demarcating of nature's abundance into finite pieces of private property ensues, the tension between abundance and scarcity mounts in Locke's texts; note the qualification at the end of this explanation of private ownership: "For this *Labor* being the unquestionable Property of the Laborer, no Man but he can have a right to what that is once joined to, *at least where there is enough, and as good, left in common for others*" (section 27, my emphasis). An economy of scarcity emerges as more and more property is enclosed; Locke is conflicted about the effects of this on one's natural right to own private property, a right he had delimited as justifiable only in nature's economy of abundance.

Temporally, this economy of scarcity functions in ways that align with the spatial initiation of finitude and limits. The temporal dimension surfaces in an increasing—and apparently inevitable—desire for more durable, lasting goods. This desire will find its final expression in the invention of money, an invention that complicates the abundance/scarcity dynamics considerably and about which Locke is openly conflicted. But we can locate the origin of this desire for more durable, lasting goods in Locke's subtle preference for complex, future-oriented labor and its direct expression, enclosed and cultivated land, over their lesser counterparts.

As we have seen, Locke distinguishes two forms of labor and appears to prefer that which both encloses land and functions in a temporal horizon of the future—e.g., he continually justifies the cultivation of land, an act of labor that requires a stable concept of the future, as the labor of civilized society. In the final sections of his chapter on property, Locke clearly ranks this future-oriented form of labor over forms that complete themselves immediately in the act of labor. This preference, which ultimately assumes the force of a normative value judgment in Locke's text, is grounded in these final sections in the future-oriented labor's ability to control the overriding ontological prohibition of waste.

A hallmark of this kind of labor is the way that it achieves its end product only after a complex chain of carefully designed acts. The end product is not reducible to any single act, but is achieved externally to each act within the chain. For example, the production of a potato emerges from the entire chain of fertilizing, planting, irrigating, tending, and innumerable other activities: the potato emerges externally to each of these singular acts. This is how we discern this labor's enactment of a concept of the future: no singular act produces the potato, but each act operates within the assured concept that a future product will emerge externally to its individual activity. Because it appears to involve more complex design and thereby greater intentionality than that sort of labor which achieves its end more immediately, this future-oriented labor can control the amount that it produces.

To the contrary, Locke claims that the more immediate form of labor tends to overstep the boundaries of the prohibition of waste, gathering and hunting more than it can use. While he does not justify this claim explicitly, we can assume that it is the lack of a concept of the future, compounded by the failure to enclose and cultivate land, which leads this immediate form of labor to these infractions of nature's law. Doubly limitless, this immediate form of labor does not operate within the temporal or spatial orders that Locke valorizes: it is little wonder that it cannot properly control its use. And for this, the laborer must submit to the punishment warranted by the law of nature, rationality bound by utility: "if they perished, in his Possession, without their due use . . . he offended against the common Law of Nature, and was liable to be punished" (section 37). The examples at hand in Locke's texts here are, tellingly, fruit and venison—the sustenance of those "wild Indians of America." It is the Native Americans' failure to enter into more complex forms of labor that renders their lands vulnerable to confiscation. It is their failure to enclose their lands for cultivation and thereby labor according to a concept of the future, which more effectively subdues nature to the rational laws of utility, that ultimately justifies the European genocide of their race.

But at the same time, the introduction of the futural mode of temporality complicates this valorization of one form of labor over the other. The reason that future-oriented labor can obey the imperative of utility more strictly— namely, that it can produce goods with greater intentionality, which in turn allows the ability to store them, to trade them for other necessary goods, and to make them more durable—also becomes a temptation to overstep the boundaries of that utility.

▼ ▼ ▼

Locke makes it clear over and over that the limit to all labor upon land is that there should still be enough left over for others: one must not enclose more than one can use, and in this way one will not infringe upon the abundance available to others' use. But as his (prescient, albeit disavowed) anxiety about overpopulation and thus overdevelopment increases, Locke begins to argue explicitly that nature and God command humans to work productively, cultivate land, and own private property: as God commands humans to labor, "subduing or cultivating the Earth, and having Dominion . . . are joined together. . . . And the Condition of Humane Life, which requires Labor and Materials to work on, necessarily introduces *private Possessions*" (section 35). Across sections 40–51, he argues that cultivated land increases the value of land not only for the individual proprietor, but for the whole of humanity: products such as bread, wine, and leather are self-evidently more valuable than the grains, grapes, and skins out of which they are produced. Cultivating land *per se* does not thereby decrease nature's abundance; to the contrary, it increases it: "he who appropriates land to himself by his labor does not lessen but increase the common stock of mankind" (section 37).[7] He even argues that uncultivated land disobeys God's and nature's command, and is of such little value in and of itself that "Land that is left wholly to Nature . . . is called, as indeed it is, '*waste*'" (section 42).

The waste prohibition thereby comes full circle: it is now human, social labor that tethers nature's raw materials to the law of utility, rendering nature

35

itself wasteful. And, in an even more bizarre twist of logic, the apparent scarcity introduced by private property actually renders nature more abundant than ever. But the law of utility, which is of paramount importance and value in Locke's system, remains firmly intact: the abundance produced by labor is tightly controlled and thus useful. The further complication of these dynamics through the introduction of money must not shake this foundation.

Locke simultaneously romanticizes the times of pre-monetary exchange and valorizes the introduction of money as the move toward civilized development and progress. As we have seen, the valorization of future-oriented labor and cultivated land sparks and cultivates a desire for the expression of this future temporality—namely, more durable goods. Exchange of goods thereby grows out of this desire for durability, a desire that Locke locates in the state of nature: in the chapter on the state of nature, Locke expresses some nostalgia for "the Promises and Bargains for Truck, etc., between the two Men in the Desert Island, mentioned by *Garcilasso De la vega,* in his history of *Peru,* or between a *Swiss* and an *Indian* in the Woods of *America*" (section 14). But this later valorization of future-oriented labor and cultivated land, the marks of civilized society, intensifies this desire for durability and complicates the modes it finds for its expression through the introduction of private property. The desire for durable goods finally leads human societies—inevitably—toward the invention of money, introducing a yet more complex relation to utility.[8]

Locke explains the shift to moneyed exchange explicitly in the mode of temporality: "The greatest part of *things really useful* to the Life of Man . . . *are* generally things *of short duration* . . . ; Gold, Silver, and Diamonds, are things, that Fancy or Agreement has put the Value on, more than real Use and the necessary Support of Life" (section 46). Money, the eventual systematic expression of these agreeable metals and stones, initiates a mode of ownership that is no longer tethered by immediate utility. It extends itself indefinitely into the future, introducing hoarding into the socio-economic arena. Locke even goes on to justify this activity of hoarding: "he invaded not the Right of others; he might heap as much of these durable things as he pleased; the *exceeding of the bounds of his* just *Property* not lying in the largeness of his Possession, but the perishing of anything uselessly in it" (section 46).

Functioning as a kind of second order of infinity over and above the infinity of nature's abundance that private property reduces to finitude, money, with its utter durability, appears to transcend the mandate of utility altogether. It introduces its own order of logic into the registers of scarcity, abundance, and utility, leading man "to enlarge his Possessions beyond the use of his Family, and a plentiful supply to its Consumption" (section 48), an impulse that Locke insists is necessary and unavoidable: "Find out something that has the *Use and Value of Money* amongst his Neighbors, you shall see the same Man will begin presently to *enlarge* his *Possessions*" (section 49). Money exceeds the order of value grounded by utility.

Again emphasizing Locke's historical and socio-economic perspective, specifically as a mercantilist here, MacPherson argues that Locke conceives of money, and of the land owned by money, as capital. Hoarding is actually not the properly rational response to money, because it takes money out of the circulation of exchange, money's proper home. Functioning as capital, money is a commodity, but one which acquires its value through exchange, rather than use. Money thereby introduces a different order of value into systems of exchange, allowing the possibility of endless growth (for example, via interest), rather than instrumental use, as its proper 'endpoint.' MacPherson argues that the introduction of money allows Locke to grant moral and rational grounds to the practice of accumulation—i.e., he argues that Locke, finally, "provides a positive moral basis for capitalist society" (1962, 221).[9]

Cultures of phallicized whiteness are grounded in the constitutive and categorical exclusion of useless expenditure. While Locke attempts to maintain the absolute reign of utility by reasserting a different kind of 'use' in the functions of money as capital, the fundamental tension between systems of value based in utility and those grounded in endless expenditure threatens utility's domination. This tension worsens as politics of race, sexual difference, and sexuality compound this nascent politics of class (and, less explicitly, religion) that we find in Locke's texts. While money appears in Locke's texts to be the inevitable outgrowth of utility's preference for future-oriented labor, cultivated land, and private property, it also introduces an order of value that may not be reducible to the final judgment of utility. The introduction of money appears to render utility's closed system rather fragile, a phenomenon and tension that will resurface repeatedly across the following chapters.

The sort of worldview that we find in Locke is thereby one dominated by the twin logics of property and utility. Labor, which man must undertake due to an ontological lack, connects these twin logics: it encloses the world and one's self into units of private property and then, elevated into the form of money, invites reason to overstep utility's boundary and hoard more property than one can use. Labor initiates the twin expressions of the logic of the limit: enclosure and prohibition. We ought not own more than we can use; yet, true to the dynamic of desire grounded in lack, we are drawn toward transgressing the fundamental prohibition of waste proclaimed by nature's law, reason. Labor develops into a system of expression that appears to twist the dynamics of scarcity and abundance beyond the reach of utility, while simultaneously using utility to judge all acts within it: one's labor must be deemed useful if one is to enter into the desired life of propertied abundance, a possibility that will always be scarce in advanced capitalist cultures of phallicized whiteness.

The Emergence of the Individual, the Political Category of Phallicized Whiteness

Locke's normative model for the liberal individual thereby becomes he who is bound by his ability to labor within a concept of the future sufficient to stake out a piece of land as property. While Cynthia Willett gives Locke credit for trying to articulate a middle-class resistance to "the leisure class and its idle games," she nonetheless argues that Locke remains entrapped by a conception of rationality "in terms of the English middle-class appreciation for the market value of productive labor and property" (2001, 71). Not only are his concepts of rationality shaped by these historical preferences, but his concepts of man's condition—man's desire, destiny, labor, and individuality—all carry these historical preferences into universalized discourses that continue to serve as the bedrock of many of our cultural assumptions and practices. Although Locke's politics were moderately progressive for the late seventeenth century, the lasting damage of these concepts still haunts our political quandaries and the very frameworks through which we continue to seek redress.

The logic of limit as enclosure, as the ways that the state of society becomes demarcated from—and always preferred over, even while romanticizing—the state of nature, continuously rewrites itself in several registers across the political histories of the U.S. It fundamentally grounds our understanding of the individual as the person who is clearly demarcated from nature. The individual becomes that 'civilized' man who takes his natural origin, as an enclosed body that is a product of God's labor, and produces private property that is enclosed into durable forms which persist into and even control the future. From this critical enclosure of the world and the self, written in the register of property, other modern epistemologies and political projects easily attach themselves to this clear and distinct unit, the individual. (Adam Smith, for example, quickly comes to mind.) The individual, carved out of nature through productive labor and conceiving the world and himself on the model of appropriating private property, emerges as the cornerstone of political theories and practices in cultures of phallicized whiteness.

▼ ▼ ▼

The individual thereby comes to function as an ahistorical unit defined by its productive labor's distancing relation to the state of nature, not by any historico-political forces. (With his unhistorical thinking, Locke acts perfectly as a liberal individual.) Classical liberalism writes the individual as the (allegedly) neutral substratum of all political decisions, positioning it as separable from historico-political forces. In carving the individual out of both the natural and socio-historico-political landscapes, modern political and epistemological projects turn around Locke's fundamental metaphors of enclosure. The individual, that seat of political and personal subjectivity, is *enclosed* and thus cut off from all other forces circulating in the social environment. The individual effectively functions as a piece of private property, with the strange twist of owning itself, impervious to all intruders and protected by the inherent right of ownership, derived from the ontological right to one's own enclosed body.

History then is reduced to a collection of what Kelly Oliver has aptly called "discrete facts that can be known or not known, written in history books, and [that] are discontinuous with the present" (2001, 130). History is that collection of events that occurred in the past and is now tightly sealed in that past. History is simply what has happened, with no fundamental effect or influence upon what is happening now or might happen in the future. Historicity is unthought and unthinkable here. The modern rational self—the liberal individual—exists in a temporally and historically sealed vacuum, made possible by the clear disjunction between past, present, and future. Cartesian concepts of time as discrete moments that do not enter into contact or affect one another dominate this conception of the individual.[10]

The logic of the limit thereby demarcates the past sharply and neatly from the present, turning each into objects about which we can develop concepts, facts, and truths. The future, that temporal horizon initiated by preferred forms of complex labor, becomes the sole focus of intention and desire. But the future never arrives. Therefore, if historicity and 'the historical' mean reading present ideas, values, or concepts as undergoing a constant shaping and reshaping by material forces, this divorce of the past from the present effectively renders all temporal zones—past, present, future, and all permutations—ahistorical. Existence itself is radically dehistoricized. And the individual, that bastion of political activity and value, accordingly resides in a historical vacuum, untouched by historical forces—the very realm of whiteness.

This ahistorical view of history perpetuates the modern project of classical liberalism and its damages, creating a particular kind of individual. The individual becomes the locus of identity, selfhood, and subjectivity in the modern political project. Demarcated from historical existence, it also requires careful delineation from other bodies, whether persons, institutions, history, or social attitudes. This concept of the individual develops with a pronounced insistence on its neutrality, rendering specific attributes of the individual merely particular qualities that function, again, on the model of private property: characteristics such as race, gender, religion, or nationality remain at a distance from this insistently neutral individual. (I use the pronoun "it" to emphasize the function of this alleged neutrality, a dynamic that is central to the valorization of the white propertied Christian male as the subject of power in phallicized whiteness.) This insular existence, underscored by its ahistorical status, is further ensured by claims of radical autonomy, whereby the individual is the source, site, and endpoint of all actions, desires, thoughts, and behaviors: we choose what we do. And we choose it, of course, because we are rational: Kantian ethics become the proper bookend to Locke's initiating of "high modernity's"[11] schemas.

This demarcation of the individual then carves the critical division between internal and external, and its political-psychic counterpart, that between self and Other. The self is located squarely and exclusively in one's rational faculties, the natural law that, according to Locke, civilizes us into economies of labor, utility, and a strange mix of scarcity and abundance. The modern rational self is radically self-contained—enclosed. It is a sovereign self, unaffected by and independent from any thing or force external to it, whether materiality or the Other. Assuming it exercises rationality appropriately, this self is radically autonomous, choosing its own place in the world. (Pointing to America, Locke insists that civilized men are free to leave society.) It does not heed any call of the Other. It is effectively autogenous, existing in a pre-Hegelian philosophical world.[12]

Utility and its epistemological counterpart, instrumentality, subsequently become the operative conceptions of power in this schema of the liberal individual as the self. Autonomous, autogenous, and ahistorical, the modern rational individual is in full control of its self. Its power is thereby something that it owns and wields, as it chooses. Power is not some force that might shape the individual without its assent or, at a minimum, its acknowledgment. It is something that an individual, even if in the form of an individual state, wields intentionally. It can still use this power legitimately or illegitimately, but that is a matter of choice. The individual controls power and the ways that it affects the world: this is its expression of freedom. Accordingly, the role of the law becomes to vigilantly protect this ahistorical unit, the individual, from the discriminations and violences of historical vicissitudes. The role of the law is to protect the individual's power, the seat of its freedom. We are far from Foucaultian ideas that perhaps power and history constitute the ways we view and experience the world, shaping our categories and embedding us in this very notion of the individual as autonomous, autogenous, and ahistorical. The liberal individual, untouched by material, political, and historical conditions, is a neutral substratum that freely wields its power as it chooses: this is the liberal sovereignty and mastery of freedom.

Because the individual is this neutral substratum, differences may or may not attach themselves to it. But those differences are cast into that inconsequential space of material conditions along with history and the Other. The odd twist of self-ownership surfaces more fully here. Following Locke's metaphors of enclosure, the individual is enclosed and sealed off not only from all historical and social forces in the environment, but also from the very attributes of difference within itself. While specific attributes that constitute "difference" in North American culture continuously shift, with new categories emerging and old ones receding, the particular vector of difference that matters depends on our historical location, and all its complexities.[13] Consequently, these attributes do not fundamentally affect the neutrality of the modern individual. These differences occur at the level of the body and history, realms of existence that do not touch the self-contained individual. The neutral individual relates to these differences through the models of enclosure and ownership. It experiences these discrete parts of itself (e.g., race, gender, religion, nationality) as one owns a variety of objects in economies of (scarce) private property: one chooses when one wishes to purchase, own, display, or wear such objects as one freely desires. The unnerving influence of power surfaces, however, as we realize that this free choice becomes the exclusive power of the subject position valorized in cultures of phallicized whiteness, the white propertied Christian (straight) male[14] who determines when, how, and which differences matter.

Neutrality thus functions as the conceptual glue of the modern political project of classical liberalism. It allows the model of ownership to take hold as the dominant conception of selfhood: one's true self resides in a neutral space and from that space one owns one's power, one's freedom, and one's attributes. Just as the capitalist fantasy still convinces us today that we choose and control our private property, the neutral individual also resides in a self-enclosed, self-contained space that hovers above these matters. Just as the kind of car an American drives today supposedly does not affect the kind of person that he or she is, so too the rational and therefore neutral individual resides in a space that transcends material conditions and their entrapments. Differences between individuals, whether of race or religion or gender or nationality or sexuality, become a mere matter of ownership—i.e., what one has and has not chosen to own. And as the inherent rights of private property imply, one consequently has the right to protect or dispense with one's property: the individual is free to choose how to wield its power and how to respond to these (inconsequential) differences. Not to have this ability—i.e., not to be able to choose and control when and how one's gender, race, nationality, sexuality, or religion matters—signifies a lack of individualism, a lack of power, a lack of civility.[15]

The individual thus becomes the proprietor of its differences and the various, discrete rights obtaining to them. The logic of enclosure and de-marcation, expressing the logic of the limit here, grounds the conceptions of difference itself in these schemas of classical liberalism. One owns—en-closes—one's differences and, additionally, the differences themselves are dis-crete—demarcated—from one another. The language of rights derives from the overarching model of ownership, just as we find it developed out of the fundamental right to one's own enclosed body in Locke's text. The modern project of liberal individualism thereby reads difference as that which is, can be, or ought to be demarcated, delimited, enclosed—and owned.

When I turn to contemporary debates around affirmative action below, I will return to several dynamics that have emerged here. First of all, the liberal individual exists as a neutral substratum to which differences, caused by history and materiality (the body), attach themselves. Equality conse-quently resides in that neutral substratum of the individual and we access it only by stripping away the merely historical attributes of difference: equality and neutrality mutually constitute one another. Consequently, those who cannot abstract from merely historical attributes of difference (e.g., race and gender) will be read as unequal to those for whom these historical differences do not matter.[16] Secondly, freedom is understood as the expression of power, over which one has conscious and rational control. Power, framed as a tool that one wields, is derived from the model of instrumental reason. And, finally, the liberal individual experiences differences such as race, gender, religion, and nationality as attributes that it owns. It consequently exercises rights over them such as those derived from the inherent right of ownership that Locke locates in the natural imperative to labor: the language of rights assumes, thrives in, and thereby perpetuates an economy of scarcity, the economy in which debates around affirmative action are firmly entrenched.

Each of these colludes to give phallicized whiteness the necessary tools to maintain the white propertied Christian (straight) male as the valorized subject in power. Functioning through the rhetoric of neutrality, this specific subject disavows its historical and material conditioning and thereby gains the power to determine when, how, and which differences matter. Grounded in the fundamental value of neutrality, difference should not matter; hence, for example, contemporary rhetorics of color-blindness dominate discourses about the desired endpoint of a 'just'—and therefore raceless—society.[17] However, in those circumstances in which difference insists on its existence (i.e., circumstances in which 'minorities' or the disenfranchised insist on their rights, voices, and even votes), the decisions about when, how, and which differences matter will remain in the power of the neutral individual, the subject in power—and the one who is free.

Dividing and Conquering Racial and Sexual Difference

Across the Atlantic and roughly two centuries after Locke's writing of his *Second Treatise,* the post-bellum United States entered into some of the nastiest parts of U.S. history. The operative nexus of racial and sexual difference surfaced with great clarity: black men were lynched on false allegations of raping white women. These allegations, rarely if ever pursued, sufficed as ample cause for castration, dismemberment, burning at the stake, hanging. This horrific violence set the scene for two dynamics to emerge explicitly and continue with great force into the early twenty-first-century United States psyche: the sexualizing of racial difference and the racializing of sexual difference.[18] The propertied Christian white male (straight) body[19] alone remained unmarked, positioned not only as the politically and economically superior subject, but also as the rational, benevolent patriarch in whose hands the security of all bodies rested. Women and non-white men were accordingly positioned below him, most often pitted against one another through the fear of alleged aggression and manipulation, as a great deal of twentieth-century African American literature shows all too graphically.[20]

The brutal and ugly underbelly of modernity thus surfaced. A period that emerged philosophically as the triumph of rationality and politically as the victory of representative democracy and its liberal individual, modernity was also the period of the birth of global capitalism and its counterparts of colonialism and slavery.[21] Many of the modern categories that we see at work in Locke's texts emerged in the post-bellum United States with a defensive tenacity that bred political, cultural, psychic, and physical violence. For example, as political categories such as freedom and individualism began to be broadened through the emancipation of slaves, other structures of modernity asserted themselves to shape the exact contours and limits of the *kinds* of emergent freedoms and rights that would develop. Namely, as the battles around the Fifteenth Amendment and suffragist movements showed, racial and sexual difference emerged as primary fields of signification through which entry to the precious categories of freedom and individual rights had to be negotiated. The categories of race and gender were being forged in the explicit terms of legal and political documents.

If one was raced or sexed, one had to fight—against other marked (raced, sexed) bodies—for one's entry into these categories. But the fight turned on evidence of a specific form of rationality. Or, to put it in the language of race and sexual difference, it turned on one's ability to approximate maleness *or* whiteness, the two social categories that govern the epistemological category of 'proper rationality' and, dialectically, the social category of property ownership. The disjunction of approximating either maleness or whiteness ensured that no set of marked bodies would achieve 'true' freedom or individuality: only the white male occupied both positions of power, maleness and whiteness.[22] The seduction of freedom thereby became the seduction of phallicized whiteness. Consequently, raced and sexed bodies found themselves fighting against one another in a battle that neither of them could ultimately win: the terms were set by an external 'overseer.'

This historical scene almost perfectly enacts the logic of power that both Nietzsche and Foucault diagnose so clearly: as the structures of modernity began to be contested philosophically (by Hegel and post-Hegelians, particularly Marx) and politically (by Emancipation), the less codified social and political structures emerged with greater clarity and rigidity to control the kinds of political subjectivities that could emerge.[23] As freedom and individual rights, which had been acclaimed as universal, began to be exposed as materially narrow and politically construed concepts applicable only to a small section of society, the broader and more vaguely articulated structures of racism and sexism began their slow processes of codification. And the singular standard for the legibility of that emergent political subjectivity of individual freedom remained the same: a propertied Christian white (straight) man, the singular subject position that inhabits both maleness and whiteness—and proper rationality.

Broad cultural structures of race and sexual difference thus surface as a complicated nexus of power relations in post-bellum practices such as mis-cegenation, the one-drop rule, and lynching. In these practices, the inter-sections of race and sex produce a confusing conflation of values that serve as smoke screens to obfuscate the protected, unmarked subject position of the white man. Values such as purity, virginity, and passivity are written on the female body as inherent qualities. In what should appear as an obvious contraposition, values such as bestiality, aggression, and uncivilized nature are written on the black body. The black female body, left in the wreckage of embodying these contradictory 'natural' traits, becomes a general aberra-tion that is treated with confusion and fear. And the white male body emerges as the unmarked, normative mode of subjectivity. Or, to put this in the terms above, the white male body solidifies his position as the modern man—the rational, transcendental man in control of both nature and history. The mode of rationality that defines high modernity—namely, as instru-mental, transcendental, and detached from history—expresses itself directly in the mode of subjectivity inhabited by white propertied Christian (straight) men in the post-bellum United States. It is what enables and ensures their power over nature and the social field of relations, and their subsequent freedom.

The Logic of the Unlimited Body

How does the white male propertied Christian (straight) body circulate as this unmarked, unseen, and thus powerful body? How does it inhabit this mode of rationality and emerge as an unlimited body?

First of all, I want to emphasize that this demarcation of social differ-ences occurs at the level of the body. Despite high modernity's disavowal of embodiment, the body continues to be the site of racial, sexual, and even class, religious, and nationalist differentiation. Embodiment itself is not deemed a philosophical category in high modernity, despite Locke's empir-icist epistemology.[24] The singular function and significance of embodiment is its role as the negative counterpart, and thus appropriate limit, to rationality. To discuss embodiment in and of itself, without deriving it through this binary logic, is not only impossible but unthinkable, as is evident in the ongoing post-Hegelian attempts to do so in European philosophy. Embodiment is a fundamental and constitutive blind spot, a disavowal that enacts the logic of the limit by assuming rationality's ability to delimit the intelligible from the sensible. It subsequently renders much of modernity's epistemological and political projects possible: transcendental truth, objectivity, universal freedom, individualism, and the language of rights are all conditioned by a disavowal of the body.

But this disavowal of embodiment also fundamentally structures phallicized whiteness—the nexus of categories, structures, and values at work in the subjectivity of white male propertied (straight) Christianity. The disavowal of embodiment grants phallicized whiteness the power to perpetrate racial and sexual violence in western cultures. One owns one's body, and this mode of relating to it as private property allows one to dispense with it, to disavow its meaningful existence in one's life or the world. How do embodiment and its disavowal lie at the heart of philosophical high modernity and its concept of freedom, the subjectivity of phallicized whiteness, and the political power of each of these? And how are these enactments of the logic of the limit?

▼ ▼ ▼

The differences that we find carved into female and non-white bodies in the post-bellum era of the U.S. effectively distinguish discrete kinds of bodies. Female, black, brown, non-Christian, yellow, poor bodies are delimited on the basis of their bodily appearances. They are trapped in and by their bodies: they do not exercise proper authority of ownership over them. Someone or some other force owns these bodies. This entrapment by their bodily characteristics imposes brutal limitations upon their freedom and their individuality: they are not free to do as they please and, perhaps more damningly, they are read as *kinds* of bodies, not as individuals. The logic of the limit functions in at least two ways here: it carves discrete differences into specific bodies, delimiting them as different from others (e.g., raced bodies are discrete and different from sexed bodies); and it simultaneously delimits the freedom and individuality accorded to those different bodies.

To the contrary, the white male Christian propertied (straight) body appears wholly unaffected. He is neither reduced to his bodily characteristics, nor limited in his freedom or individuality. He owns his body, properly controlling its power in the social world. The white male Christian propertied (straight) body speaks, acts, and desires not on behalf of his sex, race, class, or religion (or sexuality), but exclusively on behalf of himself—the autonomous individual. He is not bound to or limited by the *kind* of body he inhabits, if he properly inhabits or is affected by materiality at all. How does this work? How does phallicized whiteness inhabit the body in such a way as to ensure that it transcends the body and becomes a 'subject,' while non-white bodies are fully reducible to the body and thus objects or abjected others? How does phallicized whiteness's deployment of cultural and discursive practices ensure a continued fascination with the body of *others,* while simultaneously marking out the space of 'the disembodied' or transcendent as the space of power? How are embodiment and disembodiment functioning in these philosophical and socio-political deployments of phallicized whiteness?

In his provocative book *White,* Richard Dyer argues that whiteness in the modern world gains its hegemonic power through its disembodiment. Following the pattern of privileged subject positions (masculinity, the middle class, heterosexuality, Protestant Christianity in the contemporary U.S.), whiteness functions largely through its invisibility, through its disavowal of race itself: one is not white in the U.S., one is just a person. Whiteness poses as the universal and naturalized 'order of things.' Whiteness is not a color or a race; it is just human. It just *is,* as the history of western metaphysics easily shows. In mutually grounding gestures, it renders itself both invisible and ubiquitous. These dynamics then sediment one another: the more transparent and invisible whiteness becomes, the more normalized and omnipresent it becomes, and so on. But at the core of this disavowal of race, whiteness operates as the universal, unmarked signifier through its disavowal of embodiment itself. Echoing Lacan's phallus, whiteness functions through its remaining veiled. And a primary site of this veiling is its ontological denial of embodiment itself.

Dyer develops this dynamic in the specific register of representation. Bringing the role of religion, as a signifying field on which 'whiteness' is constituted, more explicitly into play, Dyer turns to the white ideal of (straight) masculinity, the figure of Christ. As the savior of a religion fraught with somatophobia, Christ represents that incomprehensible fusion of the divine and the human—or the spirit and the body. As Dyer develops it, the principle of incarnation, which sets Christianity apart from other monotheistic religions, is to be *in* the body but not *of* it—to suffer the temptations of the flesh but always to transcend them into the purified realms of spirit.

47

Christ *appears* in the world as a body, but ultimately stands in a realm that transcends it. To put it in the language of Protestant capitalism which it eventually grounds, Christ properly owns his body.

This tension, a Lacanian splitting, is what distinguishes whiteness and maleness from their counterparts of "non-whiteness" and "non-maleness," the signifiers of racial and sexual difference in our binary symbolic. Rather than fastening on more "feminine" traits of Christ or his teachings (for example, his doctrines of peace or championing of the meek and humble; his washing the feet of the lowly and fallen), white male propertied heterosexuality in U.S. culture has idealized the specific trait of Christ's transcendent relation to corporeality. With this transcendence as their structuring, regulative ideal, whiteness and maleness can come together in white male heterosexuality to engage this struggle between spirit and body with the assurance of ultimately transcending the body and winning the struggle. In his idealized form, the white propertied male is in the body, but is not ultimately captured or constrained by it (and hence is never at fault or slandered for submitting to it).[25] He stands in a place that transcends the messiness of materiality.

Effectively disembodied, the white male propertied (straight)—and, as we now see yet more explicitly, Christian—body is unlimited by any bodily characteristic, rendering his freedom and individuality limitless. Moreover, because this subjectivity is one unencumbered by material differences, it inhabits the most treasured subject position of classical liberalism, neutrality. The logic of the limit again operates doubly here: as the delimitation of difference that is written as discrete differences into non-white, non-male, non-propertied, non-Christian (and non-straight) bodies; and as the very possibility of delimiting the material realm from that of neutral, universal, rational subjectivity. Not tethered to a body, the white male propertied Christian (straight) body cannot be delimited: it is a free and autonomous individual, neutralized from and unencumbered by all material effects of power or history.

The liberal individual and the subject position of phallicized whiteness stand in the same neutral space—transcending material effects of power or history, irreducible to the limits of the body. The limits that George W. Bush thinks freedom ought to have, as the bumper sticker proclaims, pertain only to specific kinds of bodies.

The Limits of (Talking about) Affirmative Action

In two cases that came before the U.S. Supreme Court in April 2003 involving affirmative action in the admissions policies of the University of Michigan, attorney Kirk Kolbo grounds the plaintiff's arguments in one basic category: "individuals with the right of equal protection" (*Grutter v. Bollinger* 2003). He embellishes on this category throughout both cases, referring to it as a constitutional right, "promise" (*Grutter*, 3), and "command" (*Grutter*, 4) that protects "innocent people" (*Gratz v. Bollinger* 2003, 19) from discrimination. From this point of departure, Kolbo locates the debate in these cases as one between individual and group rights, a frame that conservative critics of affirmative action seem to have sedimented, perhaps through the authority of sheer repetition, as one that must be addressed: neither of the respondents in the two cases veers from this framework in their defenses of the University of Michigan's admissions policies.[26]

This shared frame of the individual and his or her rights to equality may emerge, though not explicitly, from a fundamental agreement among all represented in the testimonies before the Supreme Court in these two cases. While it is not clear that both sides, or the Justices, agree with the individual vs. group rights frame, no one in these proceedings contests the desired endpoint of democracy in the United States—namely, that day when "race will be a totally irrelevant factor in all decisions" (*Grutter*, 50). This value and uncontested mark of progress is held up as "the day that we all look forward to" (*Gratz*, 50), celebrated at various points by each voice in the two cases. And because this is the shared, formative assumption, much of the disagreement between the two sides subsequently focuses on whether race-neutral or race-conscious means are the best way to achieve this end of a raceless, *neutral* society.

I want to ask a few questions about the categories at work in these recent cases and in affirmative action policies and debates more broadly. The operative categories of these laws and policies exemplify both the classical liberal model of politics and politics in cultures of phallicized whiteness. I thereby offer this example of affirmative action as a way of synthesizing these two schemas, showing how the politics of classical liberalism necessarily breeds a culture of phallicized whiteness. This means that the culture of the contemporary U.S., grounded historically, politically, epistemologically, economically, and psychologically in classical liberalism, protects the dominant subject position of phallicized whiteness, Christian propertied white straight men (and varying permutations and emphases of these attributes). The two systems of classical liberalism and phallicized whiteness share the same fundamental conceptual schema, the neutral individual. And this fundamental concept also grounds the debates around affirmative action. Therefore, the further we enmesh ourselves in the terms and dynamics of debates around affirmative action, the further we will perpetuate the protection of the subject position of phallicized whiteness. In other words, affirmative action will never rid the U.S. of racism, or of any other system of oppression that works itself out in cultures of phallicized whiteness.

▼ ▼ ▼

The issue of affirmative action nonetheless continues to be one of the most contentious and complicated of contemporary political debates in the U.S. I do not pretend to have sufficiently plumbed the depths of that debate, particularly in its legal specificities and historical nuances, to offer a specialist's view here. Rather, again in the spirit of Bataille, a more general accounting of its operative categories may expose some of its constitutive blind spots, while also indicating routes out of and beyond those pitfalls. It may help us to dislodge ourselves not only from these debates, but more importantly from the violences they are now inflicting upon our social fabric.

Despite what our arrogant late-twentieth-century minds might like to tell us, affirmative action is not a new idea or phenomenon. The first Civil Rights Act in the U.S. emerges, unsurprisingly, in 1866. Following the Thirteenth Amendment, which prohibits slavery and, by implication, confers unspecified civil rights on freed slaves, the Civil Rights Act "declares all persons born or naturalized in the U.S., excluding Indians not taxed, to be citizens; [and] guarantees individual citizens the right to purchase, lease, sell, hold, and convey real and personal property, and to make and enforce contracts" (Belz 1991, 309). It does not prohibit private discrimination. Nor does it mention any social category other than those associated with the ownership of private property, that civilizing concept which ushers in Locke's state of society. It is not until Roosevelt's 1941 Executive Order 8802 that social categories are specified as in need of protection—namely, "race, creed, color or national origin" (Belz 1991, 310). But it is worth noting that this order, along with the onslaught of executive orders and laws in the latter half of the twentieth century, is modeled on the National Labor Relations Act of 1935, which prohibits employment discrimination against union members. The social category whose name we dare not speak now, class, seems to precede and shape our understandings of other categories of difference that are codified.[27]

The contemporary terms that have dominated public debates around affirmative action—and, one could argue, around race and gender—were set clearly in Kennedy's Executive Order 10925. Written in March 1961, just after Kennedy took office, this text gave us the actual terms that have since become so loaded and fraught with controversy. (The terms only appear once in the 4,500-word decree.) Also establishing the President's Commission on Equal Employment Opportunity, the order addresses the obligations of contractors working with the government: "The contractor will take affirmative action to ensure that applicants are employed, and employees are treated during their employment, *without regard* to their race, creed, color, or national origin" (Mills 1994, 5, my emphasis). This is the first utterance of those two words "affirmative action." I am, however, more interested in the two words I italicized above, "without regard."

In the careful phrasing of this order and of Title VII of the Civil Rights Act that follows in 1964 (in which the category of sex is added to the list), we see politicians attempting to walk the line between protection from discrimination and preferential treatment, the fine line that has only become more confusing as the contentious voices around it have grown louder and louder in the post-Reagan U.S. With an eye to Southern politicians in this civil rights era, who later stage a record eighty-two-day filibuster against the Civil Rights Act, Kennedy takes refuge in the much hallowed and protected concept of classical liberalism, the individual.[28]

The concept of the individual should function as a bulwark against the inappropriate uses of these various categories of difference, which are attached to it in (merely) historical ways. The judgment of how the individual is functioning as an individual—i.e., as a neutral individual untainted by differences such as race, religion, sex, or national origin—should serve as the baseline against which to determine whether discrimination or preference is being enacted. The terms of the laws, policies, and heated social debates were set: the function of the law is to protect the neutral individual from political, historical, and material conditions that might infringe upon its inherent right to express itself, its power, its freedom. The constituent concepts of classical liberalism find their full-blown expression here. And by the time Reagan is elected in 1979 with his promises to halt affirmative action, his language comes as little surprise: "We must not allow the noble concept of equal opportunity to be distorted into federal guidelines or quotas which require race, ethnicity, or sex—rather than ability and qualifications—to be the principal factor in hiring or education" (Mills 1994, 17). The neutral individual and its native abilities and qualifications must be protected.

The model of ownership regarding difference thereby dominates our political imaginations. While the specificities of the various categories and their historical emergences and recessions is worth noting (e.g., sex is a late addition; race and color, as well as religion and creed, are separated; ethnic origin seems to replace national origin; most of all, class is never mentioned, despite its originary role in both Locke's thinking and the 1935 National Labor Relations Act), the dominant category at work in this system is the same category that grounds classical liberalism and phallicized whiteness: the neutral individual stands as the alpha and omega of all deliberations. All other differences, whether of religion, race, sex, or some other attribute, are reduced to hindrances of the individual's right to cultivate its native talents. The law must protect and ensure equal opportunity, another focal category of affirmative action debates, so that each individual—as an individual—will have this right to develop. And this will only occur if the neutrality that is necessary to the balance of equality is obtained and ensured.

This understanding of the law as the vehicle to ensure and protect the neutrality of the individual seems to function on all sides (well, both sides, in the binary U.S.) of the political spectrum. Whether one supports or criticizes affirmative action, the endpoint is never questioned—namely, the creation of a society that views individuals as individuals. No one questions the desirability, much less the ontological possibility, of a color-blind or gender-blind society (or a religion-blind or national origin–blind one, although these are almost unthinkable and increasingly unspeakable in 2003).[29] But perhaps this is because the rhetoric of blindness and the desirability of neutrality is endemic to cultures of phallicized whiteness, circulating as an unspoken assumption about human nature and the state of society, and functioning as a critical tool of power to ensure the dominance of phallicized whiteness's subject position. Phallicized whiteness functions through erasing itself. Its power derives from its invisibility. And this power grants it the right to determine which, when, and how differences matter. Neutrality is one of phallicized whiteness's most effective tools.

To obtain this desired neutrality requires the assumptions about history and power that we have already encountered in the constitution of the liberal individual. It requires that one exclude history, through a willful act of power, from one's deliberations. In this Aristotelian reading of the individual as the neutral substratum to which differences attach themselves, differences are understood as historical accidents. They are ontologically connected to the problem of materiality and emerge as burdens upon one's 'natural' neutrality due to history's failings. The history of racism in the U.S., for example, demands or demanded (depending on one's politics) that we pay attention to race in the late twentieth century so that we could arrive at a time when we would not have to pay attention to it. (Note the ring of utopia, and its ahistorical space, in these longings for "the day that we all look forward to" [*Gratz,* 50].) Whether we think we have paid too much, too little, or just enough attention to race depends, among other things, on whether we view history as a discrete collection of facts written in obscure and boring books or as constitutive forces that shape our everyday lives, thoughts, and identities.

The shifts in decisions about affirmative action handed down by the Supreme Court can be mapped along such lines of shifting views of history. The law was once approached as something that should remedy past discrimination in its broadest forms; its approved scope has narrowed to carefully identified instances of discrimination, as the parameters of affirmative action have been getting smaller and smaller since the passage of Title VII of the 1964 Civil Rights Act. The 1987 decision in *Johnson v. Transportation Agency, Santa Clara,* for example, declares that racial and gender preferences are justified in order "to overcome underrepresentation rather than as a remedy for past discrimination" (Belz 1991, 312). The move toward a focus on underrepresentation, which is gauged on the basis of the contemporary demography of the local population, narrows the view of history at work in the scope of the law. This decision marks a shift that has resulted in a telescoping of the law toward that desired ahistorical space of neutrality.[30]

In the 2003 rulings of the Supreme Court on the two cases regarding admission to the University of Michigan, various appeals to historical scope shape the majority opinions. While it rejected the undergraduate admissions system contested in *Gratz v. Bollinger,* the court upheld the practices of the law school primarily because it found these practices to operate within an acceptable historical scope. The court found that the law school's admission practices were tailored narrowly enough to ensure that each applicant was treated as an individual, rather than as a representative of his or her race. Put in terms of historical scope, the admission practices are legally acceptable for two fundamental reasons: (1) they treat race as one of many characteristics that distinguish individuals, rather than as a historical system of inequality that the law must correct; in turn, this maintains the sanctity of the category of the individual as an ahistorical space; (2) when addressing historical conditions, the admission practices direct themselves to the immediate future; e.g., the Court cites the need for diversity in globalized marketplaces and explicitly states that this aspect of the university's admissions policies must be limited in time and should no longer exist in twenty-five years. If we read these decisions through the angle of their historical scope, we find a very carefully choreographed dance around the acceptable 'amount' of history that should affect institutional or legal judgments of an individual. We find, in turn, a very careful negotiation of the limits of phallicized whiteness's most precious category, the ahistorical and thereby neutral individual.

We must then ask the difficult and painful question of whether the law, with its own grounding in a neutrality that attempts to attenuate the effects of history, is the appropriate space in which to attempt to remedy the violences of systems of oppression. How can a system that reads history as accidents, which are external to the ontology of subjectivity and therefore must be overcome, function as a judge of when and whether historical violence has been remedied? How can a system that grounds itself in the apolitical, ahistorical, a-material realm of the neutral individual claim to resolve violent differences of power, history, and materiality?

Iris Marion Young argues that advocates of affirmative action must shift the categories of their positions away from the myths of neutrality if they are to address the power differentials (of racism or sexism) that they are aiming to resist. Offering compelling evidence from arenas such as standardized testing in education and systems of judgment in employment settings, Young shows that neutrality is impossible when assessing merit (1990, 200–214). She thereby argues for a retooling of the concept of equality away from its grounding in neutrality. Developing a process of "democratic decisionmaking," Young argues against the myth of objectivity and, implicitly drawing on feminist standpoint theory, argues for the inclusion of many voices in determining standards of judgment. As she urges us away from neutrality and its restricted reading of difference as a burden, she suggests that "equality . . . is sometimes better served by differential treatment" (1990, 195).

Young thereby uncovers the unnecessary and invidious connection between neutrality and equality.[31] In tying equality to neutrality, the framework of classical liberalism requires the erasure of history, power, and differences for the maintenance of freedom and equality. But what if history, power, and differences cannot be erased? What if they are the ontological conditions in which humans exist? Or, even worse, what if the lure of erasing them—or of acting as if they can be erased—is a fundamental tool of phallicized whiteness, one that will always perpetuate its domination?

In trying to divorce our conceptions of equality from neutrality, I suggest that we historicize the categories themselves. Rather than assuming that equality can only be achieved in ahistorical vacuums where differences are eliminated and power neutralized, perhaps we should approach the concept of equality as one that has developed through historical struggles of power. As a modern category, the radical notion of the equality of all humans allegedly emerged as a tool in the struggle against monarchies and aristocracies (or so the narrative of liberalism tells us). This was not a neutral or ahistorical vacuum. Nor was it an economic vacuum. Rather, this concept of equality emerged in the seventeenth century as a political and economic appeal to a natural ontology that social conditions were not upholding: equality was politically conceived as a natural category.

Despite the telescoping toward smaller and smaller purviews of history in affirmative action rulings by the Supreme Court, we can trace the effects of historical change in these contemporary debates. True to its seventeenth-century roots, the shifts in how we conceptualize equality seem to occur primarily along economic lines. Namely, whether we understand equality as a natural given that must be protected by the law or as a natural right that the law ought to achieve shifts and changes as the economic climate of the country shifts and changes. Contention over affirmative action emerges most acutely in weaker economies. As Nicolaus Mills argues, "An improved economy is the most obvious answer. So long as jobs are scarce, so long as there are limited scholarships and limited places for the college students who need them, affirmative action will remain a battleground" (1994, 32–33). And William Julius Wilson agrees that debates about affirmative action, and about race and racism more generally, will never be solved if they continue to be played out "as a zero-sum game in which one side's gain is the other side's loss" (Mills 1994, 33).

But the zero-sum game appears to be the only playing ground of advanced capitalist cultures of phallicized whiteness. Locke shows how economics of scarcity are endemic to human economic exchange. This scarcity is then codified in the structures of capitalism. It is not surprising, then, that debates about affirmative action continually shift as the arena in which this scarcity plays itself out also shifts. As Iris Marion Young again shows, arguments about merit occur where the scarcity is most explicit—i.e., in the highest-level jobs and their professional educational systems: law schools, medical schools, military academies. True to the twisted dynamics of scarcity and abundance, access to jobs that will yield economically abundant lives will always be scarce in capitalist cultures. And contention over admission to such abundance—i.e., debate that is cast in the terms of the social meaning and existence of equality—will consequently remain heated.

If we cast this dynamic, in which scarcity determines the site of contention over the existence of equality, in the terms and dynamics of phallicized whiteness, we begin to see how the focus of affirmative action debates increasingly becomes the protection of that ideal of whiteness—namely, disembodiment—and the social ontology that constitutes it. To put it more crassly, the site of contention in affirmative action policies and laws has shifted from 'body-work' toward 'head-work'—i.e., from union contracts to admission to the most elite universities, law schools, medical schools, and military academies. For cultures of phallicized whiteness, it is not only that these positions, clearly the positions of power in U.S. culture, are to be reserved and protected for white Protestant straight males, but that there is a kind of ontological perversion in the very idea of anyone else doing this kind of work.

Recall that, for Locke, the state of nature develops into two kinds of rational beings in its post-monetary stage: the lesser rationality of industrious and useful appropriation via one's labor and the full rationality of unlimited accumulation via the capital of money and land. The latter of these, the fully rational capitalist, grounds Locke's concept of the individual. Accordingly, it is equality amongst these individuals that the law must protect. When affirmative action policies begin to facilitate the entrance of humans with 'lesser rationality' into realms of culture designated only for those with 'full rationality,' the very ontology of phallicized whiteness becomes threatened: the disembodied state of the intellect is no longer pure white and, more threatening, the 'body' of culture threatens to disappear. The question 'who will do the nasty work?' is not only a question of sheer economic privilege in advanced capitalism, but one of ontological necessity for the structures of phallicized whiteness: disembodied and transcendent phallicized whiteness cannot perform embodied tasks. It is too "free" to do so.

The concept of equality that we inherit from Locke rests on a classed, raced, and sexed ontology of the world and of different kinds of human rationality. Materially and economically birthed, it is both a modern and a white concept and it functions to protect the values of those social systems. To assume that working toward a neutral space in which differences among humans no longer matter will alter this concept of equality is to fail to grasp how these cultures of modernity, capitalism, and whiteness wield the illusion of neutrality, while relying on a social ontology of difference. Until the laws of the U.S. shed these fundamental presuppositions of individualism and equality as ahistorical concepts, they will not provide effective routes to achieving parity in the distribution of capitalism's scarce access to economies of abundance.

IS THE MIRROR RACIST?

Interrogating the Space of Whiteness

2

That invisibility to which I refer occurs because of a particular disposition of the eyes of those with whom I come in contact. A matter of the construction of their *inner* eyes, those eyes with which they look through their physical eyes upon reality.
—RALPH ELLISON,
Invisible Man

In "Love Thy Neighbor? No, Thanks!" Slavoj Žižek (1998) begins with some general musings on the bad press that psychoanalytic approaches to racism enjoy these days. Arguing against these critiques of "psychological reductionism" and an "abstract-psychologistic approach," Žižek persuades us in his ever-entertaining ways that the psychoanalytic frame is exactly the lens that can diagnose the machinations of racism in northern-western cultures and, by exposing their internal inconsistencies, presumably help us to disrupt them. I agree with Žižek and much of the recent work in the intersections of psychoanalysis and race[1] that the dynamics of psychoanalysis have much to offer to readings of race and racism in contemporary settings of Eurocentric cultures—particularly the dead-end, circular readings of social constructionism.[2] However, I also suggest that these lenses of psychoanalysis have much to tell us about white inhabitants of these cultural symbolics of phallicized whiteness and, more particularly, some of the silent assumptions about space and embodiment which constitute that whiteness. Psychoanalysis may be an appropriate lens for diagnosing our cultural racism exactly because it enacts some of the central dynamics which sediment that racism.

Of course, in carving out a space that I refer to as 'our cultural symbolic,' I am already at odds with most Lacanians' understandings of 'the symbolic.' While I understand that Lacan was attempting to unravel the structures of signification and dynamics of subjectivation that occur within the symbolic, I wish to speak of this symbolic as a historicized and particular phenomenon. Referring to 'our cultural symbolic,' I am referring more specifically to the symbolic that dominates cultures of phallicized whiteness and structures signifiers in a way that gives disproportionate and abusive power to some persons—some bodies—over others. Following out Lacanian dynamics of signification and subjectivation, I am reading 'our cultural symbolic' as a process that signifies some bodies as more powerful, more valuable, and more meaningful than others—namely, those white male straight Christian propertied bodies that we have already encountered in the emergence of the neutral liberal individual.

In reading race through psychoanalysis, therefore, I wish to follow not only Žižek's suggestions, but also those of Frantz Fanon. Fanon reads his place as a black man in a white world fundamentally through psychoanalysis, which he frames as dominating the western psyche, both culturally and individually. As Fanon describes his experiences and those of his fellow colonized Antilleans, he shows how "the racial drama" (1967, 150) that occurs when the black man comes into contact with white culture is due, in part, to a clash of psychic developments. For example, Fanon claims that the black familial constellation cannot be mapped through the Oedipal complex; therefore, when the black man comes into contact with white culture, where authority can be read through the Oedipal drama, a neurosis and conflict over authority occurs in the black psyche.[3] He thus reads psychoanalytic models as both describing and constituting western (Eurocentric) symbolics. And he gains his critical distance from these models, a distance that is vital to his survival and his sanity, through recognizing them as specific to historical and cultural formations.

If we wish to interrupt the logics of racism that are embedded in our cultural symbolic of phallicized whiteness, perhaps we should follow Fanon's insights and begin interrogating that very model of psychic development. That is, if the psychoanalytic model dominates our cultural notions of authority, law, language, and subjectivity, then perhaps an interrogation of some of its logics will expose some of the conceptions and dynamics endemic to

forms of racism in our culture. Specifically, an interrogation of Lacan's accounts of ego-formation may expose some of the latent logics about space
and embodiment that undergird forms of white supremacist racism within
our culture—logics that are reducible to a logic of the limit, written here in
the registers of boundaries and containment.

Interrogating Optics

To begin, I offer a fairly banal observation: we live in a culture obsessed
with and driven by images. The Nike slogan "Image is everything" captivates
our faculties of judgment across the political spectrum. From the religious
right to the queerest left, this cultural fixation with images is constantly read
as indicating some state of grand transition—whether toward further deca-
dence or more excessive and celebratory 'liberation.' But I suggest that these
judgments are, at best, superficial: they operate on the faulty presupposition
that this obsession with images is something new. As we see in Lacan's
accounts of ego-formation as a bodily experience, the field of signifiers that
constitutes our cultural symbolic—and thereby grounds our senses of authority and law—is conjoined with the visual field in a relation that is framed
as ontological. From his insight into this connection, Lacan tells his inter-
locutors in the 1953–54 Seminar, "I cannot urge you too strongly to a meditation on optics" (1988, 76). I wish to follow this suggestion, even if it may
lead us, with irony abounding, into one of Lacan's central blind spots.

I am focusing on Lacan's accounts of ego-formation, primarily in his
short essay on the mirror stage and his 1953–54 Seminar, as exemplary
performances of the ocular-centric sensibilities and dynamics that dominate
our contemporary culture. My focus is on the role of optics and optical
metaphors in these discussions of ego-formation. In both his early account
of the mirror stage and the more complicated, later accounts of 'the inverted
bouquet,' Lacan relies over and over on the dynamics of sight, images, re-
fractions, and reflections to give him the tools to decipher processes of ego-
formation and interplays between the imaginary and the symbolic. An ontology of the visual seems to ground his conceptions of ego-formation.

While this ontology affords him provocative insights into the conjoining
of sight and hearing, especially of speech (two senses and realms that, in
appearing ontologically separate, have caused much despair and bewilder-
ment in the western tradition, particularly in the twentieth century), it may
also betray the fact that his accounts are historically and culturally specific,
springing from an ocular-centric and scopophilic culture—i.e., from a culture

already structured by an obsession with images.[4] And, while this offers great explanatory and therapeutic power to that culture, it can simultaneously enact a violence against bodies both within and outside that culture. If images and the beholding of images—the styles, perspectives, rhythms, desires of beholding images—constitute one of the fundamental poles structuring the interplays between the imaginary and the symbolic, then one's significance within that cultural symbolic will likely be shaped and informed by the way one *looks*—both how one appears and how one beholds others' appearances. This grounding in the visual field thus issues into specific conceptions of space and embodiment—conceptions that may have more than coincidental resonance with dominant forms of racism in cultures of phallicized whiteness, where political values are enacted on the basis of *how bodies look*.[5]

▼ ▼ ▼

Through this lens of optics, I explore three aspects—one epistemological, one semiotic, and one psycho-ontological—of Lacan's accounts of ego-formation and their connections to race, particularly in their conceptions of space and embodiment, in a phallic, white supremacist symbolic.

Epistemologically, Lacan's account of ego-formation is a historically and culturally specific account that, in claiming itself universal, enacts its own whiteness (and maleness and heterosexuality, as feminists have shown). Echoing Hortense Spillers's argument that this "universal sound" (1996, 87) of psychoanalysis is connected to its disavowal of race and racism, I suggest that Lacan's accounts, despite their radical edges, continue to circulate within traditional forms of western subjectivity—forms that hinge on implicit claims to universality.[6] While much excellent work has been done to argue that psychoanalysis is not ahistorical, Lacan's discourse nonetheless implies, in an appropriately Hegelian trace, a universal structure—even if it is within the dynamic of historical or developmental change.[7] There may be historicity and change in Lacan's discourse, but it always follows and claims a universal structure. Working within this traditional landscape of universality, Lacan's accounts have drawn on and assumed a certain amount of ideological power that makes their explanatory power difficult to resist. However, if they also enact—and sediment—a racism that poses as structurally endemic to our cultural symbolic, then we must discover ways out of and beyond Lacan's accounts. This epistemological quandary around universality is thus not separated from larger political and ontological troubles.[8]

Semiotically, I perform a style of reading that allows what Maia Boswell has called "an unnoticed politics of race" (1999, 110) in Lacan's texts to surface. The omission of racial difference as a significant dynamic from La-can's accounts of ego-formation gives us an exemplary performance of how our white supremacist cultural symbolic perpetuates its racism through the very omission of race.[9] In his essay on the mirror stage and the 1953–54 Seminar, race is never mentioned. Such omissions are, as we have seen, hallmarks of whiteness's obliviousness to race—an obliviousness that both supports the flourishing of white privilege and perpetuates white supremacist racism. For Lacan, this omission of race allows an account of ego-formation that enacts conceptions of space and embodiment which, as enactments of the logic of the limit, undergird racist structures of politics, meaning, and subjectivity. In giving no attention to the ways that racial difference is sig-nified in the processes of ego-formation, Lacan enacts one of the central blind spots of a racist symbolic.[10] What occurs in Lacan's accounts of ego-formation is thereby also one of the most effective tools perpetuating ra-cism—namely, the omission of race from the field of signifiers.

Finally, as the larger psycho-ontological knot that reaches beyond the scope of this chapter and speaks to the overarching theme of this text as a whole, Lacan's accounts enact the conceptions of space and embodiment that support the dominant forms of racism found in our scopophilic culture. Interrogating Lacan's accounts, I generally ask whether ego-formation within an image-centered culture necessarily breeds raced subjectivities—and thus a pervasive form of racism that we find in cultures of phallicized whiteness. While I focus on the interpellation of images at work in Lacan's accounts, I am also interrogating the conceptions of space that allow this scopocentric and racist symbolic to emerge. In a more general excavation of the dominant models of vision in contemporary French theorists, Kelly Oliver argues that the conception of vision at work in Lacan's texts "imagines space as essen-tially empty and objects (or subjects) in space as points separated by the distance between them" (2001, 171). I want to investigate how that concep-tion of space allows Lacan to work out a logic of the limit that sediments not only a specific model of subject-formation, but also a cultural symbolic of phallicized whiteness.

This ontological conception of space as empty drives Lacan to conceive of bodies, and subjects, as entities demarcated from that empty space. Op-erating as boundaries that contain these entities, the logic of the limit func-tions here as the necessary condition for ego- and subject-formation: one cannot become a subject if one cannot properly demarcate oneself from the ontological emptiness of space. A subject is consequently he or she who is properly contained, a dynamic that is constitutive of a racist (and sexist), white supremacist symbolic. I focus here on two effects of this fundamental assumption: the emergence of this subject as one who is shaped according to the dynamics of distance, and subsequently cathected primarily through aggression and autonomy (not unlike the liberal, neutral individual);[11] and the hypostatizing of vision as the sense through which we ought to behold the world, due to its ability to demarcate bodies and subjects clearly and distinctly.

If this model of ego-formation, and more importantly its attendant notions of vision and space, enact the dominant models of subject-formation in cultures of phallicized whiteness, then dislodging racism from its biologized and visual moorings is, as Stuart Hall suggests, perhaps the most crucial, even if most difficult, strategy of anti-racist politics (Hall 1996b). Such a strategy will, furthermore, involve unhinging ourselves from the kinds of subjectivity that Lacan's accounts describe, accounts that continue to function in phallicized white cultures as normative, prescriptive, and ideologically interpellating. We thus need to interrogate the Lacanian reliance on optics insofar as it maps a symbolic that seduces us culturally. As we have seen in the emergence and continued dominance of liberal individualism, cultures of phallicized whiteness are deeply invested in the atomistic subjectivity that emerges from Lacan's accounts. And, while Lacan conjoins this subjectivity ontologically with aggression, it has historically also been conjoined with white supremacist racism. Therefore, if this atomistic, aggressive subjectivity is also a racist one, then we need to interrupt, interrogate, and redeploy this interpellation of images, and the attendant conceptions of space, in which it is grounded—both so that we can better use psychoanalysis through realizing its limits and, more generally, so that we can disrupt the phallicized white supremacist symbolic that is grounded in the visual field.

Embodying an Ego in a Scopophilic World

Lacan begins to diagnose how our subjectivity always already embodies cultural images in his work on the mirror stage, which he locates developmentally as preceding the infant's entrance into language and into the Oedipal complex. He argues that, between the ages of six and eighteen months, a fundamental transition occurs in the psychic development of the infant. Through the discovery of his[12] image reflected in the mirror, the infant encounters his first dyad, which later gets transcribed into the dyad of self-other. He thereby enters, through a moment of primary alienation and 'splitting' that will mark the entirety of his psychic life, the world of intersubjectivity. At the same time, the infant enters into an 'identification,' which Lacan defines as "the transformation that takes place in the subject when he assumes an *image*" (1977, 2, my emphasis). In a fundamental moment of both recognition and misrecognition (*méconnaissance*), the infant sees himself as both the subject before the mirror and the object reflected in the mirror.[13] This play between self and other initiates him into the endless and simultaneous processes of identity-formation and identification with the Other, the locus of the law in the symbolic field of signifiers.[14] Thus, in a primary moment of both narcissism and alienation, the infant takes his first step, in playing with the image of himself, toward forming an identity—a meaningful identity, a culturally legible identity.

Explicating these preverbal processes of identity-formation and identification, Lacan quickly turns to the function of embodiment in this emergence of the ego. He describes the infant's discovery of his mirrored image as the gathering of a fragmented sense of his body as 'bits and pieces' into a sense of wholeness, the *Gestalt* (1977, 2). Relating the infant for the first time to its external "reality" (1977, 4), the mirrored image bridges "the *Innenwelt* and *Umwelt*" (1977, 4). The image gathers the fragmented body, which the infant has experienced only as discrete parts (e.g., as hunger in the stomach, as suckling of the mouth, as pain in a finger, as tickling of a foot), into a whole, cohesive body. Through the recognition of his own image, the infant, according to Lacan, begins to conceive of himself as a whole body and, consequently, begins to read the outside world as also inhabited by other whole bodies: the infant moves from an isolated awareness of discrete phenomena to a more cohesive awareness of a whole environment, a larger space.

But, while it may be conceived as ontologically empty, this is not a psychically empty space. Through his move from his fragmented *Innenwelt* to a cohesive *Umwelt*, the infant discovers an *Umwelt* inhabited by other figures, other bodies. And he learns to read these bodies through the only tool at his disposal—through the primary narcissism of and splitting from his own image and the (often aggressive) fantasy life that it spawns.

In an interesting nod toward scientific objectivity, Lacan elaborates on the dynamics of this move into the *Umwelt* through references to "biological experimentation" (1977, 3). Relying on a biological parallel between birds, insects, and humans, Lacan suggests that the infant's recognition of his own image as a *Gestalt* stimulates his development as a social (and sexual, as he develops further in the 1953–54 Seminar) being of a certain species, just as it does for the female pigeon and migratory locust. In recognizing himself, the infant simultaneously recognizes a human being, a larger category to which he belongs and toward which he aspires: he desires to be this whole image. Granted, this belonging will always be conflictual due to the infant's primary alienation and narcissism, but Lacan posits the formation of an aggressive ego as the ontological status of the human ego.[15] Without exploring the nuances of the content of the reflected image, Lacan asserts that the infant's sheer sight of his own image places him in the—presumably universal and formal—social world of his species. Or so Lacan—and his examples—would have it.

▼ ▼ ▼

In fastening on the mirrored image as the site of primary identity-formation and identification, Lacan frames the primary psychic sense of the body—and, subsequently, of the self—as it is seen. Sight is what orders the infantile sense of the self in the world. Sight, providing a doubled spatial orientation that divides the inner world from the outer world and the outer world from one's body, gives an ordering principle to the infant's chaotic relation to the world and to himself. Sight allows the infant to begin constructing a sense of himself as a self—a self with an interior that is separate from other selves. Sight ushers the infant into the social world of the *Umwelt*. Sight, the sense we might associate most with the imaginary, grounds the infant's corporeal relation to the realm of the symbolic, the space of language. What thorny knots can we unravel here to grasp the role of visibility in Lacan's accounts of ego-formation?

In his 1953–54 Seminar, Lacan offers the model of the inverted bouquet as "a substitute for the mirror-stage" (1988, 74) to articulate further the relations between the real, the imaginary, and the symbolic. Placing the dynamics of ego-formation within the dynamics of optics, questions of reflection, refraction, convergent rays, and divergent rays give Lacan tools "to illustrate . . . what follows on from the strict intrication of the imaginary world and the real world in the psychic economy" (1988, 78). As he develops this model and all its possible permutations, we begin to see that the determining factor for whether one sees real or virtual images is the position of the eye. If the eye is closer, farther, to the left or to the right of the concave mirror, it will not behold the illusory image of the vase as containing the inverted bouquet of flowers. The position of the eye determines whether one sees the illusion, which is, with an appropriate touch of irony, itself an image of a 'normal' vase holding flowers.

Casting this model into the questions of ego-formation, Lacan compares the imaginary vase containing the real bouquet of flowers—which is an optical illusion—to the image of the body in the mirror stage. The image of the body introduces the infant to imaginary space; literally, the image he beholds is a virtual image that he sees where it is not, in the mirror. It thereby allows the infant to distinguish between his outer and inner worlds, spatializing him as a container (vase) that contains his inner world (flowers).[16] This image, which Lacan also calls the *Urbild*, is thus what allows the ego to begin to develop and take on its functions of distinguishing between inner and outer worlds and between one's self and others. As Lacan explains later in the seminar, "[t]his means that the human ego is founded on the basis of the imaginary relation" (1988, 115). The ego emerges on the plane of the imaginary through the infant's beholding of his corporeal image, which in turn forms his primary narcissism. But, again, what conditions the possibility of this beholding?

Returning to Lacan's development of the inverted bouquet model, he emphasizes that "[f]or there to be an illusion, for there to be a world constituted . . . one condition must be fulfilled—as I have said, the eye must be in a specific position" (1988, 80). It must be in a specific position physically, inside the cone of the concave mirror, and psychically, 'inside' the symbolic—or, less metaphorically, positioned in a space of legibility within the symbolic. As he continues and bares yet further his resonances with classic western notions of subjectivity, Lacan tells us flatly that "the eye is here, as so often, symbolic of the subject" (1988, 80). He then goes on to explicate some of the implications of this model:

> It means that, in the relation of the imaginary and the real, and in the constitution of the world such as results from it, everything relies on the position of the subject. And the position of the subject—you should know, I've been repeating it for long enough—is essentially characterised by its place in the symbolic world, in other words in the world of speech. (1988, 80)

It is thus through the interpellation of the symbolic that the imaginary and real come to make sense.[17] It is through the interpellation of the symbolic that the infant beholds his image and begins to form his ego. Consequently, the sort of ego (fragile, functional, volatile, porous, impermeable) that an infant forms depends already on the space of the symbolic that he inhabits. Moreover, the frame of spatiality for understanding this formation of the ego is one of containment: the ego 'contains' the subject's inner life—interestingly, just as the body 'contains' the subject. Both, it seems, are optical illusions.

▼ ▼ ▼

We may now return to Lacan's accounts of the mirror stage and ask further about the nuances of the images that the infant beholds. Clearly, this image of himself carries great significance in Lacan's account of ego-formation. But, asking in the voice of Ralph Ellison that initiated this chapter (not in the voice of cognitive scientists), what is it that the infant sees? Are we to assume that all human infants 'see' the same formal image? Or, to grant Lacan some sense of his own historical location, are we at least to assume that all human infants in the "overdeveloped world"[18] see the same formal image?

Lacan appears to give this formal gaze some content when he describes the experience of this stage "as a temporal dialectic that decisively projects the formation of the individual into history" (1977, 4). This would seem to open Lacan's account to the historical location and cultural content—to the interpellation of the symbolic—of the images reflected in the infant's mirror. However, as we see in the remainder of his discussion, this projection of the individual into history refers to the newly formed ego's temporal anticipation of fantasies and fears, which seem to dominate the development of a primarily narcissistic, split, and aggressive ego. (This temporality mostly assumes the posture of the future anterior, a temporality fundamental to cultures of phallicized whiteness.) The projection of the individual into history refers to the temporal complexity enacted by the individual's fantasy life, not to the historical location of the culturally coded—symbolic—images that are reflected in the infant's mirror play.

We are thus forced to ask that which Lacan's account seems unable to frame: what is it that the infant 'sees'? What visual marker dominates our cultural image of the body and allows the infant to behold his image as an image of wholeness? What visual marker dominates our symbolic's signifying of the body? Just as blind spots often operate, the answer seems so obvious that it need not be stated: we see, with the 'inner' eyes of our cultural symbolic, a body bound by skin. The body of the infant's mirrored image is a flattened, two-dimensional mass that is bound and contained by skin. This specific, epidermal image sets very specific dynamics into play—between spaces, between persons, between cultures. The body bound by skin, which Lacan fails to note as significant, dominates the ways that we signify bodies in our cultural symbolic fields. And, in what is more than a coincidence, it also enacts a primary conception of space and embodiment that grounds some of our symbolic's contemporary forms of racism.

Unraveling the Morphology of Contained Bodies

If our primary identity is formed through an image of the body as bound and contained by skin, a very specific kind of space is thereby enacted in this mirror stage.[19] Space is immediately structured through the dynamics of containment and distance: the skin contains the body; the body, now as a whole, contains identity; and the distance between bodies, a distance structured by one's placement in the symbolic, determines the relations between them.[20] The crucial move from the infant's *Innenwelt* of 'bits and pieces' to his *Umwelt* of the *Gestalt* is made possible by the gathering of his body into a whole—by the appearance of his body as it is contained by its skin. It is this skin that gives the body a strict boundary, thus setting it apart from the surrounding larger space, which it begins to read as socially mapped rather than merely 'empty.' It is in this setting apart from other 'bodies' that the infant enters into the dynamics of his identity-formation and begins to develop into a legible subject.[21]

While Lacan underscores the role of separation in his description of the image as the first instance of alienation, he underestimates the role that this distinction from other bodies and from the larger space plays in this identity-formation. It is not only that the infant recognizes for the first time that he lives in a whole body, but also that this whole body is distinct from and separable from other whole bodies (particularly the care-giving body). It is this distinction from other whole bodies that registers him as an 'individual' and thus as a meaningful identity within our cultural symbolic. Distinction from the other plays a primary role in our identity-formations, and a discrete body contained by skin allows such identification to occur.

Consequently, this space of containment plays into a space of distance. In a quintessentially Cartesian grid of relations, it is the distance between distinct bodies that both determines and depicts the relations between bodies within our cultural symbolic. For example, as Sandra Bartky (1988) (among other feminists) has shown, the distance between male and female bodies in contemporary work settings in North America bespeaks the kinds of power relations between these bodies. When the infant grasps his image as a whole body that is thereby distinct from other bodies, he thus enters the culturally structured space of intersubjectivity, where dynamics of distance define social relations. Dynamics of distance, in fact, become a primary mapping of power in the cultural symbolic.

Just as the 'eye' must be located 'inside' the symbolic to behold the illusion that the vase is holding the flowers, so too the location of one's body—a body rendered legible through its container, skin—in the symbolic is manifested in the distance it maintains *vis-à-vis* other bodies: whether one sits with one's legs sprawled or nicely closed, whether one touches another during speech, whether one stands closer to or farther from another, and—in perhaps the quintessential control of distance by the visual—whether one engages the eyes of another. All of these bespeak the subtle, bodily codings of power in a cultural symbolic. Reading these codes properly can become a matter of security and violence, of sanity and insanity, of life and death. And the ability to read them depends on one's location 'inside' the symbolic, which may itself involve a process of finding, recognizing, or even resigning oneself to that location.

▼ ▼ ▼

When the infant grasps his image as a whole body that is thereby distinct from other bodies, he thus enters the cultural field of relations, which operates not only through a dynamics of containment and distance, but also through a dynamics of power—a power that is structured primarily through mastery. The infant learns to move through the world as a discrete and strictly contained mass, internalizing the cultural fact that it is in being cohesively contained that one gains identity, subjectivity, value, and power. The space between bodies is accordingly read as negative space—space awaiting the formative power of containment. It is space in need of delimitation. Only a whole body can master this negative space and contain it, delimiting and mapping the social relations that obtain within it.[22]

To speak of whole bodies as those with cultural meaning and value is thus to suggest that only bodies which are properly delimited can function with authority in this symbolic. Bodies that exceed their boundaries, messy bodies with uncontrollable fluids,[23] bodies with too much passion or fire in the soul all become bodies that are in need of control, in need of proper limits. These excessive bodies need to contain themselves. They cannot function as separable individuals if they are not properly contained. They cannot function as valuable members of the economy of atomistic relations if they are not properly delimited. But how can a body that is not contained find the capacity to contain itself? How can a body that is not whole shape itself into a whole body? The double bind of mastery and its disembodied dynamic thus asserts itself.

If it is only whole, contained bodies that can shape negative space into mapped, socialized space, then it seems that the question of 'wholeness' has totalized the social, political space. That is, if only whole bodies determine

69

what bodies are whole (and thus valuable) and what are not (and thus in need of control, by other whole bodies), then the claim to wholeness is circular and self-justifying, if not tautologous: whole bodies are the bodies that proclaim other bodies as not-whole—as unlimited, uncontained, even unhinged. As a field of mastery, the logic of containment totalizes the field of social relations through proclaiming itself as the only—allegedly ontological—logic of embodiment itself. To be contained and limited is the only way that bodies can become proper individuals—or legible subjects.

The Phallic Field as the Visual Field: Mastery in the Register of Visibility

We may get a better sense of how this dynamic of mastery plays itself out in the logic of containment if we return to the field that grounds Lacan's account—the field of the visual. And the structure that dominates it—the phallus.

The logic of the phallus, which for Lacan becomes the law of the symbolic that "speaks man" (*ça parle*) or places him in his particular location in the symbolic, is conjoined with the logic of the visual.[24] Lacan reads the phallus as possessing the power of the copula, elevating it to the signifier of signifiers. In the language of traditional western metaphysics, the phallus becomes what structures Being, and thus beings. In a play of embodiment, disembodiment, and representation that itself exemplifies the functioning of the phallus, Lacan reads the symbolic act of the logical copula through the physical act of sexual copulation and thereby installs a particular criterion as the indication of the power of the phallus: visibility.[25] The visual field becomes a primary arena in which the phallus shapes power in the symbolic field—i.e., how bodies look correlates with how and where they are located in the symbolic field.

Referring to the ancient rituals and frescoes of the Villa of Mysteries in Pompeii, however, Lacan reminds us that the veiling and unveiling of the phallus assume mythical proportions (1977, 285). He thereby emphasizes that the phallus masters and controls—contains and shapes—the visual field through itself remaining veiled. The phallus does not function in the symbolic field directly or immediately. It must undergo constant mediation to enact its desire—through language and its transformation of an object into a signifier, through property, through the exchange of women (as Irigaray develops), or through this very play of visibility in the symbolic field it dominates. The phallus dominates and shapes the modes of acceptable visibility through itself remaining veiled. It is unseen.

The way bodies appear thus reemerges as a primary mapping of social power. Mastery in this dynamic of containment operates through the control of visibility—a control that is exercised without touch, without physical contact. The phallus determines the limitations of bodies—how bodies are contained—through the kind of visibility that they display. Only those 'whole bodies' simply appear. Only those whole bodies are easily, clearly, and distinctly seen simply as they are—as human bodies (only coincidentally carrying power and value). Most bodies (and the sheer disparity in numbers indicates the hegemony at play here) have to locate themselves somewhere on the spectrum from invisibility to hyper-visibility. These are those out-of-control bodies, the ones that cannot contain themselves and must heed the proper limits and boundaries set out for them. Their submission to the limits enforced by 'whole bodies' surfaces in the way they appear: to overstep one's boundaries is to look bad.

▼ ▼ ▼

Out of this field of the visual as the field of social power, many feminists and other anti-racist theorists have focused on the dynamics of visibility as a primary site of mastery and domination—for both sexual and racial differentiation.[26]

For example, much of the early work of Luce Irigaray exposes, in a variety of ways, this function of the phallus and the constitutive roles of vision, sight, and visibility in the register of sexual (in)difference. As she *unveils* (specifically in the Lacanian context and more broadly in cultural contexts[27]), the cultural marking of bodies as powerful or powerless turns on whether a body has or lacks the penile representation of the phallus, thus showing how the phallus structures a binary, oppositional logic of sexual (in)difference. Lacking this visual marker, femininity consequently vacillates between invisibility ("the *horror* of nothing to see" [Irigaray 1985b, 26]) and hyper-visibility (the beautiful object on display for exchange), with no cultural power other than that which she can siphon from the phallus by reflecting its image. A woman is to be either paraded as a 'trophy,' who is seen but not heard, or shamed to utter absence, awaiting the phallic gaze that will cast value upon her.

As Gwen Bergner develops, "[v]ision is instrumental in producing both racial and sexual difference" (1995, 79). In psychoanalytic terms, masquerade, projection, and representation all become the visual registers in which sexual and, less explicitly, racial differences are enacted. The field of racialized signifiers thus also appears to function through the domination of the phallus. A binary, oppositional logic of (in)difference accordingly ensues, which implies that the white supremacist symbolic is grounded in anti-black racism.[28] Race is thereby determined by one's proximity to either of the extremes, black or white, which register in different modes of visibility: the white (phallic) extreme fades into invisibility, while the other extreme is, assuming one is placed appropriately inside the symbolic, easily *seen*.

A wide range of theorists of race consequently agree with Hortense Spillers's observation that "Africanity . . . [is] the essence of visibility" (1996, 79).[29] Without reducing race to skin color, Spillers's proclamation exposes the ways that black bodies—and by extension, other raced bodies with other visual markers[30]—will never simply appear. Unlike 'whole bodies,' black bodies produce a "visual violence" (Bergner 1995, 79) in the phallic field of vision.

Historical examples of this dynamic proliferate. Ralph Ellison harrowingly describes the black man as the invisible man, never seen simply as a human (Ellison 1952). Frantz Fanon describes his experience of embodying blackness as the process of whiteness writing upon his body: "below the corporeal schema, [sketching] a historico-racial schema . . . [using] elements provided by the other, the white man, who had woven me out of a thousand details, anecdotes, stories" (1967, 111). Following from her argument that "if being is seeing for the subject, then being seen is the precise measure of existence for the object" (1991, 28), Patricia J. Williams goes on to write of the schizophrenic experiences of utter invisibility as a black law student and paralyzing hyper-visibility as a black law professor.[31] And the majority of work by bell hooks, an extraordinary reader of visual culture, diagnoses this dangerous terrain of visibility for black women in the U.S., where black female bodies are seen as alluring objects or the exotic Other, but never simply as other humans (hooks 1990, 1992, 1995). It is clear: the way raced bodies *look* is certainly not in their own control.

Images of Authority

The sexing and racing of bodies thus occurs primarily in the ways that they appear—or, more exactly, fail to appear. And the ways that they appear are dominated by the phallic field of representation. Bodies appear as they are interpellated by the symbolic law. The functionings of the phallus, and particularly the emergence and transmission of authority, consequently become sites requiring further inquiry. To make this inquiry, I return again to the site of ego-formation—the formation of that much prized and needed container for the subject.

Referring to the 'bits and pieces' of the infant's *Innenwelt* in Lacan's mirror stage, Fanon describes how, for the black male body, "the fragments have been put together again by another self" (1967, 109). His image of his own body, a foundational site for his ego- and subject-formation, is interpellated by the cultural symbolic in which it is located. The black infant attempts to gather himself into a 'whole body,' but can only see himself as he is seen by the white racist world and its phallicized symbolic. Only by taking on the limits and proper modes of visibility of the phallic field of white supremacy can he cobble together an image of himself and form himself into a functioning, legible subject. But what fragments does he see? The stereotypes are all too easy to list: hyper-sexed, out of control, angry, ignorant, violent, deaf and dumb, even cannibalistic (Fanon 1967, 120). The black male body becomes legible when he sees the world and himself from the proper location of his 'eye' inside the symbolic—in spaces of inferiority. As Patricia J. Williams writes, "[B]lacks in a white society are conditioned from infancy to see in themselves only what others, who despise them, see" (1991, 62).[32]

Whole bodies, which by now we can begin to read as white and male bodies, are thus not the only legible subjects in the symbolic. Raced and sexed bodies are certainly legible. Indeed, we might even say that they are too legible, their legibility far preceding any actual act, speech, even thought or desire. If the symbolic law "speaks man," it speaks raced and sexed bodies more loudly and with a deafening repetition—a repetition that threatens paralysis of these bodies in any attempt to become individuals.[33] In a culture in which play before the television often precedes any play before the mirror, this interpellation of the symbolic assumes frightening proportions.

▼ ▼ ▼

The symbolic thus speaks all of us, regulating our identity-formations through the social mapping of power that is written across our bodies. The very relation between the infant and his own image is already interpellated by this symbolic and its figurations of authority.[34] In a phallicized white symbolic, this means that particular bodies are always already coded as powerful and (most) others are not: white male (straight) propertied Christian bodies carry authority, which they 'must' (dutifully, perhaps) exert upon all those other unruly bodies out of control. (U.S. foreign policy and its 'duty to make the world safe for democracy' ring a little too loudly here.) In Lacanian terms, the infant's image of himself is interpellated by the images of authority in the larger space of the symbolic. As Elizabeth Grosz explains, "the laws and prohibitions of the symbolic field must be culturally repre-sented or embodied for the child by some authority figure" (1990, 47). It is in learning to read these bodies of authority that the newly developing ego learns to read his proper location in the symbolic field.[35]

The conjoining of sight and speech here takes on the racialized and sexualized mapping of power that we have already seen in the dynamics of visibility. Returning to the inverted bouquet, Lacan explains that "the incli-nation of the plane mirror [must be] governed by the voice of the other" (1988, 140). It is the voice of authority that places the eye so that it can see the desired optical illusion—of an ego containing a subject. To become a legible subject in the symbolic, the infant must heed the call of the voice of authority. While authority ranges far beyond any strictly legalistic meaning for Lacan, it does connote a proper meaning, a proper comportment and embodiment of culturally legible codes, regulations, logics, rhythms, styles, systems, and values. It certainly means entering language through the proper grammar, the proper units of meaning, the proper cadence and syntax and style of speech. It means speaking in the proper voice.

Again, the sexing and racing of bodies emerges—this time in the register of voices. The trophy wife is, just as good children are, seen but not heard. The 'male answer syndrome' produces male students who blurt answers to things they have never heard of and female students who cannot speak their wisdom. Black, Latino, and many immigrant communities develop dialects that risk cultural illegibility in an effort to shun white authority. It is only white male bodies whose voices are heard clearly and distinctly, speaking in calm rationality even as they proclaim bigotry and hatred.

Authority thus functions as an efficient closed economy, transmitting like to like in exemplary performances of the Law of the Same. The phallus is not just the phallus—it is a white phallus. Or, as Kalpana Seshadri-Crooks develops through her reading of Mary Ellen Goodman's pioneering work on racial identification (Goodman 1952), wherein white four-year-olds both readily identify as white and readily dismiss the color of their own skin (fixated on the 'color' of black children's skin), "the discourse of whiteness can be said to function as a condition of dominant subjectivity: it inserts the subject into the symbolic order" (1998, 358).

The Liberal Individualism of Lacan's Ego: Autonomy, Scarcity, Desire

We have already encountered the ways that whiteness gains its hegemonic power through its disavowal of race, its own invisibility, and ultimately its own disembodiment. It is this invisibility that renders whiteness ubiquitous, the universal signifier—the same position that the phallus holds in Lacan's account of the symbolic. Echoing Lacan's phallus, whiteness functions through its remaining veiled. And a primary site of this veiling is its ontological denial of embodiment itself. The body becomes, just as it is in Lacan's accounts of ego-formation in a phallic symbolic, an optical illusion. It is the body that recognizes itself as an optical illusion that can subsequently control the visual field, the field of optics.[36] (And we wonder why modern philosophers were so enamored with the emergent field of optics.) Other bodies are 'too real'—too fleshy to recognize that the field of appearances, which is the field of social power, is a game of optics. Other bodies' 'eyes' have not inhabited the 'proper' space of the symbolic that renders this recognition of optical illusions possible.

As Dyer draws this game of optics out in the specific register of representation, the ideal of white male heterosexuality emerges in the figure of Christ, who inhabits precisely the space of the symbolic that allows the recognition of optical illusions: the principle of incarnation is to be *in* the body but not *of* it. This tension between the flesh and the spirit, an exemplary Lacanian splitting, is what distinguishes whiteness, maleness, and heterosexuality from their oppositional counterparts in the phallicized binary symbolic. (And that only oppositional counterparts are considered itself indicates the power of the phallus in this symbolic field.) With several ironic twists of apparent embodiment and transcendence, the white male heterosexual body disavows its own corporeality—its own particularity and specificity—so that it can function as the universal signifier and appear as the controlled, contained body. It recognizes its body as nothing more than an optical illusion and, accordingly, transcends it into a realm of mastery—of all bodies.

In this process of disembodiment, whiteness functions perfectly as the phallus. For whiteness, the appearance of bodies—both how they appear and that they are not 'real'—ensures the continued mastery of the symbolic field. The white straight male body appears as the 'normal' body—without marking, without distinction, perfectly contained, and, subsequently, in power. The logic of space and embodiment that insists upon reading bodies as bound by skin not only puts the visual markings of race and sex fully into play, but also perpetuates the logic of containment in which whiteness itself, as that which is perfectly contained exactly because it is not a body, thrives. Controlling its optical illusion as the body that is perfectly contained, whiteness is never where it appears: it is somewhere else, veiled beyond capture.

▼ ▼ ▼

Functioning within an ontology of contained space, Lacan's accounts of ego-formation capture the dilemma of intersubjectivity endemic to the model of liberal individualism. While Lacan points toward the dynamics of recognition and their self-splitting as necessary and constitutive of ego-formation, the fundamental autonomy of the liberal individual remains the desired *telos* of all development. The fundamental criterion of one's social legibility remains one's demarcation from all others and the social world itself. Driven by the dynamics of narcissism, the kind of recognition that Lacan idealizes remains one that is grounded in a self that is ontologically separable from all other entities.

Cynthia Willett diagnoses this dilemma as the struggle between the two dominant models of human subjectivity in western cultures since the Enlightenment: the liberal subject "who defines itself through active self-agency or possessive self-ownership and claims . . . the right to protect a private space" and "the (post-Hegelian) subject who discovers who he is through the recognition bestowed upon him by other persons" (2001, 6). As Willett also argues, these remain two sides of the same coin: each of these models of subjectivity assumes that separability from others and the social world constitutes the fundamental endpoint of all desires. Utter self-sufficiency, achieved either through will power or through transcending the recognition of others, is what humans must ultimately seek according to both of these models.

Both of these models, Locke's liberal individual and Lacan's authoritative ego, operate within an economy of scarcity that is grounded in a model of desire that can never find any external satisfaction. Both models are driven by lack, which each thinker conceives as the ontological condition of humans, and which develops further into an explicitly aggressive drive in Lacan's accounts. Furthermore, in Lacan's accounts, the symbolic cannot function without sufficient distance between and delineation of singular entities: bodies must be separate and distinct for one to call out the narcissistically cathected aggression against and toward the other. Relations between selves on both of these models subsequently function through protective gestures that must be repeated constantly. Standing out into the ontologically empty space of this aggressive and threatening social scene, one must mark one's territory and construct strong and clear borders around it. The self becomes the fortress that must be protected. And the narcissism that initiated the aggressive formation of the ego closes itself off from the wider social world into a cultural solipsism: the self must be contained and the social world must protect its fragile containment.

Desire, the dynamic that drives ego-formation and this attenuated notion of intersubjectivity for Lacan, ultimately remains trapped in this fortress of the narcissistic self. When experienced by the hegemonic subject position that finds the world to be its self-reflective mirror, this desire wallows in sameness and lashes out aggressively against all that is different. When experienced by the abjected position, this desire cannot effectively resist its submission to the violent world which abjects it. Grounded in the fundamental need for the other, this model of the self frames the world as a collection of finite beings who may violate and threaten its own small place in the world: scarcity precludes abundance; and hyper-vigilant protection forecloses any open generosity.

These are the terms of our culture, a culture of phallicized whiteness. And they are the terms I want to develop further as I turn toward possible responses to these dilemmas.

THE PLACE OF SEXUAL DIFFERENCE

Idealizing Heterosexual Desire

3

If traditionally, and as a mother, woman represents *place* for man, such a limit means that she becomes a *thing*, with some possibility of change from one historical period to another. She finds herself delineated as a thing. Moreover, the maternal-feminine also serves as an *envelope*, a *container*, the starting point from which man limits his things. The *relationship between envelope and things* constitutes one of the aporias, or the aporia, of Aristotelianism and of the philosophical systems derived from it.

—LUCE IRIGARAY,
"Sexual Difference,"
An Ethics of Sexual Difference

Every oppositional discourse will produce its outside.

—JUDITH BUTLER,
"Bodies That Matter,"
Bodies That Matter

In turning explicitly to ethical concerns in *An Ethics of Sexual Difference*, Luce Irigaray does not take the routes that many Anglo-American philosophers might assume are the proper categories or presuppositions of ethics. She does not turn, at least not explicitly, toward questions of rights or duties or even rationality or utility.[1] Rather, heeding her own call for us to "reconsider the whole problematic of *space* and *time*" (1993a, 7), she turns toward the figuration and question of 'place,' which she reads as manifesting a logic of containment—a clear expression of the logic of the limit. As a central figure that must be redeployed if we are to rethink our fundamental categories and reorient our very experiences, 'place' becomes a vexing and fascinating site through which to consider our subjectivities, particularly those subjectivities of phallicized whiteness who conceive of themselves as a 'place' in the world.

Irigaray interrogates several foundational texts from the history of western metaphysics on this question of 'place.' Casting her concerns as explicitly ethical, these essays mark a turning point in Irigaray's work, which had thus far been focused on 'interrupting' and thereby calling into question presuppositions of the phallocentric economies of western metaphysics through various strategies of deconstructive mimicry. But, as Carolyn Burke, the translator of both *An Ethics of Sexual Difference* and *This Sex Which Is Not One* from French into English, so nicely develops, Irigaray's move toward more explicit ethical concerns cannot be divorced from her prior work both in and on the language of western metaphysics.[2] While there is a subtle shift in style in these essays of *An Ethics of Sexual Difference,* in which Irigaray speaks, with puzzling irony and playful impossibility abounding, 'in her own voice,' these essays continue to call for the sort of double reading that her prior work invites. To grasp both the interruptive space she creates in various texts from the history of western philosophy and the work on and in language which these readings enact, we must read simultaneously in two manners: conceptually and performatively.[3] We must read both for *what* she is saying about the concepts, questions, or figures at hand and *how* she is saying it.

Often, we are tempted to divide these reading strategies according to a prior categorization of Irigaray's texts. This is particularly tempting in the essays of *An Ethics of Sexual Difference,* where Irigaray's styles are apparently neatly divided for us: six of the essays are 'about' or 'on' a text from the history of western philosophy and five of the essays are 'in Irigaray's own voice.' The six explicitly on other texts thus clearly call for conceptual readings of the 'matter' or problem taken up in the text and the other five call for performative readings of what Irigaray is doing with language, a language often read as more poetic and mythical than 'philosophical.' But this very divide does a real and frighteningly phallomorphic violence to Irigaray's texts.

As several theorists and astute readers of Irigaray have developed at length, Irigaray's texts call into question this very division into binary poles— a division that undergirds virtually all western metaphysical systems, grounded as it is in the basic principle of non-contradiction.[4] Such binary polarization often reduces one pole to the specular partner of the dominant pole, which effectively erases the subordinate pole as carrying any meaning other than that which it reflects back into the dominant pole. For example, in the most simple reading of non-contradiction, $x \neq -x$, the dominant pole finds its simple negation of itself reflected back to it in its specular partner; only one term is finally at work in the logical operation. To paraphrase Judith Butler, one pole serves both as grounding and condition of possibility for the other pole and, in so doing, is erased from the scene of 'meaning.'[5] In the pairing at hand in this question of reading, the conceptual readings are taken up as carrying 'philosophical' import and the performative readings, which silently allow the style of conceptual readings to emerge through reflecting the expectations of conceptual units of meaning, schemata, and grammar back to the reader, are rendered 'literary,' 'poetic,' perhaps even 'interesting'—if they are framed as meaningful in and of themselves. Across her early texts of *Speculum of the Other Woman* and *This Sex Which Is Not One*, Irigaray exposes this logic of non-difference or in-difference, in which only one term is reflected back to itself rather than interacting with another term, as the logic of sexual (in)difference that dominates western metaphysics and cultures.[6] (And so we find, early in our discussion, Irigaray's own grounding in interrupting Aristotelian logic.)

Irigaray's texts thus call us to read with two simultaneous strategies, or, perhaps more appropriately, sensibilities. While she is by no means the first to make such a plea (Nietzsche and Plato easily come to mind as historical examples), the stakes at risk in not reading her texts this way are extraordinarily high. Not to read Irigaray's texts both conceptually and performatively almost certainly ensures a reading that fails to grasp the movement and possibility of sexual difference—events that occur in language—for and toward which Irigaray writes.

I belabor this question of reading Irigaray because it is a dynamic that must be consciously at work in what follows. In choosing a style of writing that often assumes the form of commentary, I have already delimited the kinds of readings that I can produce here. Although not impossible, it is extremely difficult to convey a conceptual and performative reading simultaneously in an exegetical voice. Nor is it simple to convey these readings simultaneously in a voice of philosophy that continues to labor under the grammar of teleology, where sentences and paragraphs and essays are supposed "to get to the point," to borrow Carolyn Burke's ironically performative phrase (1994, 253). As Burke has discussed as one of the primary trials in translating Irigaray's texts, our dominant grammar of teleology mitigates against the kind of performative work Irigaray is doing in language; it mitigates, rather unsurprisingly, in favor of the conceptual—i.e., phallicized— readings.

I belabor the question of reading to call explicit attention to the kind of readings offered here and the vacillation between conceptual and performative modes. I will also return to this question of styles of reading at the end of this chapter as itself a site that indicates the place of 'place' in Irigaray's own texts: what does it mean that Irigaray's texts beckon her readers never to stay 'in place'? Is this fluid back-and-forth chiasmus sufficient to disrupt the Aristotelian notion of place and the logic of the limit that constitutes it? Or might it reinstall us within that logic while appearing to disrupt it?

The following readings of Irigaray's texts, primarily those from *An Ethics of Sexual Difference* and *Sexes and Genealogies*, explore both her diagnosis of how the logic of the limit circumscribes the concept of space in Aristotelian metaphysics and her suggestions about ways to move beyond such a logic, and thereby recuperate the sexual difference that it suppresses. The readings develop in three registers: 1) Irigaray's reading of Book Four of Aristotle's *Physics*, where she locates a fundamental *aporia* in western metaphysics and its dominant conception of place as structured by a logic of containment, which subsequently suppresses sexual difference; 2) Irigaray's own sense of how it is that place must be reconfigured (particularly in the figure of woman), if the phallocentric economy of space-time is to be redeployed; and 3) how Irigaray's suggestive figures of touch, mucus, chiasmus, lips, and angels perform, or gesture toward, this sort of redeployment. Following these three, I will then turn toward her own styles of reading as deconstructive mimicry and interpolation to discern the sort of 'place' that is already enacted in that style of reading, asking the difficult question of whether Irigaray finally reinstalls—precisely in the dynamics of desire and sexuality—the logic of the limit that she hopes to displace.

Aristotle, Place, and the Interval of Desire

Irigaray approaches Aristotle's text through one of the tropes that dominate late modern western philosophy, the dynamic of desire. While we can trace desire through various texts of ancient Greece (Plato's are surely among the most erotic of texts), the kind of desire that is grounded in a 'deep' subjectivity is distinctly late modern, having its roots most easily in texts of Hegel and various early-nineteenth-century Romantics (Schiller, Schelling, Schopenhauer).[7] When Irigaray brings this question to Aristotle's texts, therefore, multiple interpolations are at play. To list some of these in a general and oversimplified historical trajectory: the high modern models of the self as rational, or at least potentially rational; the Enlightenment models of the liberal neutral individual as separable from society and culture, with attendant rights and duties; the phenomenological models of the subject as a repository of history, struggling with self-consciousness and intentionality; the psychoanalytic models of the psyche as a site under siege by history, unconscious drives, and misperceived boundaries; even the post-structuralist readings of the self as a phantasm produced through some of these prior

81

models; and several others. Consequently, while Aristotle speaks of man (*sic*) as naturally desiring to know in the opening line of his *Metaphysics,* in his texts he is not working with the same senses of man, nature, desire, or knowing that Irigaray brings to bear. This is not to argue that Irigaray presents us with a 'misreading' of Aristotle's *Physics;* I do not want to perpetuate the sort of naive ahistoricism that often lurks behind such a claim for a hermeneutics of transparency. But I do wish to call attention to the kinds of conceptual and historical investments that her readings of this text already embody and enact.

While it would be fascinating to take up each of these conceptions of the self and read the effects it produces and the traces it leaves in Irigaray's readings of Aristotle, opening each of these texts to the rich historicity that constitutes these dialogues, I must limit myself to one. (In my own performative mode, I must contain and limit myself if I am to make any sense.) I focus primarily on psychoanalysis—a voice that, despite much excellent work on its presence in Irigaray's texts, still tends to be overlooked in discussions of philosophically trained and oriented readers.[8] More specifically, I will focus on the presence of Lacanian concepts and styles of approach—on Lacan's 'voice'—in Irigaray's own approach to the questions she brings to Aristotle. While the essays of *An Ethics of Sexual Difference* are sprinkled with references to Freud, Irigaray does not offer any explicit discussion of Lacan.[9] And yet several of his conceptual tools are at work in her texts—e.g., she draws on the broadly psychoanalytic dynamics of sublimation and the more specifically Lacanian conceptions of morphology in her readings of Aristotle. Focusing on this 'voice' of Lacan in Irigaray's texts may lead us toward a productive juncture of struggle and tension in her attempts to create, and the very possibilities of creating, a different place for the feminine and sexual difference.

Returning then to Irigaray's general approach through the dynamics of desire, we can hear her frame Aristotle's discussion of place as an ethical concern in her lamentation in "Sexual Difference," the essay that opens *An Ethics of Sexual Difference,* that there is "no double desire" (1993a, 9) between man and woman in western metaphysics and, consequently, western cultures.[10] Read as the spectral pole that reflects the desire of the dominant term back to itself in strict cohesion with the law of non-contradiction, the feminine can only reflect (phallic) desire, not produce or conceive it. There is no chiasmus. And if there is no chiasmus, there cannot be any ethical parity in the navigation of social power. We thus hear a faint reverberation of Irigaray's desire in her reading of Aristotle through desire—a desire for "a double loop in which each can go toward the other and come back to itself" (1993a, 9).

By framing it as a discussion of desire, Irigaray brings questions of movement and asymmetry to Book Four of Aristotle's *Physics*. If desire "occupies or designates the place of the *interval*" (1993a, 8), then we must ask, with Irigaray, how that interval is crossed.[11] We must ask who or what is crossing and from where—questions implicit in Aristotle's discussion of place. This general orientation toward the interval of desire also offers a provocative reading of Aristotle's insistence that we must approach the question of place through the dynamic of motion.

If part of Aristotle's orientation toward motion is a more subtle orientation toward desire, then the kinds of 'things' that he discusses in this *Physics* include sentient 'things,' or what we might more aptly call 'bodies.' From this perspective, any reading of Book Four that presumes the discussion is only about 'physical things,' with no sense of sentient things that (to employ twentieth-century language) intend to move, excludes some of the primary sensibilities shaping Aristotle's discussion. He is focusing not only on things that move, but also on bodies that move and bodies that initiate movement. The question of place is a question of motion, a question of how bodies move from one place to another; it thus invites a focus on bodies that have the principle of motion in them—i.e., active bodies, desiring bodies. Moreover, putting the *Physics* in conversation with the larger context of texts such as the *Metaphysics* and *De Anima* and the respective discussions of the self-moved mover or Prime Mover, we might even argue that Aristotle's concerns culminate in an orientation toward moving bodies and how they move.[12] Irigaray's orientation toward desire thus seems both to bring her questions about the asymmetry of desire to Aristotle's text and, simultaneously, to enrich our readings of Aristotle as focused on both physical and 'meta-' or 'extra-' physical (in post-psychoanalytic language, 'psychic') bodies in his discussion of motion and place.

Aristotle's 'Place' and the Logic of Containment: A Brief Exegesis

When Aristotle observes that we would not even consider the question of place "if it had not been that some motion existed, some motion across place" (211a12),[13] he frames motion as the primary category through which all other questions of physics (space, time, place) are approached. He elaborates the two species of this sort of motion as "on the one hand as 'carrying' (*phora*), and on the other hand as growth and decrease" (211a15) and proceeds to focus primarily on 'carrying' or 'locomotion' (*phora*). For Irigaray, this already enacts a dynamic of sexual (in)difference through the focus on the motion that moves from one 'place' toward another, implying an asymmetrical activity and unilateral teleology as the primary ways to approach the question of place. Prior to these distinctions, Aristotle adds onto his enumeration of various characteristics of place, as an explicitly marked textual afterthought that a twentieth-century hermeneutics might read as 'the real motivation' behind his conceptions,[14] "the distinction of up and down" (211a4, fifth characteristic). Putting these together, we see that Aristotle focuses his discussion of place on vertical movements of bodies from one place to another.

The most simple—and certainly too simple—reading of such a movement through the register of sexual difference would be to suggest that this is clearly the phallicized movement of sexual penetration. Read in its 'proper' heterosexual manifestation, this translates morphologically to the erect (and thus active) penis 'moving into' the empty (and thus passive) space of the vagina. This morphological or physical connection certainly does ring in Irigaray's readings.[15] And it is important, even if dangerously reductive, to note how easily the morphological register presents itself to our contemporary ears; this both accentuates our own location in a phallicized, heterosexual, and white symbolic and distances us from the ancient Greek symbolic, wherein positions of active penetration and passive receptivity would not be coded exclusively as masculine and feminine, respectively.[16] This morphological reduction, however, is not where Irigaray leaves or leads her discussion. Rather, to grasp Irigaray's metaphysical diagnosis of what this focus on vertical locomotion implies for ethical subjectivity, we must move further into Aristotle's readings of place as a vessel.

Without reducing Aristotle's discussion to this specific movement of penetration, Irigaray does focus on the dynamics of activity and passivity. She raises the ethical question of the conditions of possibility for activity, a characteristic we late moderns associate with subjectivity and the Greeks, at a minimum, associate with citizenship. This condition of possibility is place—for a thing to move, for it to have the principle of movement in it, it must be 'in place.' Carefully distinguishing the relation of thing to place from part to whole (see chapter 3 of *Physics*), Aristotle continues to distinguish a body moving "in" another body from a body moving "with" another body (see 211a34–211b5); accordingly, things move "in" place and parts move "with" wholes.[17] The fundamental distinction between the two relations and movements is separability.

Throughout the first section of Book Four, Aristotle shows over and over how place is distinct and separable from bodies. Consistently returning to his exemplar, the vessel (*angeion/angos*), Aristotle reads place through a logic of containment. He states this clearly in the first possibility of place at the beginning of chapter 4: "Place is what contains or surrounds (*periechon*) that of which it is the place" (210b35). But it is strictly the sort of containment that is "separate and touching" (211a32) with the body it contains or surrounds or embraces, and it is here that Irigaray raises her most pointed questions for Aristotle. Continuing this line, Aristotle describes the relation of body to place as when the body "is immediately 'in' the surrounding body (*periechontos somatos*) [by filling the body] to its inner limits" (211a32). This is Aristotle's most precise definition of place as a vessel, a definition that Irigaray diagnoses as "not complex enough" (1993a, 41).

As the condition that allows a body to exist "in the world" (211a24), place is what allows for locomotion (*phora*). A body can move if it is 'in place,' if it is contained. *Phora* implies not only its primary meaning, "a carrying" (and particularly as a metaphor, "to carry across"), but also senses of bringing forth or giving: place is therefore that which 'brings forth' a body—giving the principle of activity, allowing or even inciting it to desire. The text also notes, parenthetically, "By the surrounding body (*periechontos somatos*), I mean the motion that is the carrying through space (*phora*)" (212a7). Place, as that which limits (*peirainô*) a body, is what then brings the body forth into motion. But the container, the limiting and surrounding body, itself must remain unmoved.

Reading the space between the boundaries of the vessel, which he calls "an interval" (212a10) that is "*regarded* as empty" (212a13, my italics), Aristotle argues that bodies move 'in place' because place itself does not move: *phora* is the carrying of bodies across the interval that can occur 'in' (because of) the surrounding body (*periechontos somatos*) that is place. Bodies can move because they are 'in' place (*phora*). The rich possibilities of the Greek *en* (in) are helpful here. When used with the dative case, which is the form in these passages of Aristotle, *en* can connote the spatial sense of one body being 'in' another or the state or condition of a body; the temporal sense of duration or future orientation; and, finally, the logical sense of sufficiency, whereby relations of body to its principle or *archê* are implied. In this latter sense, bodies are 'in' place in the sense that place is what grants the contained body the principle of activity. Place functions not only spatially, but also—and perhaps more importantly—ontologically. And the primary characteristic of this possibility of granting a body the principle of activity is that place should be both separable and motionless: place is "an immovable vessel (*angeion/ angos*)" (212a15), "motionless" just as the whole river is motionless *vis-à-vis* the moving boat (212a15–19). "Hence we conclude that *the innermost motionless limits of what contains is place*" (212a20). And, through Irigaray's eyes, we can begin to see that the unspoken morphological exemplar for such a model of place is the womb (see 1993a, 43).

Contained Subjectivity

As Irigaray develops Aristotle's conception of place, she performs the role of the feminine as place: she brings out the ways that "place in this context always constitutes an inside" (1993a, 42). 'Place' directs us toward that which is contained. What matters is what is inside—not what is excluded, left outside, uncontained or perhaps even uncontainable. What matters is not the container itself. The trajectory of concern and interest is directed, just as it was in Lacan's model of the inverted bouquet (a model literally fashioned on the logic of the vessel; "vase" is one of the primary meanings of *angos*), toward that which is contained, which becomes a basic criterion of evaluation: if it is contained (limited, *periechontos*), then it can move (*phora*); if it can move (particularly across), it must be desiring; if it is desiring, it is valuable. One must exist 'inside' a place (a vessel, a womb, a vase, an ego, an individual subjectivity, a world that contains rather than rejects) if one is to develop as a desiring being. And place is that which gives or brings forth desire.

In focusing our attention on the inside, Aristotle approaches the question of place from the situation of one who is (at least potentially) in place, from the perspective of one who is contained. He reads the dynamics of the vessel only through its teleological orientation toward containment, bringing the synonymous meanings of *peras* and *telos* as ends or goals together. For Aristotle, a vessel is only functioning as an actual vessel when it is containing something: an empty vessel is only a potential vessel. In insisting on this teleological orientation, Aristotle effectively erases the possibility that the vessel could function in a non-teleological or even a 'doubly teleological' way. To speak in Irigaray's language and desire, Aristotle erases the possibility of a chiasmus, a teleology oriented toward containing another that might turn back upon itself and contain itself or be contained. Or, to shift us toward her questioning, perhaps Aristotle effectively erases the possibility *that we could read* the vessel in any way other than through this strictly teleological function and still read it as a 'vessel.'

To be that which is 'inside,' a body must have bodies that are exterior to it. As Aristotle puts it, "If then a body is surrounded or contained by another body outside it, this body is in place, but if not, then not" (212a32). As he elaborates, this means that, "whenever a thing is a continuum of homogeneous parts" (212b5), those parts are only potentially in place; it is only when "the parts are separated but in contact, as in a heap, [that] they are in a place actually" (212b6).[18] It is thus only through contact with exterior bodies that are separable from it that a body is in place, rather than only a part of a whole (body, which would need in turn to be in place).[19]

Given that Irigaray frames her discussion of Aristotle through the dynamic of desire, a Hegelian-Lacanian interpolation of the dynamics of recognition may both help us to better understand Aristotle's discussion of interiority/exteriority and direct us toward Irigaray's reading; it will also begin to orient us toward Lacan's 'voice' in Irigaray's text. For Hegel, the basic structure of recognition, which he places at the heart of the quest for self-consciousness in the *Phenomenology of Spirit*, is grounded in the possibility of being recognized by another. In the infamous master-slave dialectic, consciousness can only move toward self-consciousness through 'coming out of itself' to be recognized by another consciousness. It is only as it exists for-another that consciousness can return to itself as existing in-and-for-itself. (Whether this return is ever possible opens a different kind of question, one that Lacan seems to answer in his reading of the subject as ontologically narcissistic and aggressive.) The exterior is essential to the possibility of consciousness developing (in Hegelian parlance, articulating) its interiority: without the exterior, there is no interior; the exterior 'gives place to' the interior.

Lacan then complicates this dynamic of recognition considerably. We have already seen how an external image is the primary requirement for ego-formation, a formation that is ontologically grounded in misrecognition (*méconnaissance*) and functions to contain the interiority of subjectivity. (In many ways, Lacan's mirror stage can be read as a developmental casting of Hegel's master-slave dialectic, wherein consciousness is at war with its own perceptions of reality to develop into self-consciousness.) This reliance on exteriority for the development of interiority is then further complicated in the general psychoanalytic conceptions of sublimation and repression, which are also deemed essential apparatuses for the constructions of coherent interior subjectivities.

At their most extreme operations, sublimation and repression (both of which can be understood as deep acts of memory) are the mechanisms that allow an ego to incorporate—interiorize—traumatic external events so that it will not be paralyzed by them.[20] These traumatic external events can range from physical violence to the everyday, psychic alienation from the Other. At the core of all of these events, the psyche is returned to that primary site of loss—the loss of the mother. Alienation from the other, and ontological alienation from the Other, are projections of this primary site of loss, the loss of the mother (leading Elizabeth Grosz to write this as the loss of the (m)other [Grosz 1990, chapter 3]). Morphologically, this is the loss of the womb. Ontologically, in Aristotle's language, it is the loss of place.

These deep acts of memory thus become convoluted ways of constantly returning to that primary site of loss so that it can be incorporated and internalized and thereby effectively 'not lost.'[21] It can be remembered—and thus recuperated. The return to that site of loss, externalized through acts of sublimation and repression, enables a psyche to revisit it nostalgically, lamenting its loss and thereby recathecting its connection (albeit a severed connection) to it. In this grieving, the psyche thereby attempts to bring closure—in an act that is necessarily repeated over and over and thus never fully closed—to this primary loss, this primary hole and tear in one's relation to the world. The alienation is an ontological alienation and the closure, necessarily refracted through the convolutions of memory's hermeneutics, can never be complete. But in enabling the psyche to revisit the 'place of places,' these acts of deep memory nonetheless provide a profound experience of one's origin and thus of one's place in the world.[22]

But how can one do this if one is not given this gift of exteriority, the gift of "being received" that Nietzsche speaks through Zarathustra?[23] "How is an inside to be sublimated, remembered?" (Irigaray 1993a, 42). And without sublimation or memory, without an exterior that allows this relation to an interior, without returning to the primary site of loss without identifying *as* that primary site of loss (for some other desiring body), how is one to develop an interiority at all? Without having a 'place,' how can one become a body that moves, a body that desires, an actual (or whole) body at all? How can one become a subject, much less an autonomous individual?

A Hermeneutics of Morphology

Irigaray reads Aristotle's discussion of place to locate the site at which this exemplary text of western, phallocentric metaphysics "tak[es] from the feminine the tissue or texture of spatiality" (1993a, 11). As we see in this brief exegesis, the logic of containment dominates Aristotle's approach to the question of place. And, less surprisingly, the "immovable vessel" (212a15) accordingly dominates his physical descriptions. But he never fully turns to reflect upon the ways that these physical descriptions are also behaving as textual analogies for a metaphysics that goes unquestioned. The vessel is assumed as the 'natural' exemplar of a metaphysics that is concerned with principles of motion, desire, knowledge, and being. According to such a logic of deduction, wherein physical examples are drawn from metaphysical precepts, Aristotle never turns to interrogate the ways that his physical exemplar, the vessel, itself shapes (pun intended) his discussion through the analogical relation it draws between his metaphysical account and the physical world in which it operates. He never wonders how his reliance on the vessel, as the primary frame for his understanding of 'place,' itself shapes his understanding of place: he never questions how his physics might shape his metaphysics.

If we read Aristotle's texts performatively and not only conceptually, we begin to see how it is in this precise *aporia* between the physical and the metaphysical that Irigaray opens Aristotle's text to the play of sexual (in)difference at work within it. She reads this *aporia* as exemplary of the carefully contained, carefully bound work that phallocentric metaphysics cuts into its delimited areas of study. While one can certainly deduce physical relations from metaphysical arguments in Aristotelian logic, Irigaray diagnoses these two dimensions, physics and metaphysics, as "dislocated" (1993a, 36) from one another.[24]

Logical deduction is not the sort of 'passage between' that Irigaray desires. It assumes and reinscribes a fundamental space or gap between the two areas: to deduce one (physical) concept from another set of (metaphysical) concepts is to ensure the division between the two sets. The kind of connection drawn through a logical deduction emphasizes the distinction between the two sets of concepts. It implies a difference in kind between them, a difference that is rendered sharper and clearer as deduction reasserts the distinct qualities of the sets of concepts. A primary effect of the logical act of deduction is to draw explicit attention to the clear and distinct boundaries of the concepts involved: deduction ensures that the concepts are clearly contained, with distinct and firm boundaries. The space between the concepts thus becomes an essential part of this process of delineation: deduction ensures that a fundamental space or gap remains between the two sets of concepts. It enacts the logic of the limit.

In Irigaray's reading of Aristotle, this fundamental space or gap between physics and metaphysics remains uncrossed and uncrossable. Logical deduction ensures that the sets of concepts cannot 'touch,' much less blend porously into one another in ways that are not logically mappable, logically containable. This particular *aporia* thus performs the very meaning of *aporia*, "no way." It performs the very inability of Aristotelian metaphysics to deal with the problem of "ways," the problem of passage. Deduction is unilateral and teleological, reasserting separation, not connection, between the concepts. It does not and cannot account for how one concept might affect or subtly shade into the meaning of another. Because it is the fundamental blind spot of Aristotle's reading of place, Irigaray reads this *aporia* between the physical and the metaphysical as the site of the suppression and effective erasure of the feminine and, subsequently, of sexual difference itself.

When she turns to the figure of the womb, Irigaray refers to her own turning (in a moment of textual self-consciousness that is common in Irigaray's texts, if not in Aristotle's) as a working out of "the analogy with the relation between the sexes" (1993a, 43). In an interesting textual pause, wherein she seems to gesture toward the role of psychoanalysis's voice in her texts, Irigaray playfully questions (parenthetically, as ever) her borrowing from Freud,[25] while proceeding to perform the psychoanalytically inspired style of reading that has already been at work throughout the entire essay: she reads Aristotle morphologically.

This lens of morphology is present throughout her essay (and throughout the majority of her texts). It is what drives her insistence that Aristotle's "definition of vessel is not complex enough" (1993a, 41). For Irigaray, morphology allows her to move back and forth between the registers of, in psychoanalytic terms, the symbolic and the imaginary. In Aristotle's language, morphology bridges metaphysics and physics, enabling her both to read the metaphysical in its physical registers and, the truly unthinkable in Aristotelian logic, to read the physical back into the metaphysical.[26] In understanding morphology as the ways that concepts shape bodies and bodies shape concepts, Irigaray moves in and out, back and forth, crossing the (allegedly impermeable) boundaries of bodily-conceptual inscriptions—and *performing* the resignifying of the very blind spot that she locates in Aristotle's text.

Out of this performance, the womb emerges as the morphological ex-

emplar of Aristotle's place, that "innermost motionless limits of what contains" (212a20). Read through our contemporary symbolic's phallocentric
lenses, the womb is that place of places, that receptacle of receptacles. It is
the very site of desire, serving as "place itself . . . that toward which there is
locomotion" (1993a, 39). It is the alpha and the omega of the only sexual
act for a phallicized sexuality, heterosexual penetration, and the phallicized
male body that is served by that act.[27] It is both the site of origin and the
site of loss: it both gives birth to the desired child and envelops the male
sexual organ in his nostalgic return to the site of his primary birth and loss.
It physically (both reproductively and sexually) and psychically contains and
gives place to the phallicized body. And it is also what dominates the phallicized reading of female sexuality, according to which "the female sex (organ)
is . . . *vessel*" (1993a, 43) and womanhood is determined by her relation (potential, actual, distanced, near, impossible, rejected) to motherhood, to the
womb.

Following the basic premise (of Greek temples and Lacanian psychoanalysis) that the phallus must be veiled if it is to exercise its power, Aristotle's
concept of place seems to be a veiled reading of the womb as the exemplar
of places. It follows then that women and men stand in a different relation
to place—and subsequently to movement, desire, and subjectivity itself. This
is the site of ethics. If the womb is the exemplar of place, then woman and
femininity are configured in ways that mirror the configuring of place: the
innermost motionless boundary of that contained body which can move. The
feminine is configured as that which allows active bodies to move, desiring
bodies to act, male bodies to desire. One must be contained to desire; yet
she is the container, not the contained. As we saw in the brief discussion of
sublimation, woman is denied an externalized representation of place—she
is the place of places, place itself, not that desiring body that is in place.

What Does Irigaray Want?

This brings us then to the extraordinarily tricky and complex question
of Irigaray's desire. If woman is place itself, if the feminine is configured as
the site that incites desire but does not desire itself, the question of Irigaray's
desire brings us 'inside' (in a performance of the difficulty at hand) the very
suppression of sexual difference itself.

In her reading of Aristotle, and of Spinoza later, a sort of lamentation
emerges in Irigaray's voice: she laments the erasure of the very possibility of
feminine subjectivity. Even more so, she laments that this erasure serves as

the necessary condition for masculine subjectivity to emerge in this phalli-cized conception of place: for male bodies to become active, desiring subjects, female bodies must contain them and 'give them place'; for female bodies to serve as containers, they must be passive receptacles for some other (male) body's desire, not desiring bodies in and of themselves. It is a unilateral, strictly teleological relation. The logic of containment, which dominates Aristotelian conceptions of place and the subsequent models of subjectivity, ethics, and power that emerge out of it, becomes both the site of and the vehicle for the suppression and erasure of the feminine—and of sexual difference.

Out of her lamentation, Irigaray longs for a possible recuperating of the feminine. And while she sees, perhaps more clearly than any other reader of the history of western philosophy has yet seen, that this will not be any task of simple repair, her desires are—as she knows they inevitably must be—shaped by these same dynamics, these same logics of containment and de-limitation. Irigaray calls, over and over in figure after figure, for a 'place' for woman. We read her lamenting the impossibility of woman's sublimating her own primary sense of loss, the very act that allows man to move out into the world and find his place in it: "In this possible nonsublimation of herself, and by herself, woman always tends *toward* without any return to herself as the place where something positive can be elaborated" (1993a, 9). Either locked up in and by his desire or threatening as the unlimited, lim-itless lack of a 'proper' place, she has no place and is no subject. And without her subjectivity, there is no possibility for an ethical world.

Calling for the construction or reconstruction of a world in which an ethical subjectivity could exist (1993a, 17), Irigaray struggles with her vexed relation to this logic of containment. As the very site of the suppression of sexual difference, it nonetheless calls to her as the site of possible recuper-ation. We hear this hope in her own language: "for an ethics of sexual difference to come into being, we must constitute a possible place for each sex, body, and flesh to inhabit" (1993a, 17–18). In these kinds of callings, lamentations, and hopes, it is not the logic of place as conceived through containment and limits that she seeks to disrupt. She calls, rather, for ways that this place can be opened and changed so that both women and men can inhabit 'it.' She articulates this desire fairly directly, pleading for "[a] world that must be created or re-created so that man and woman may once again or at last live together, meet, and sometimes inhabit the same place" (1993a, 17). But how is this not yet another call for the erasure of sexual difference, hoping to place women and men in the same place, a place of sameness? Would such a world of ethical parity and sexual difference not require a radical reworking of the very possibility of a 'same place'?

Listening to these lamentations, hopes, and desires, my question for Irigaray is fairly direct: if the conception of place as contained by limits is the site of the suppression of sexual difference, why continue to work within its grasp as we attempt to create an ethics of sexual difference? Why perpetuate the logic of containment in an effort to create, perhaps for the first time, an ethics of sexual difference? If the logic of containment is at the core of sexist phallocentric conceptions of sexual difference—conceptions that are actually conceptions of indifference—just as the logic of containment is at the core of racist conceptions of racial (in)difference, must we not find ways out of and beyond this very logic of the limit if we are to radically (re)conceive sexual and racial difference?

Irigaray's Intervals—and Desires

I do not want to suggest that Irigaray is simply 'wrong' as she moves toward answering her own desires. I do not mean to suggest that although she is an amazing reader and diagnostician of the fundamental blind spot of sexual difference in the history of western philosophy, she fails then to move beyond her own critique and diagnosis. The very demand that she offer an 'answer' to these subtle and complex dynamics would be itself a performance of the teleological systems she is seeking to disrupt.

Rather, I call our attention again to a mode of performative reading to sensitize us to the kinds of openings Irigaray creates in her very critiques. In her interpolative strategies of reading Aristotle, to stay with the example at hand, Irigaray disrupts the possibility of reading some singular foundation (back) into Aristotle's texts.[28] When she reads Aristotle's discussion of place through a morphological lens, the emergent deep resonances with a woman's womb *do* something to Aristotle's texts. The registers multiply, perhaps endlessly—even perhaps limitlessly. What we might have read as an abstracted discussion of the way place, time, space, and motion interact suddenly takes on profound ethical and political meanings. What we might have read as an abstracted discussion of metaphysics, concerning only philosophers (or, in our early-twenty-first-century scene of demarcated specialization, perhaps only scholars of Aristotle), suddenly becomes a discussion of the ways women's bodies, and subsequently men's bodies, are shaped by long, deeply embedded historical concepts. This suddenly becomes a discussion of the struggles toward, and possible impossibility of, feminine subjectivity.[29]

Her readings open multiple levels of meaning. In reading for the erasure of the feminine (a strategy she never hides), Irigaray opens a 'gap' in these texts: an interval that had not been there surfaces and offers itself to us as readers. Focusing on the possibility of feminine subjectivity in Irigaray's reading of Aristotle, Tina Chanter describes this textual gap as a historicizing effect, "creating an interval . . . between what women have always been and what they could become" (1995, 152). Several kinds of intervals emerge: it is a textual interval, both literalized in Irigaray's signature use of ellipses, parentheticals, and italics and also enacted as a space between what had been assumed in Aristotle's text and what now surfaces in Irigaray's reading; it is an ontological interval, opening the space in which a feminine voice and morphology might be imagined and deployed; and it is a historical interval, opening the possibility of a future that is not determined by the past. Finally, it is the interval of desire—that opening which invites desire to play within it, inciting desire to cross it.

In opening this textual interval, Irigaray opens the question of the possibility of desire. If desire, as she has told us, "occupies or designates the place of the interval" (1993a, 8), then the possibility of such an interval must be opened for there to be desire. There must be a space between two bodies if there is to be an interval that incites attraction, that invites the crossing that is desire. As Irigaray indicates in a provocatively quick nod to Aristophanes' myth in Plato's *Symposium,* the myth of the 'circle-people' paralyzes desire because it does not offer "a space between him and her" (1993c, 46).[30] A space, an interval, is the site of desire. But there must be two bodies— two different and differing bodies—for such a space to exist. (And thus we see how sheer logical deduction, while creating a space, cannot create desire: it assumes and enacts only one active pole or 'desiring body,' not two, in its unilateral teleology; the kind of space it creates is uncrossable.)

There is no feminine body in Irigaray's eyes. There is only the specular partner of narcissistic reflection of the self-same. In attempting to conceive a feminine morphology, Irigaray does not leap toward the daunting task of creating a female body that is not dominated by the phallocentric logics of the Same. That is an impossible and suspiciously phallomorphic task, assuming the possibility of leaping beyond historical context and into ontologically separated spaces of being. Rather, she opens a space, an interval that invites the desire to conceive of such a body, to conceive and birth it through imagination. She opens a 'place' that will, in an Aristotelian sense of place, 'bring forth' this imagining. But unlike Aristotle's "immovable vessel" (212a15), Irigaray's textual intervals seem to be moving constantly, shifting and playing with the questions and dynamics and voices at hand. She is not opening toward a feminine as yet another womb: she is opening an interval in which an imagining of a different and differing feminine morphology might emerge.[31]

While Irigaray sees that she should not reinscribe the same sort of spatiality that we find in the Aristotelian 'place' of a motionless vessel or the Lacanian 'whole bodies' that are properly bound by skin, this figure of the interval nonetheless haunts Irigaray's own imaginings. As I developed in the Lacanian models of ego-formation, a logic of containment orients the space between bodies as 'negative' space, empty space in *need* of delimitation. Aristotle discounts the possibility that the interval between the place and the body contained is "empty," even though it is regarded in this manner.[32] For him, the constitution of this interval seems to be an ontological relation of principles (of potentiality and actuality, to use his language from the *Metaphysics*), rather than a spatial one. In both models, however, the interval persists as the configuration of a teleology that is oriented unilaterally— toward containment. The figure of the interval, whether conceived spatially or ontologically, implies a negative space that is awaiting formation, lacking and in need of containment. It does not exert its own force. It is a space that needs to be crossed, and that can be crossed only in one direction. This orientation of spatiality has served as the site of the suppression of the feminine, of sexual difference, and (although quite differently) of racial difference. We must then ask of Irigaray's openings of textual, ontological, and historical intervals: is this an empty interval that can only be crossed in one direction? Is this an interval of empty space that is in need of containment— of boundaries, formation, delimitation?

From Touch to Angels: Mucus, Lips, and Thresholds

Irigaray seems to conclude her reading of Aristotle fairly directly with the claim that woman's "issue is how to trace the limits of place herself so as to be able to situate herself therein and welcome the other there" (1993a, 35). She seems to conclude that the problem is the asymmetry that has not allowed the feminine any 'proper' place, rather than the possibility that such an asymmetry is endemic to this very conception of place. All her lamentations over the absence of, and her implicit calls for the creation of, a chiasmus thus hinge on the creation of a 'place' for woman: "If she is to be able to contain, to envelop, she must have her own envelope" (1993a, 35). It seems as if, rather than disrupting the very logic of containment implied in this conception of place, Irigaray wants a place to be made for woman: "If desire is to subsist, a double place is necessary, a double envelope" (1993a, 48).

But these apparent conclusions are produced by a reading that is executed exclusively at the conceptual level. A more performative reading brings us in touch with a whole other register of these essays and her work more broadly.

In much of her early work, particularly *This Sex Which Is Not One*, Irigaray valorizes the morphology of 'touch' as a way to exceed the phallocentric symbolic that is so deeply grounded in the visual. Essays that are now classics of her early work, "This Sex Which Is Not One" and "When Our Lips Speak Together," perform what Judith Butler has called "an eros of surfaces" (1993, 46), an eroticism that refuses the polarity of penetration-containment as the *telos* of all erotic acts. Drawing on "the geography of her pleasure" (1985b, 28), Irigaray writes in the very modes she describes—self-contradictory, setting off "in all directions" (1985b, 29), her words "never identical with anything" (1985b, 29), speaking meanings that are "contiguous" (1985b, 29), not clear or distinct or transparent—or delimited. Her language "touches upon" (1985b, 29) itself, writing gaps and pauses and intervals into our reading ears with her infamous ellipses, folding back into and drawing upon the sheer materiality of her utterances, eliciting visceral responses that tingle in bodies rather than solidifying in (phallic) brains.[33]

She writes a feminine morphology that is not phallicized in the essays of *This Sex Which Is Not One*, blurring boundaries of insides and outsides, of what she means and how she says it, of the conceptual and performative registers of her own texts. By the time we arrive at the final essay, "When Our Lips Speak Together," our own bodies may have undergone what Tamsin Lorraine calls a "perceptual training" (1999, 88–89, 233), leaving us open to Irigaray's subtle plays of touch, fluids, mucus, and lips that are always half-open and half-self-touching. We are ready not merely to read and analyze and conceptualize her language: we are ready to do it, to live it, to embody it.

Irigaray's valorization of touch, which is at the heart of her figures of lips and mucus, performs an attempt to imagine a new cultural symbolic, a symbolic toward which Irigaray is always writing, and toward which she writes with a particular historical sensibility in these essays. As Penelope Deutscher has developed at some length, Irigaray writes toward a future that is, in its enactment of sexual difference, impossible in this world's political and philosophical structures: "a politics anticipating difference" (2002, 1).

And in these early writings particularly, she writes toward a symbolic that clearly does not yet exist, one that would not reduce multiplicity to singularity, or difference to sameness. This would be a symbolic not grounded in the visual and its attendant logics of external relations and containment. It begins to articulate a morphology that would not fall into the unilateral, asymmetrical teleology that she diagnoses in Aristotle. Consequently, many readers of Irigaray have celebrated this bodily figuration of touch as ushering us into a spatiality that does not divide bodies into clear and distinct, contained vessels.[34]

The work of Elizabeth Grosz in *Volatile Bodies*, particularly the essay "Sexed Bodies," draws out the ways that Irigaray's valorization of mucus, as that which confuses corporeal boundaries and limits, invites us to radically reimagine sexuality itself, particularly the normative roles of heterosexuality that infect all of our lived experiences. Writing in the register of subjectivity and interpersonal relations, Tamsin Lorraine's developments of Irigaray's figures of fluids, lips, and thresholds capture much of the general celebration and hope found in these morphological figurations. In Irigaray's "threshold of the lips, which are strangers to dichotomy and oppositions" (Irigaray 1993a, 18), Lorraine finds a model of relation in which two bodies, "neither active nor passive, [can] . . . shape each other without clear distinction between the two, and yet without losing the trace of their difference" (Lorraine 1999, 38).[35] Lorraine articulates the ideal of a spatiality that is not divided by an asymmetrical polarity into clearly demarcated subjects and objects: touch disallows the division of bodies into 'contained vessels,' while maintaining a difference that allows a subjectivity grounded in connection, rather than distinction, to emerge.[36] Touch, particularly figured through mucus, creates a space in which to imagine interpersonal relations that are not configured through the binary of subject-object which emerges out of the logic of containment and dominates our concepts of ethics. Touch provides Irigaray with a model of embodiment and spatiality that allows for non-oppositional difference to thrive as the site of non-discrete, non-contained subjectivity.

I am deeply sympathetic to this quest and hope for imagining a spatiality not grounded in the logic of containment. However, I am also frustrated by the ways that touch becomes an ending point, rather than a starting point, for imagining a morphology of sexual difference. In the discussions that valorize touch to reorient embodiment and usher us into a spatiality that does not erase difference in the ways that the spatiality of containment and penetration does, a specific model of touch seems to be at work. There are, of course, many forms of touch that we can easily enumerate from our lived experiences: the friendly pat on the back; the slightly different pat on the butt that we see with humorous repetition in male professional sports; the pleading pull of a child on a mother's arm; the long and tight embrace of loved ones long separated; the erotic caresses between lovers that often penetrate various orifices and involve various organs; the aggressive "brush" against a buttock or breast that signifies unwanted sexual advances; the violent slap of a face or even crashing of skulls. These are all viable instances of 'touch.' But none of these are the kinds of touch invoked in Irigaray's texts. None of these fits the kind of touch that Irigaray valorizes as ushering us into a reimagining of spatiality.

An unspoken, specific sort of touch circulates in Irigaray's texts. They assume a kind of touch that involves bodies in a mutual shaping to which each has consented and from which each benefits. Bodies thus emerge from this experience of touch changed, and yet still themselves. Different, but still intact. Truly different. Two examples are helpful. The one Irigaray develops most explicitly is that of maternal touch, wherein a kind of mutual loving is celebrated as structuring this touch that is nothing but nurturing and beneficial to all involved. The other is less explicit in Irigaray's texts, but involves a sort of romanticized model of amorous touch between women, of which nineteenth-century notions of "Boston marriages" and early 1970s models of strictly egalitarian and consensual lesbian relations emerge as simple historical examples. In both of these models, an idealizing and even a romanticizing of a certain kind of touch is at work—a romanticizing that betrays the sort of tame, domesticated homoeroticism that is palatable to Irigaray.[37] While this kind of idealizing might be helpful in stirring our imaginations, it seems insufficient to sustain and support our work in reconfiguring spatiality, and thereby reconfiguring ethics.[38]

Irigaray articulates this dynamic of 'touch' further in the later works that have been translated as *An Ethics of Sexual Difference* and *Sexes and Genealogies,* particularly as she turns to the figure of angels. Angels become for Irigaray a fascinating mode of bodily comportment that allows bilateral passage between the divine and the mortal—the very *aporia* of Aristotelian metaphysics. Angels cross back and forth, to and fro, through the threshold of thresholds. They perform, in their own bodies, a sort of chiasmus, opening for Irigaray a figuration through which to imagine a chiasmus of sexually different beings. For Irigaray, angels cross and recross the interval, "transgress[ing] all enclosures in their speed, tell[ing] of the passage between the envelope of God and that of the world" (1993a, 16). Speaking in "gesture . . . [they] tell of another incarnation, another parousia of the body . . . [in their] movement, posture, the coming-and-going between the two" (1993a, 16). They are mediators, "endlessly reopening the enclosure of the universe, of universes, identities, the unfolding of actions, of history" (1993a, 15). And, most telling of all, angels "pass through the envelope(s) or container(s) . . . never remain[ing] enclosed in a place, [but also] never immobile" (1993a, 15).

Angels appear to embody and enact, for Irigaray, a placeless desire, a movement back and forth across the interval of intervals, the gap between the divine and the mortal. Angels cross this interval, leaving both poles both intact and changed by their crossing. Their movement leads Irigaray into the sort of reimagining of bodies, desire, and space that our ethics of dominance, mastery, and sexual indifference desperately needs. As long as we continue to forget angels, Irigaray suggests, we will remain tragically trapped in sexually undifferentiated bodies that can never cross a threshold without forming it into a definitive place—the sorts of embodiment and spatiality that render ethics of mutual codetermination and alterity ontologically impossible.

But what sorts of bodies does Irigaray behold in these angels? In "Belief Itself," one of her most prolonged discussions of angels and devils, Irigaray turns to angels as, again, ushering us into a spatiality that is, to invoke her reading of Freud's Little Ernst, not structured through the 'reel of mastery' that allows Little Ernst to control (believe he is controlling) the presence and absence of his mother. With the string of his reel, Little Ernst believes[39] that he controls, and passes back and forth across, the threshold to his first dwelling place, his primary site of loss, his mother's womb. He believes, as Irigaray writes, that in his *fort-da* game he masters the possibility of "return[ing] into her, [moving] back into the lost paradise where she shelters him and feeds him with and through her/their container" (1993c, 34). It is an exemplary performance of his proper relation to his own (Aristotelian) place. But in this game of hide and seek, "the son plays with himself alone" (1993c, 34), performing the self-enclosed economy of narcissism (and aggression) that is the law of the self-same. Irigaray's turn to angels exposes this 'closed economy' through the angels' enactment of a 'real,' not falsely believed, crossing of thresholds.

Irigaray vacillates between two embodiments of angels: a Rilkean sense of angels as white, light, semi-transparent, pure,[40] and of a questionable sex

(1993c, 35); and the Exodus account from the Hebrew Bible of angels as "neither God, nor men nor women, nor beasts," but "sphinxes" (1993c, 45). In the first embodiment, of lightness, whiteness, and semi-transparency, angels are mediators between this world and "beyond the horizon" (1993c, 35). Primarily moving vertically, "the angels come down and go up, go up and come down, in a vertical mediation" (1993c, 36) that rather eerily echoes Aristotle's exemplary motion for his interrogation of place and that in our ears (which we share with Irigaray) has a decidedly sexual ring of penetration, traditionally associated with heterosexual intercourse. In the second embodiment, of neither human nor animal nor God, a more Heideggerian sensibility emerges in two angels who sit face to face and thereby "shelter what may take place" and "guard the presence of God" (1993c, 44): these two angels give place to the advent of God in the human world and the unimagined future that would materialize therein. Irigaray's angels thus move up and down, carrying messages across the uncrossable threshold, and give place to "the presence of God" (1993c, 44). Are these not figures Aristotle might have imagined?

In the Greek etymology of angels, *angelos,* a double resonance emerges that enriches the tensions which haunt Irigaray's deployment of angels (*anges*) in her attempts to imagine a different and differing morphology, and an ethical symbolic. The first resonance is in the most basic meaning of *angelos,* messenger. This is certainly the meaning that intrigues Irigaray, as we see in her essays "Belief Itself" and "Sexual Difference," as well as her reading of Diotima in "Sorcerer Love," where she suggests that Plato misguides the intermediary comportment that Diotima offers to the discussion of love. Angels are messengers that cross all thresholds—between divine and mortal, human and animal, and even man and woman. "From beyond the angel returns with inaudible or unheard of words in the here and now" (1993c, 36). But there is also a phonetic resonance in *angelos* with *angos* or *angeion,* the terms Aristotle used to connote "vessel" in his discussion of place. These two words, *angelos* and *angos,* are the only Greek terms that begin with an alpha and a double gamma. Merging this phonetic resonance with the basic meaning of "messenger," we may hear subtle ways in which an Aristotelian sense of place, as conceived through containment, boundaries, and limits, haunts and limits Irigaray's attempts to imagine beyond it.

If Irigaray's angels are vessels that carry messages across (primarily vertical) thresholds, how do they differ from Aristotle's place (*phora*) that functions because it is limited and contained (*periechontos*)? If her angels are half-animal and half-human, but still serving to give place to the presence of the divine, how are they not functioning as the boundaries and limits that allow particular bodies to materialize? In either instantiation, boundaries, vessels, and limits function either to carry something across a threshold or to bring some body into existence—the very characteristics, functions, and problematics Irigaray diagnosed as suppressing the feminine and sexual difference in Aristotle's discussion of place.

Irigaray thus leaves us with two kinds of space in her musings on angels: a vertical threshold that angels cross back and forth and the 'place' created between two facing angels, in which the divine can emerge. A figure of an interval, whether as a threshold or as a place in between, surfaces in both. An interval frames these 'imaginings' of differing morphologies. It almost seems that Irigaray, despite her keen suspicion of such moves, wishes to solve the *aporia* of Aristotelian metaphysics through turning to a morphology that can criss-cross the threshold and an interval that would produce a place for bodies other than phallically active ones. But the fundamental frame of the interval, which emerges out of a logic of containment and delimitation, persists, just as it does in her very style of reading. This frame may itself *limit* Irigaray's imaginings.

Reading at the Limits: Idealizing Heterosexuality

In relation to the spatiality of mastery that structures Little Ernst's *fort-da* game, Irigaray suggests that angels disrupt his easy play of domination because they embody a place that is "at the limits of known spatiality" (1993c, 42). She continues, insisting that we must "rethink and rebuild the whole scene of representation [if] the angels [are to] find a home" (1993c, 42). And the way to do this is not to reduce them to our known spatiality of grids and places, but to "note the moment when they pass by" (1993c, 42)—to behold them at our limits.

This presents us with a final way to read Irigaray's texts and, more particularly, her style, the theme with which I began. The introduction of limits focuses the similarities in the variety of configurations we have encountered that manifest a logic of containment. Limits function centrally in Aristotelian concepts of place, where the proper place (*phora*) is that which is limited or contained (*periechon*); in Little Ernst's *fort-da* game, where the limits of presence/absence are tightly (even if fictively) controlled; and in the Lacanian reliance on the visual space of bodies bound by skin and thereby distanced from one another. The introduction of limits also focuses both of the ways that Irigaray reads texts from the history of western philosophy and, most importantly, the *places* in which this style of reading positions her.

While Irigaray's style of reading has been characterized (by her as well) as a style of deconstructive mimicry, it is also a style of interpolation. Irigaray often writes in a literal style of interpolation, where we find parts of texts interspersed with her own musings, implications, exclusions, questions, sometimes even exclamations. (Her discussion of Aristotle on place is an easy example of this kind of text.) She interrupts these texts. And her interruptions both place limits on the texts, literally in the form of her insertions, and expose the limits that are already operative in the very constitution of the texts. That is, she both carves 'limits' internally into the texts and exposes the constitutive exclusions that are necessary to the very construction of the texts. As Judith Butler puts it, she explores "how the borders are secured" (1993, 37).

On the one hand, following Husserl for example, it might seem as if some moment of exclusion is the necessary condition for any system of signifiers. In this vein, we are always already 'making sense' due to the function of limits: this is the very condition of finitude and, as we find in Husserl, the very structure of intentionality and choice.[41] But on the other hand, the exposure of exclusionary limits in texts from the history of western philosophy also disrupts the very kinds of claims made in and by the texts themselves.

Whether they are set forth by Plato, Aristotle, Descartes, Spinoza, Kant, Hegel, or even Heidegger, systems of metaphysics, including even those that are most porous or might not claim the name "system" for themselves, necessarily claim some universality, echoing the 'universal sound' that we have already encountered in psychoanalysis. Indeed, they often claim an ontological status in the very writing of their 'logics.' When Irigaray exposes the primary exclusion of the feminine as the enabling condition for these systems, she thereby calls into question their universal or even ontological status. She calls into question, in the language of Hegel and Bataille, the totalizing grasp of these closed systems. Through exposing this 'outer' limit of these systems—as a limit that is necessary to their very function as systems—Irigaray resituates philosophy itself as a historicized discourse that is ontologically grounded in exclusion.

But, as Butler warns, it is dangerous to read this "as the necessary and founding violence of any truth-regime. . . . [We must] resist that theoretical gesture of pathos in which exclusions are simply affirmed as sad necessities of signification" (1993, 53). Irigaray can leave us neither in sheer lamentation nor in secure recuperation. The exposure of these necessary and constitutive limits as the site of the suppression of the feminine presents western philosophy with the task of reconfiguring its very relation to limits—to limits, to finitude, to infinity, to place and space and time and philosophy's very mode of conceptual thinking. As Irigaray tells us over and over, the whole scene of representation, the whole economy of space-time, must be radically reconceived, reconfigured, reimagined. And, following our sustained excursion here into the question of place, this means we must retread and reimagine our relations to and with limits.

▼ ▼ ▼

Irigaray writes both at the limits of these texts and for the limits of these texts. She tracks down, spies out, unearths these limits. Configured as the feminine that is rendered unrepresentable, she exposes that constitutive outside which allows, through the disavowal of it, the 'inside' of the various metaphysical presuppositions and systems to operate. But where does this position her? Her interpolative deconstructive mimicries simultaneously carve her own limits and 'place' 'inside' these texts, and play and toy with these limits, turning them back upon themselves. How does this combined style of interpolative deconstructive mimicry affect her imaginative essays on future figurations of the feminine? In what 'place' do Irigaray's texts locate Irigaray?

In both of her styles of reading, the interpolative, deconstructive mimicry and the creative imaginings of impossible morphologies, Irigaray speaks and writes from some 'place.' We have already explored an example of the former at length here. To add another, well-known example, she mimics the constitutive exclusionary limits in her reading of Freud in *Speculum* in an effort to turn them back upon themselves, leading Freud's text to "eat its own tail" as it lands in an endless stream of self-contradictions: she 'penetrates' and enters Freud's text. In the imaginative texts we have encountered here, both the early figures of lips, touch, and mucus and the later figures of angels, she attempts to transgress the limit of phallicized signification[42] and speak the unspeakable: she speaks in a futural voice opening toward a femininity not yet imagined here. It readily appears that the latter of these is the more provocative, the less easily pinned down. But I am arguing that it, also, locates her in some 'place'—a contained, delimited, demarcated place. Judith Butler argues that Irigaray is repeatedly placing "the feminine [as] 'always' the outside, and the outside [as] 'always' the feminine" (1993, 48), a strategy that only reinscribes, rather than resisting, the centralizing power of the phallus and its marginalizing erasure of the feminine. Writing this in the register of limits and place, I argue that these interpolative, deconstructive, and imaginative strategies position her in some 'place' that is delimited and emerges as meaningful because it, too, is finally contained.

Again, this contained 'place' emerges more clearly in her texts on the history of western philosophy, which are the texts that Butler diagnoses as "penetrative" (1993, 45). Although Irigaray's voice moves constantly in these texts, enacting textually the differing/deferring mode of the impossible sexual difference toward which she writes,[43] we can nonetheless demarcate the contours of the place from which she writes. This leads Butler to argue that these texts are at odds with "the rigorously anti-penetrative eros of surfaces that appears in [her] 'When Our Lips Speak Together'" (1985b, 45–46). She thereby faults Irigaray for not living up to her own imagination. Or, in the terms with which I began this essay, Butler reads Irigaray as allowing her conceptual readings to gain an upper hand against her performative texts—a classic problem of phallocentric metaphysics. However, if we disallow this disjuncture and read her conceptual and performative texts—or her interpolative deconstructive mimicry and her creative imaginings—as conjoined, we may realize that the two styles of text do not emerge from radically distinct places or voices. We may subsequently uncover dynamics in Irigaray's texts that delimit her project of writing toward an impossible sexual difference.

▼ ▼ ▼

Two fundamental and related moves haunt and limit Irigaray's efforts to resist the marginalizing erasure of the feminine and its subsequent ethics of mastery, control, and sameness. Both have been diagnosed as emerging in Irigaray's later texts: the increasing idealization of the heterosexual couple and the increasing move toward idealization itself. The emergent heterosexism is most often dated from the 1996 publication of *I Love to You*, where she locates the heterosexual couple as the fundamental unit of sociality.[44] As Deutscher develops with great subtlety, Irigaray falls short of her own textual aims and strategies here, reasserting a kind of essentialism[45] that reads the heterosocial/heterosexual as the privileged site of (potential) difference and, oppositionally, the homosocial/homosexual as the privileged site of self-sameness. Drawing on Derrida's texts on friendship and narcissism, Deutscher compellingly argues that Irigaray "reinstates the belief that the other can be stably identified and known" (2002, 138), a belief that situates sexual difference as something that has already occurred, rather than something yet to be imagined and created. As Deutscher writes succinctly, "once she affirms sexual difference as the privileged site of difference, . . . she returns to an identification of difference that we might wish to see left more in suspense" (2002, 137).

Deutscher proceeds to suggest that perhaps we can "deemphasize the exaggeratedly heterosexual imagery in Irigaray's recent work" (2002, 139) if we read it as an intentional response to historical conditions, which do in fact privilege heterosexuality as the social relation *par excellence.*[46] But I argue that Irigaray's increased heteronormativity is actually connected to her increased move away from historicized conditions and toward transcendent idealized states—those states in which cultures of phallicized whiteness thrive. And, more damningly, I also argue that we can see this movement already in her 1980 lecture, "Belief Itself," and its meditation on angels.

As indicated in my prior reading, the figures of angels in this text echo Aristotelian notions of place almost perfectly: vessels that carry messages across vertical thresholds, particularly the threshold of thresholds between God and man. Despite Irigaray's pleas to the contrary, these figures read all too easily as always already inscribed in predetermined, predictable tasks designated by the power of powers, God. They traverse the fields of the eternal and the historical, the transcendent and the material; but they ultimately find their meaning in the first elements of these pairs, the transcendent space of the heavenly messages they convey. Irigaray ultimately places them in this transcendent space in her idealizing of them as a figure to mime (not to mimic) in our attempts to imagine sexual difference. As Cynthia Willett writes, "She presents her angels as though they were untouched by the struggles of the material world" (2001, 152).

These characteristics become clearer through the stark contrasts with the figures of self-touching, half-open lips and mucus that clings to all surfaces from "This Sex Which Is Not One" and "When Our Lips Speak Together." As I developed above, these figures blur all boundaries, opening us toward possibilities of sociality irreducible to delimited bodies and the ethics of mastery, control, and self-sameness that ensues. Aristotelian notions of place, and the logic of the limit that they enact, have little purchase here. Written three years earlier than the lecture on angels, these texts also notably flirt with homoeroticism.[47] But in so doing, they also flirt with a doubled essentialism: lesbianism as the ideal of egalitarian relations and its precondition, women as inherently egalitarian. The homosocial/homosexual is the perfect site of egalitarianism in these texts because it is already read as the site of sameness-dressed-as-equality. The evidence of this is her conflation of women's auto-eroticism and homosexuality: to love oneself is already to love the same, and to love the same is the act of homosexuality. There is no queer pleasure here, despite the tantalizing descriptions of the auto-eroticism of female morphologies. The move toward angels and away from these half-open, self-touching wet lips is perhaps less radical than we might have thought at first.

Cynthia Willett argues that Irigaray's heterosexism comes explicitly at the expense of all other forms of difference—racial, national, religious, and, of utmost concern to Willett's project, class (2001, 150–51). When Irigaray fixes on heterosexuality as the site of difference, she reinscribes sexual difference as the only horizon of difference that matters. Amplifying that reading, I argue that Irigaray's heteronormative perspective enacts the oppositional logic that, despite all her aims and intentions, she cannot escape. The move toward angels and away from half-open, self-touching, wet lips is not thereby accidental or a radical break. And the increasingly explicit heterosexism of her recent work is just that—increasingly explicit. It is not, however, a radical departure from her conception of difference—namely, as demarcated and oppositional.

To say that the figure of angels enacts an Aristotelian sense of place in a way that the earlier figures of lips and mucus disrupt it is to say that the figure of angels enacts the logic of the limit. These vessels-as-angels are delimitable, albeit bizarrely so. One last index of this delimited state brings the question of Irigaray's 'place' fully into view: the angels reside in an ahistorical place. Both ontologically and textually, these angels do not exist in historical time for Irigaray: ontologically, we can only glimpse them and hear their message at "the moment when they pass by" and "at the limits of known spatiality" (1993a, 42), a fleeting moment that escapes our spatio-temporal existence; textually, they function in Irigaray's lecture as an ideal to be sought but never caught, existing in a space that transcends the text's own abilities to articulate it. Irigaray only points toward the kinds of effects the angels can have, should we learn to hear and see them. The angels never enter historical time. And this seems to be why Irigaray finds them so powerful.[48]

So, what is the connection between her heteronormativity and this idealization of ahistorical beings? I suggest that they function dialectically, mutually grounding one another: the heterosexual poses as the ahistorical site of difference and the power of the transcendent ahistorical articulates itself in the ideal of heterosexuality. Each compounds the other to allow a subtle logic of the limit to reinstall itself in the very spaces of Irigaray's texts where she seems most ready to unhinge it: heterosexuality functions through the careful, oppositional demarcation of difference; and one must delimit the ahistorical clearly from the historical in order to idealize a transcendent, ahistorical state. The increasingly explicit heterosexism diagnosed in Irigaray's recent texts (post-1996) is thereby a perpetuation of this prior move toward figures that are both more contained and less historicized. The vessels-as-angels reinstall the logic of containment, which in turn grounds the logic of opposition that is at the heart of phallocentrism: bodies must be contained if they are to be legible to an oppositional, dyadic logic. And the idealized, ahistorical ontology of these vessels-as-angels compounds the idealization of that oppositional logic. The apparently increased idealization of heterosexuality in Irigaray's texts is thereby only a further expression of a dynamic already at work in her texts, the very dynamic that reinscribes the problems of the oppositional, dyadic, phallicized logic of difference, particularly when idealized. Heterosexuality emerges not as something radically new in Irigaray's texts, but as the most forceful expression of the logic of difference as that which is delimited. And, despite her idealization of angels as beings to mime, it seems her texts are finally historicized, placing her in the very place that the logics of phallicized whiteness attempt to place all of us: the endless desire for that idealized heterosexuality.

All of this results in an increasing cannibalism of differences, where differences (racial, class, religious, national) must mirror the perfectly delimited opposition of heterosexuality. When Butler warns that "every oppositional discourse will produce its outside" (1993, 52), we must read this founding gesture toward ahistorical heterosexism in Irigaray's text as it excludes historicized differences that do not function according to the logic of delimitation. The radically limitless, as a performative force that might invite an uncontained reimagining of spatiality and embodiment, does not surface in Irigaray's texts.

Or what Bataille might call "the formless."

And we might call "queer pleasures."

PART TWO

Moving toward Resistance:
A Politics without
a Future

FREE TO BE QUEER

Queer to Be Free

4

Freedom's just another word for nothin' left to lose.
—JANIS JOPLIN, "Me and Bobby McGee"

Something becomes an other; this other is itself somewhat; therefore it likewise becomes an other, and so on ad infinitum.
—G. W. F. HEGEL, *Hegel's Logic*, section 93

What we must work on, it seems to me, is not so much to liberate our desires but to make ourselves infinitely more susceptible to pleasure.
—MICHEL FOUCAULT, "Friendship as a Way of Life"

It's hard to be queer all the time. And besides, I *do* like Hegel.
—JUDITH BUTLER, *Artforum*, 1992

I taped that last epigraph to the cover of my copy of Hegel's *Phenomenology of Spirit* in 1993. I was intensely involved at the time in two of the most transformative experiences of my life: writing a dissertation, on Hegel and Foucault; and coming out, to myself, to my friends and family, to the world. And I could not even begin to fathom how the two might be connected. What did the dialectical structure of Hegel's approach to historical experience have to do with the rapid shortening of my hair and hilarious donning of combat boots? What did Foucault's constant attempts to break from Hegelian historicity (or my attempts to argue for them) have to do with trips to Washington, D.C., and New York City for various gay pride events?[1] The quip from the ascendant star of queer theory at that moment, Judy Butler (as she had refigured her own name to avoid the very abstract theorizing I was involved in), offered some comfort, even if only in the form of playful self-irony. As it turns out, that may have been the perfect, if not only, form of comfort available.

I do not want to let go of that playfulness or the decentering effects of any hearty self-irony worthy of the name. If anything, I want to exaggerate and cultivate both of them. Although it takes a particular set of muscles to be playful with the gravity of Hegel,[2] I am going to attempt a brief parody of a classically Hegelian retrospective style here and suggest a few connections between these two experiences that simultaneously dominated my life. The parody emerges from the doubly forced character of these connections: the connections are forced by the logic of this text (specifically, its need to introduce sexuality into our discussion), a dynamic Hegel disavowed in his own texts and I readily admit; and, secondly, the connections are forced by my own desire for some self-consciousness, a dynamic Hegel readily admitted and even valorized as the quintessential human desire, and one whose assumptions of subject- and essentializing-identity-formation I wish now to disavow.

To reduce things perhaps too far, I learned two fundamental things from Hegel that I can now read, in classically Hegelian retrospection, back into this collusion of my experiences in the early '90s: the development of a self is always already dependent on and constituted by an other; and experience and consciousness are historicized. Hegel orients both of these dynamics teleologically through the logic of desire, rendering a self that has the possibility of total self-consciousness and, accordingly, a historical experience that also can achieve self-consciousness, particularly regarding its moment in the grander narrative of Spirit's unfolding. These two constellations offer fruitful lenses to my experiences as a queer white lesbian in this culture of phallicized whiteness in advanced capitalism, and this is part of what I want to develop here. What does it mean, particularly amidst all the turbulent noise contesting the meaning of "queer," to be queer in this time and place? Against what Other is this category constituted? What is this historicized category and what, if any, demarcated set of experiences does it call into existence? Can this category offer a politics and ethics of resistance, which Foucault figured as a politics and ethics of freedom? If so, what kinds? How do they work? How can we cultivate them? The final parody may be in using Hegelian tools to uncover queer dynamics—now, that would be funny.

So much for the autobiographical introduction, a genre that queer theory seems to have inherited from its feminist roots and which I hope to trouble more thoroughly.[3]

The pressing question at stake here centers on the ethical and political possibilities of freedom, questions central to both Hegel and Foucault, and to the more general trajectory of this text. As we have seen in my development of the liberal project, the dominant concept of freedom functioning in cultures of phallicized whiteness frames freedom as an ontological condition of humanity: humans are ontologically free, and we find ample evidence of this in their innate ability to transform the world of nature into one of human utility—to work. One is free because one is human, and one is human because one works; therefore, one is free because one works. And nothing, not history, politics, or power differentials, should affect this ontological ability to be free. In this crass shorthand, we can glimpse how Hitler's program of National Socialist anti-Semitism and xenophobia pushed this liberal conception to its limits, perverting and twisting it into the infamous "Arbeit Macht Frei." The genocide undertaken under the auspices of that slogan indelibly marks a period of horrific violence in western culture—one we cannot forget. Its inversion of the liberal project's notions of freedom calls us to interrogate those notions all the more critically and vigilantly. If the connection between freedom and labor has been used to justify the attempted genocide of an entire race, then the connection itself warrants a thorough revamping.

To cast this discussion of phallicized whiteness and the logic of the limit in the terms of freedom then calls me back to the dangers of any totalizing critique. As several readers of early drafts of this manuscript have chided me, I do not want to critique the liberal project so categorically that we cannot recuperate anything beneficial from it. The concept of freedom is worth salvaging, even if it means reworking some of the fundamental, and often unconscious, values of this culture. Beyond the modern notions of freedom as liberation or transcendence, the concept of freedom still appears to harbor radically transformative power within our lives: it still appears capable of moving us from the fears and anxieties endemic to economies of scarcity toward the joys and generosities of economies of abundance. In what follows, I want to move toward what such transformations might mean by, first, undertaking a critical discussion of the dominant concept of freedom in phallicized whiteness through the specific angle of sexuality. The field of experience that frames us most explicitly as subjects of desire, sexuality is also the field of experience in which some of our culture's most intense anxieties are cathected and in which the model of freedom as liberation is presented most forcefully.

Unraveling the Self-Other Dynamic: Politics of Tolerance, Ethics of Alterity

Across the preceding three chapters, we have seen how a logic of the limit shapes the meanings of difference, and subsequently of sameness and subjectivity, in cultures of phallicized whiteness. Whether the carving of the liberal, neutral individual out of the state of nature through its demarcation of private property, the racializing of bodies according to their visual epidermal delimitations, or the suppression of sexual difference through the logic of containment, a logic of the limit is at work in the classing, racing, and sexing of bodies. And a logic of the limit also emerges in the guise of heterosexism in Irigaray's own texts, a guise that may be one of the most forceful expressions of the logic of the limit and its firm installation of oppositional logics and politics.

Each of these constellations, in expressing the logic of the limit, grounds a specific notion of subjectivity—namely, a concept of the self as constituted against an Other. Insofar as the self is that which is clearly demarcated and contained, the process of subjectivation becomes one of demarcating the world in which the self resides. Others consequently are read in their approximation of this demarcation—e.g., according to whether they, too, are 'whole bodies' and subsequently subjects in control of their world. Class, race, and sexual difference are read through the ability to contain oneself and wholeness becomes a primary index of cultural legibility. Bodies that are 'not whole' are read in precisely this way—through the negation of wholeness. No body is read as less than whole without that entailing a pejorative, and often politically violent, judgment against it: limitlessness is not legible, much less a valued characteristic. Consequently, even to become an Other requires an insertion into this logic of containment and its attendant narcissism, even if negatively.

It is helpful, therefore, to cast this discussion of the logic of the limit in these terms of self and Other as we attempt to understand the conceptions of freedom at work within it. Many theorists in the late twentieth century have approached the dilemmas of both subjectivity and ethics through the guise of alterity. Drawing on a variety of figures, ranging from Levinas, Heidegger, Sartre to Lacan, Irigaray, Derrida, these discussions have centered on how to approach the Other without the violence of domination, domestication, or assimilation.[4] How can we develop ourselves as free subjects in dialogue with others without endangering, colonizing, or containing the freedom of that Other? The dilemma appears to pit freedom against engagement with others, resulting in concepts that frame freedom as the transcendence of material dialogue with Others—a move that, in historical terms, we could frame as the Kantian culmination of the Lockean aversion to Others. But, as we see in the texts of Hegel that often lurk behind and within these discussions, contact with the Other is necessary to the development of one's self: solipsistic freedom is only ever a sharply curtailed experience of freedom in the world. The task thereby becomes one of cultivating freedom and Otherness simultaneously.

To develop these dynamics, and the problematic politics of freedom that emerge out of them, I locate them in the Kantian-Hegelian heritage of the subject-object split in which they implicitly stand and the self-Other split which subsequently emerges upon the introduction of desire.

▼ ▼ ▼

Beyond the role of contradiction and opposition in the dialectic, a generally Hegelian sense of negation as that which is grounded in delimitation still dominates late-twentieth-century post-structuralist attempts to think difference—including both Lacan's and Irigaray's.[5] While many mid- and late-twentieth-century theorists have read contradiction as the core of Hegelian dialectics (i.e., the infamous thesis-antithesis reading of the dialectic), this does not render a full sense of Hegelian negation, which is not captive to contradiction. Hegel certainly agrees with and perpetuates Aristotle's principle of non-contradiction, showing how contradictory, oppositional dyads produce the sharpest and clearest form of articulation in his dialectic. But contradiction is an ideal—and thus materially rare, if not impossible—form of negation that does not function as a Kantian regulative ideal in Hegel's dialectic; to the contrary, it is the most simple, and thus most abstracted, form of negation. It is, in an inversion of the Cartesian predisposition toward clarity as the site of truth, the most boring form of negation because it is the clearest. To limit Hegelian negation to this singular fastening on contradictory negation is to sever it from its resources to articulate the subtleties and nuances of historical human experience. It is to preclude it from articulating historicity. It is to preclude reading Hegelian negation as a subtle breaking away from high modernity's ahistorical logic of clear and distinct limits toward a logic of limits that allows for ambiguity and fluidity in its mutually codetermining relata.

Hegelian negation is most interesting and most fruitful where it is most subtle and often ambiguous—namely, in its orientation toward and role within the emergent *Aufhebung* (sublation).[6] Hegelian *Aufhebung*, as a site of simultaneous cancellation of difference and elevation of it into relation, articulates the ways that the limits, functioning as boundaries that apparently distinguish bodies into discrete units, simultaneously "yield to the reality of mutual codetermination" (Cornell 1992, 15), as Drucilla Cornell aptly phrases it. Limit, as the site of determinate negation, articulates how entities are simultaneously distinguished and connected: it is the site of individuation, the site of identity forming through its relation with otherness.

As Hegel explicitly discusses in the *Science of Logic*, "every determinate being . . . determines itself as an other" (1969, 118). Serving as the fundamental negation upon which one's consciousness as a being rests, the limit allows for individuation. As the limit is internalized beyond superficial considerations, consciousness realizes that it is dialectically both Self and Other. (In Lacan's reading of the mirror image and Irigaray's language of reading Aristotle, consciousness realizes its dependency on the Other to 'give it place,' to delimit it; as Lacan and Aristotle focus on the contained body as the 'telos' or 'proper meaning' of spatiality, Hegel similarly focuses on the role that otherness plays in the formation of the subject, a teleology that is not simply reversible.) The function of limits as internalized into constitutive, distinguishing marks of one's identity thus becomes the necessary condition for identity-formation itself.

The Kantian dilemma of a subject-object split thus loses foothold in Hegelian negation, wherein identity and difference (subject and object; self and other) are codetermined in the shared site of the limit. Functioning as a boundary, limit provides the Hegelian dialectic with that determinate negation which ontologically connects self and other in the very site of their differentiation. It may also appear to perpetuate the conception of difference that we encountered in the Lockean schemas of the neutral individual and that continues to dominate late-twentieth-century sensibilities, philosophically and politically—namely, difference as that which is or can be delimited. But in the Hegelian approach, the ambiguity of such demarcation—an ambiguity that is heightened through the dual functions of separation and connection performed by the limit—becomes the site of intrigue, rather than the site of anxiety that it is for the Lockean perspective.

This rich sense of negation thereby exposes the external standpoint of any system, such as Locke's and culminating in Kant's, of atomistic logic or strict identity politics that posits subjects/selves as ontologically separated from objects/others. But, particularly as Hegel grounds these dynamics in the register of desire, it also raises a question that has echoed across late-twentieth-century readings of his texts—namely, the question of radical otherness that I outlined briefly above. Generally, this question has focused on the dilemma of whether this ontology of mutual codetermination between subjects/selves and objects/others may actually—materially—attenuate the status of the other as Other through a centralizing, domesticating relation to the self. Crassly put, the question runs: how can the other be radically Other if it is always already—even if not explicitly or consciously—related to the self? Or, in the register of desire, how does this logic of desire not finally trap the logic of recognition in a fundamental and grounding narcissism?

My suspicion about this line of questioning is that it reinscribes the very atomistic logic of separation presented in the Kantian dilemma. That is, it assumes the same sort of ontology of separated entities at work in the Kantian split of subjects and objects. The crucial difference is that this post-Hegelian line of questioning, located in the register of desire, emerges from the perspective of 'the radical Other,' rather than the perspective of the knowing subject. Rather than a (Kantian) lamentation of the limits of the knowing subject, this line of questioning accuses that knowing subject of colonizing all that is outside of it through this totalizing grasp of ontological relatedness: the question accuses the knowing subject of overcoming all limits, of knowing no absolute limit to its own (colonizing, imperialist) desire— a desire, driven by the lack of self-consciousness, to own and contain, to swallow up difference and Otherness as it encounters it, as bell hooks argues.[7] The difference between these two viewpoints—the post-Hegelian perspective of the Other and high modernity's perspective of the self—expresses the considerable shift undertaken in discussions of ethics in contemporary feminist, race, and post-colonial theory.

To take up the explicit perspective of the self is essentially to articulate the kind of freedom that is at work in cultures of phallicized whiteness. In this schema, the Other is posited as the limits to the self's desire. As a limit, functioning here in the mode of a prohibition, the desiring self is drawn to overcome any limit or boundary to its freedom: the prohibition incites the desire to transgress the boundary and freedom becomes the freedom from prohibition. Two related dynamics emerge: colonization, which is no longer a historically or politically justifiable act; and its recent younger sibling, a politics of tolerance. In a politics of tolerance, the preferred rhetoric of the right in the contemporary U.S. but also a position with deep roots in traditions of classical liberalism, the Other is allowed a defined circumference of habitation by the self. The desiring self can no longer simply devour the Other; it must, rather, contain it. To tolerate difference is essentially to contain it, preferably without having to contact or engage it. As Wendy Brown has argued, "repugnance lies at the core of tolerance" (2002): to live one's 'difference' in an area strictly demarcated and defined by the (politically dominant) self of phallicized whiteness will never approximate freedom.[8]

This sort of realization has driven feminist, race, and post-colonial theorists to take up the perspective of the Other and undertake an ethics of alterity. This work ranges widely and merits more subtle attention than I can give to it here.[9] Whether positing the Other as the exotic, the limit of all knowability, that which cannot enter into relation and must be revered as a sacred site, or the Levinasian *face-à-face* experience that calls us into being, these attempts to open up epistemological, historical, and political spaces in which the Other can speak have become a sustained effort to break from the colonizing impulse of bland, but not innocent, tolerance. In attempting to problematize the very framework of self-Other, I hope to speak to these dialogues in some way: the self-Other framework invites an oppositional logic and its attendant model of power, domination, that are endemic to phallicized whiteness; it may not be sufficient to provide a possible site of sustainable, ethical freedom.

The critique of Hegel that asks this question of radical Otherness thereby runs the risk of again hypostatizing a substance of difference. It falls back into the very metaphysical assumptions (that identity is an atomistic substance) that undergird the metaphysics of Sameness against which it is arguing. Consequently, it risks reinscribing a subtle and insidious form of identity politics, grounded in a logical atomism of external relations, which ultimately may undermine its political aims of a liberatory ethics for all subject positions. Nonetheless, this question of totalizing grasps and the status of otherness in Hegelian dialectics is paramount, particularly when investigating the possibility of a liberatory ethic of mutual codetermination in the Hegelian sense of negation. I want to pursue it, but also attempt to avoid the metaphysics of substance, external relations, logical atomism, and identity politics that seem to follow so easily in its wake. The question of freedom is deeply implicated in this question of otherness: if the self-Other schematic cannot sufficiently avoid the containing logic of the limit, what sort of freedom does it entail? To pursue this question of the status of otherness as a question of limits, I turn to the ways that limits function within the Hegelian dialectic.

Boundaries and Prohibitions: The Concept of Freedom in the Logic of the Limit

The logic of the limit expresses itself in two fundamental registers: as boundaries that contain and as outer limits that serve as the prohibition across which one must not step. Of the same genera, these two types of limit are not wholly distinct and, as we have seen, are dialectically intertwined. But they do behave differently, accentuating different sorts of dynamics—and thereby of relations, of ethics, of politics. Limits function as boundaries in Lockean private property, individualism, and rights; Lacanian embodiment; Aristotelian physics; and Irigarayan morphology. But they also function as prohibitions in the logics of capitalist and Protestant utility and in the general psychoanalytic models of social and psychological desire that affect the Lacanian and Irigarayan readings. The latter mode, prohibition and the transgression that it incites, functions as a dominant concept of freedom in cultures of phallicized whiteness, where the self is understood through the dynamics of desire: freedom becomes the freedom from prohibitions. I turn to Hegel, therefore, for his development of both the connection and the distinction between these two instantiations: how do the modes of containment that enclose bodies and thereby race, class, and sex them relate to the dominant understanding of freedom as the freedom from prohibition?

Hegel reads human consciousness as constantly transgressing its own, self-made limitations. As we see performed in the *Phenomenology of Spirit*, consciousness is driven through the world by a lack that leads it to endlessly exceed its own, self-imposed limits. One of Reason's primary roles, particularly in its talent for synthesizing retrospective reflection with desire's future-anterior orientation (a Lacanian temporality), is to make consciousness more effective in its gathering of experience and knowledge of the world—i.e., to render consciousness self-conscious and thereby answer desire's lack. As Reason's negative thus labors *ad infinitum*, the self becomes richer and more self-conscious through its gathering of these distinguishing moments and marks, these 'limits' that it constructs and exceeds as it internalizes them. The dynamics implicated in this sort of limit are thereby not only those of a boundary that serves both to connect and distinguish the self with/from experience and Others, but also those of a limit as a prohibition, inciting desire always to exceed and transgress its self-imposed boundaries.

Limit (*Grenze*) as boundary has dominated our discussion, generally and of Hegel, thus far. In Hegel's texts, it can be seen as a neutral ground of

119

differentiation: it is what separates and also connects; and a consciousness of it allows both sides of the relation to emerge as more clearly delineated and fully articulated than a prior ignorance of such a boundary had afforded. Examples are often either physical or logical—e.g., physical boundaries of skin or fences around yards; logical boundaries between concepts or academic disciplines; and conceptual boundaries that function mentally, physically, and politically, such as borders between sovereign nations or discrete units of private property. As we move toward limit configured as prohibition, however, neutrality is no longer claimed or feasible: desire has entered the scene.

In prohibition, a limit functions dynamically within a specific act to keep one thing, positioned as desiring subject, from another, positioned as desired object: it creates an interval and incites desire, just as Aristotle and Irigaray describe. If we read Hegel's phenomenology of consciousness moving through experience as a moving through and internalizing of limits, we see how limits function in the shaping and articulating, but also the prohibiting and inciting, of desire. Driven by lack, desire always responds to what it does not or cannot have—this is how it seeks its fulfillment, endlessly. The limit still serves as the site of simultaneous connection and distinction between two entities, but the relation cannot be framed as static or symmetrical. Limits as prohibitions usher in a centralizing focus on that aspect of human life which becomes most precious to discourses of phallicized whiteness, subjectivity.

Framed in a Foucaultian approach, we can glimpse how prohibitions aid the emergence of this modern category of experience, subjectivity.[10] As Foucault traces in his first volume of *The History of Sexuality*, the modern subject emerges as a subject of desire as it responds to repressive laws. Repression sequesters specific objects, actions, and behaviors off from the acceptable, normal—even 'natural'—realm of experience. It prohibits specific things, creating taboos, which in turn incite desire for the forbidden fruits. Prohibitions exacerbate the lack that is at the heart of the modern subject's desire. And in late modernity, these prohibitive laws become increasingly codified through the arms of both clerical and secular authorities. The more codified they become, the more internalized becomes the source of transgression: the mandate emerges to submit to the laws of desire if one is to become a subject.

A primary psychic dynamic at work in this law of desire is consequently the dynamic of anxiety. Situated in a symbiotic relation with this particular conception of subjectivity as the site of desire, anxiety becomes one of the most intense and powerful emotional registers of this subject. It seems to function as a primary psychological register of phallicized whiteness in advanced capitalism, indicating the particular values at stake through its enactment: we are anxious about our most precious values. Whether one is becoming the right kind of subject or whether one can become a subject at all, for example, depends on whether one desires normal experiences, whether one has transgressed the law in appropriate ways. The process of subjectivation before the law of desire becomes a process through which the transgression of prohibitions becomes the index of one's subject position: as the phrase 'boys will be boys' tells us, white males are permitted innumerable, socially acceptable transgressions of the law (assuming they occur at the designated time of life, early adulthood[11]); but black males fill our prisons more quickly than they fill our college classrooms. This process of subjectivation via transgression, in turn, becomes fraught with anxiety: anxiety enlivens subjectivity, attuning it to the nuanced borders and contours of the law. In a passage I return to below, Foucault suggests that anxiety may be "what discourse is, when it is manifested materially, as a written or spoken object" (1972, 216). Subjectivity, at least partially constituted as an epiphenomenon of discourse, is highly cathected through anxiety. And both are enacted through the dynamic of prohibition in late modernity.

Contemporary examples of these socio-psychic dynamics appropriately emerge out of actions and behaviors that are explicitly construed in the register of desire, the central thread of this subjectivity. (In cultures of phallicized whiteness, desire is always read specifically in the register of sexuality—and, more explicitly still, of genital sexuality, a phenomenon central to our queering of freedom.[12]) For example, in the prohibitions in the U.S. around the act of sodomy, the anxiety enacted in the prohibition is not about the act itself, but about the kinds of subjectivities produced through the prohibition. The anxieties attendant to prohibitions of sodomy respond to two possible subjectivities that might emerge on either side of the act: (1) political, and potentially dangerous, subjectivities that might be produced by admitting to such an act—e.g., subjects not constrained by a sexual ethics of procreation; and (2) docile subjectivities that refuse or even denounce the act—e.g., subjects deeply constrained by a sexual ethics of procreation, with its social and religious ramifications, and generally governed by laws of repression. Accepted ways of transgressing this law, and of verbalizing such transgressions, fluctuate as the power and security of the law itself waxes and wanes. As cases regarding states' laws against sodomy continue to come before the Supreme Court, we can gauge the levels of anxiety in the U.S. regarding not only sexuality, but more importantly the internalization of the law in creating the *right* kinds of subjects of desire.[13]

Differentiated from the neutrality of limit as boundary, then, limit as prohibition is oriented asymmetrically. Whereas the doubled function of limits as boundaries between objects (to separate and connect) affects and individuates each side of the relation in a balanced, equivalent manner, the function of limits as prohibitions plays itself out in the dynamics of desire. Limits as prohibitions subsequently orient the effects of the limit, albeit not unilaterally, upon the subject as the central and centering area of concern. The kinds of objects or actions prohibited matter less than the kinds of subjects produced through the variety and stringency of the particular prohibition. Limits as prohibitions decisively orient relations toward the particular kinds of subjectivities produced through them, centering experience definitively in the perspective of the self that undergirds the twin politics of colonialism and tolerance above. And this process is, as Hegel's account of subject-formation shows, endless.

▼ ▼ ▼

The kind of limit, as both boundary and prohibition, that Hegel reads consciousness as constantly constructing and subsequently transgressing in the *Phenomenology* is thus not, and cannot become, an *absolute* limit. As Derrida develops in his early essay "From Restricted to General Economy: A Hegelianism without Reserve" (1978), these limits are always internal to human consciousness for Hegel, always those which Hegel can fold back into the dialectical grasp of Reason.[14] They most often function in two ways: immediately, as a limit that initially appears absolute to consciousness; and mediately (often narrated retrospectively), as a distinction that consciousness—lifted into Reason—has grasped, and thereby read in its true shape as a distinguishing mark within consciousness's experience of the world. Or, in the register of prohibition and language of Bataille, limits function immediately as prohibitions and mediately as transgressed prohibitions that are thereby recognized as partial or 'merely historical,' even if omnipresent.

Limits, as both boundary and prohibition, are thus essential to the dialectical grasping and articulating of experience that is the unfolding of self-consciousness: the moving through limits is the dynamic of both thinking and desiring, and constitutes the dynamic through which one becomes a (contained) subject. Consciousness thereby totalizes its grasp on experience, reading all moments as limits or negations that it can—and should—internalize as it unfolds in time. (The horizon of temporality emerges as a central structure of experience for early-twentieth-century post-Hegelian thinkers.) Again, in Irigaray's language, each limit 'gives consciousness place' through demarcating and articulating its moments of experience. Each 'contained' Other—i.e., each Other meriting the designation of Other—presents itself as a limit to be overcome by this desiring self: limits are necessary to individuation and at the same time the 'overcoming' or internalizing of limits is the movement of desire. Derrida's reading is thereby correct and there is no 'absolute limit' to this unfolding of consciousness via limits: consciousness lays claim to the totality of (possible) experience and there is no outside to desire. Desire becomes its own totalizing system. And, grounded in this logic of desire as both its point of departure and that which it attempts to sublate via Reason, Hegel's text cannot fully supersede this totalizing grasp of desire. The self, in its endless pursuit of both its own development and its freedom, will consistently reduce the Other to containment and then swallow it up whole—just as feminist, race, and post-colonial theorists fear.

The dominant concepts of freedom that emerge out of these logics of containment will thereby be ones that always keep the dominant subject position in power. If the Other is read through containment, then the recognition of the Other always occurs through that logic of subjectivation—i.e., the logic of containment. A subtle logic of narcissism reigns: each recognized Other is recognized only as contained.[15] From the perspective of the self, this contained Other appears as a limit to the self, a prohibition that it desires to transgress. And so we see the strange dialectic between limits as boundaries and limits as prohibitions. If freedom is the freedom from prohibitions, then the self is necessarily drawn to violate the Other, to erase its difference from it, to swallow it up into its own contained self.

The model of subjectivity that we find in Hegel's texts enacts the dynamics we have found operative across cultures of phallicized whiteness: contained selves that narcissistically and anxiously read Others as threats to the demarcated places in the world from which they desire. The dominant conception of freedom consequently always involves violation or, no less perniciously, ingestion of these differences. The market forces of advanced capitalism expand these powers endlessly, granting them particular efficacy as they hide the deleterious effects: difference is allegedly celebrated, as we fill our walls and CD players and kitchen cabinets with artifacts from "Other" cultures.

If we are to resist the colonizing impulse written into this contained model of desiring subjectivity, we must simultaneously interrupt and redeploy its attendant model of freedom. If the self develops through interplay with Others, which it necessarily reads as presenting limits to its desire that it must transgress in order to be free, then an oppositional dynamic between self and Other partially constitutes our notions of freedom. Logics of containment fall into oppositional politics, positioning the site where the self encounters the Other as the site of freedom's contestation and triumph—the site of liberation. Rhetorics of liberation are always rhetorics of liberated desire. To be free is to be free from this site of Otherness, to have overcome—or benevolently grown tolerant of—the Other and its infringement on the self and its desire: to be free is to be free from difference.

I want to bring these three dynamics together to bear on the task of refiguring these models of freedom and subjectivity: the self as a contained and desiring entity; the self-Other as a necessary opposition; and freedom as the transcendence of difference through transgressing prohibitive boundaries. An explicit question emerges from this constellation. It is one that faces any politics of resistance against phallicized whiteness: how to conceive of freedom without recourse to the logic of prohibition?

Free to Be Queer: The Liberation of the Homosexual Identity, Another Tool of Phallicized Whiteness

And so what does this strange signifier, "queer," have to do with these struggles for concepts of freedom? I offer three points of departure: the oppositional logic of gender (male/female) internal to heterosexuality as the naturalized norm of sexuality, and the oppositional politics (heterosexual/homosexual) emergent from it; the doubled reduction of the self to desire and of desire to fields designated as "sexual" in cultures of phallicized whiteness, particularly as driven by dynamics of prohibition; and the intricate intersections of heterosexism and white supremacist racism. The normalizing of heterosexuality presents one of phallicized whiteness's most insidious forms of domination—namely, the normalizing of our self-consciousness as subjected to the law of desire. This model of subject-formation instantiates the forms of freedom specified above: the self emerges as an intrinsic identity harboring essential desires that must be liberated from the field of social, political, or economic prohibitions in order to fulfill the lack that drives them. The field of sexuality consequently becomes the field of liberation in cultures of phallicized whiteness, particularly as it attempts to totalize the possible positions of resistance to it: the signifier 'queer' works to step outside of this totalizing logic and conceive of freedom down different rails of experience. (And it also conveniently introduces us to the last signifier in the chain constituting phallicized whiteness—'straight white propertied Protestant male.')

▼ ▼ ▼

As David Halperin describes the salient characteristics of heterosexuality, its structures echo my working hypothesis about the structures of whiteness and its domination of the signifying field. Heterosexuality functions in the same way that all privileged positions function: it hides its power. As Foucault puts it in volume 1 of *The History of Sexuality,* a text with a long and storied past in relation to queer theory and queer politics,[16] "power is tolerable only on condition that it mask a substantial part of itself. Its success is proportional to its ability to hide its own mechanisms" (1978, 86). Just as whiteness is phallicized through its necessary veiling of the phallus, so too does heterosexuality now pose as the naturalized, ontological condition of humanity, rather than as the complex deployment and repetition of historicized and politicized discourses.

This allows, as Halperin aptly describes, "a crucially *empowering* incoherence to attach to the unmarked term and concept of 'the heterosexual' " (1995, 46). He explicitly enumerates the logical contradictions that become characteristics of heterosexuality:

> They serve to define heterosexuality, implicitly and therefore all the more efficaciously, as simultaneously (1) a social norm, (2) a perfectly natural condition into which everyone is born and into which everyone grows up if no catastrophic accident interferes with normal, healthy development, (3) a highly laudable accomplishment that one is entitled to take pride in and for which one deserves no small amount of personal and social credit, and (4) a frighteningly unstable and precarious state that can easily be overthrown . . . and that therefore needs to be militantly protected, defended, and safe-guarded by a constant mobilization of social forces. (1995, 46–47)

While the terms do not match up in any perfect (dangerously Hegelian) alignment, this "empowering incoherence" of heterosexuality echoes rather loudly the "semiotic flexibility" that Dyer suggests constitutes whiteness and its domination of the social field of racial signifiers. Both operate as master signifiers, phallicizing the field of discourse in which they function. And both assume and ensure this role through the constant proliferation of contradictions in the social field that leave the dominant signifier unscathed and in power.

We find further evidence of this phallicized character of the domination of heterosexuality in the oppositional logic inherent to it and the oppositional politics emergent from it. As several feminist theorists have developed, heterosexism operates through the binarization of gender: one is either male or female, and there can be no gray area in between. To be gendered ambiguously is to be culturally illegible. A failure to signify correctly often results in psychological and physical violence, indicating the anxieties that heterosexism produces in the psycho-social fields. In fact, the conflation of heterosexuality and a binary gender system has become so entrenched that it is now embedded in the English language: Gayle Rubin argues that the lack of a clear distinction between contemporary meanings of sex as sexuality and sex as gender "reflects a cultural assumption that sexuality is reducible to sexual intercourse and that it is a function of the relations between women and men" (1993, 32). The failure to signify as *either* male *or* female challenges the oppositional logic of heterosexism, a logic which demands that humans are ontologically sexed into the binary system that it perpetuates and that, in the circular fashion endemic to closed systems, feeds it.[17] As all phallicized fields of signification operate fundamentally through a binary logic, so too does heterosexism continuously reinstall the binary gender system in which it lives.

But this binary logic functions doubly in heterosexism, effectively totalizing our conceptions of freedom through a logic of prohibition. Out of that internal oppositional logic of gender, an external oppositional politics also emerges. As the category of heterosexuality has been increasingly challenged as an ontological given of human nature in the latter part of the twentieth century, historical categories of resistance have emerged—namely, the social movements of gay and lesbian liberation and their constituents, gay men and lesbians. Drawing on the nineteenth-century category of homosexuality, men and women in the latter half of the twentieth century in overdeveloped countries began to assume the label willingly. The impulse to do so seems to have been both psychological and political; in both cases, the act involved the (allegedly) voluntary demarcation of an essential part, if not the very essence, of one's identity. Narratives of coming out, as Eve Kosofsky Sedgwick has thoroughly shown, rarely operate as they appear and the essentializing effect of gay and lesbian liberation movements place them in a space of dubious resistance. To come out is to proclaim one's identity according to the law of desire, the very law of heterosexism.

It appears then that, when threatened, heterosexuality neatly created its opposite in the political field, the category of homosexuality.[18] This is but one of several dynamics that should make us wary of the identity politics of gay/lesbian (or even gay/lesbian/bisexual/transgender, the now dangerously-close-to-domesticated "g/l/b/t") alleged resistance to heterosexism: it was formed in reaction against the dominant category of heterosexuality. Homosexuality will only ever be the Other against which heterosexuality normalizes itself, just as femaleness and non-whiteness function as the Others for the dominance of maleness and whiteness. While we need to problematize the specific concepts of freedom, and resistance, within any politics driven by the law of desire, we should already heed Nietzsche's warnings about the efficacy, and health, of reactionary politics.

Taking these structural similarities between heterosexuality and phallicized whiteness as a point of departure, I want to argue more strongly that these two systems of domination, heterosexism and white supremacist racism, functionally intersect. We know from Gayle Rubin's classic text "Thinking Sex" how systems of sexual normalization and racial normalization have intersected historically, leading Rubin to locate historical periods in which the anxieties provoked by one field find their ricochet expressions in the other field. She offers a brief legal genealogy to show how "most of the laws used [in the twentieth century] to arrest homosexuals and prostitutes come out of the Victorian campaigns against 'white slavery' " (1993, 5). She thereby shows how anti-prostitution laws framed implicitly around race (and class) develop into the legalized persecution of homosexuals.[19] Rubin uses much of this legal genealogy to show the ways that U.S. culture's present sexual morality, with its strict hierarchy of 'good' and 'bad' sexualities, functions largely in the same manner as ideological systems of racism. As she puts it, "this kind of sexual morality has more in common with ideologies of racism than with true ethics" (1993, 15). Drawing this sociological connection between race/racism and sexuality further, she also goes on to show the ways that "in modern, western, industrial societies, homosexuality has acquired much of the institutional structure of an ethnic group" (1993, 17), pointing to the demographic move of gay men and lesbians into segregated urban settings—gay ghettoes.[20]

Rubin thus indicates the ways that, as constituted through structures of legal representation and demographic shifts, the lesbian and gay subject shares central characteristics with the "raced" subject—i.e., the non-white subject—in U.S. history. One need only reflect on the targets of violence in the U.S. to deduce that homophobia and racism intersect in some frighteningly real ways.[21] More strongly still, I want to follow out these ontological and historical dynamics and argue that one set of oppressions actually functions to protect and perpetuate the other: heterosexism protects whiteness.[22] The move toward the field of the sexual as the socio-historical site in which we might reconfigure freedom is thus more than just a response to cultural norms: it is fundamental to interrupting the power of phallicized whiteness.

Heterosexism protects whiteness in the same field in which it attempts to trap resistances against it: the field of desire, which is also the site of the modern subject's constitution. Heterosexism, whiteness, and modern subjectivity all operate in the field of desire, and the lack that drives desire surfaces in the heterosexism-whiteness nexus as a lack of control, with all its violent outbursts. Writing toward the emergence of this dynamic, Dyer focuses on some of the complex alliances that have developed around whiteness and heterosexuality in our culture. He approaches these through the roles of embodiment and disembodiment in these phallicized fields that we have already encountered. He writes,

> All concepts of race are always concepts of the body and also of heterosexuality. Race is a means of categorising different types of human body which reproduce themselves. It seeks to systematise differences and to relate them to differences of character and worth. Heterosexuality is the means of ensuring, but also the site of endangering, the reproduction of these differences. (1997, 20)

As evidenced in Rubin's legal genealogies, heterosexuality often becomes the primary field of anxiety whenever whiteness appears to be threatened. Heterosexuality, particularly as it is naturalized as necessarily reproductive, is the site at which the purity of races is—or, rather, *must be*—reproduced. Anxiety about this imperative, which is absolute and non-negotiable for whiteness in its hegemonic position within white supremacist racism, often creates anxiety around heterosexuality itself. It turns out that heterosexuality—and, indeed, sexuality itself—is not very white. Once we begin to grasp these dynamics, other historical patterns become less surprising; for example, it becomes less surprising that the U.S. Congress passes a "Defense of Marriage Act" in the same decade that begins to forecast the impending minority status of whites in the U.S.[23]

But this alliance with heterosexuality seems to become whiteness's Achilles' heel. As whiteness comes to rely upon heterosexuality for the reproduction of pure whiteness (and thus ally itself, unstably and uncomfortably but also necessarily, with sexuality *per se*), its claim to the universal signifier is more and more complicated. For example, the specific anxiety over interracial heterosexuality in U.S. culture begins to unveil some of the complex relations between whiteness, purity, and embodiment, particularly as mediated through this imperative of reproductive sexuality. In short, miscegenation threatens purity; simply recall the infamous one-drop rule. As Dyer puts it, interracial heterosexuality, operating within the naturalized assumption of reproduction, "breaks the legitimation of whiteness with reference to the white body. . . . white bodies are no longer indubitably white" (1997, 25). The purity of whiteness is thus in danger precisely where it must be repro-duced. Consequently, we begin to see that whiteness is not simply allied with reproductive heterosexuality itself, but rather demands particular, 'racially pure' forms of reproductive heterosexuality: race and sexuality are not sepa-rable categories.

What is the white body to do with this need for pure reproduction? From here Dyer turns toward the gendering of heterosexuality and the ways that white masculinity follows out a very specific form of embodiment and sexual desire—the form exemplified by the figure of Christ. Through its idealization of Christ, and his capacity to be *in* the body but not *of* it, white male heterosexuality is always able to transcend the body in a successful conquering of the struggle between body and mind, flesh and spirit. More specifically, the straight white male body is able to transcend those dark, frightening but also seductive sexual desires because of his whiteness. It is his whiteness that gives him this ability to transcend the 'darkness' of his masculine, uncontrollable desire. Sexual desire itself is not very white. And thus we arrive at the conundrum that seems to spur and connect much of the anxiety within *both* racism and homophobia: "the means of reproducing whiteness [sexuality, having sex, sexual desire] are not themselves pure white" (Dyer 1997, 26). As a body that categorically cannot be reduced to its own embodiment, whiteness must disavow sexual desire, the matter *par excellence* that is wholly of the body. This disavowal of sexual desire, as an exemplary disavowal of embodiment itself, thus becomes a necessary condition for the possibility of whiteness.

The projection by whiteness of perverse, unnatural, and out-of-control desire across non-reproductive sexualities and non-white bodies follows im-mediately from this bizarre condition of possibility. There is a long and storied past to the history of projecting sexual drives as 'dark and uncon-trollable' onto non-white races in U.S. culture. In explicitly sexualized ste-reotypes, there is the myth of rape by non-white of white, which has no foothold in statistics that show rape is primarily intraracial, and the often connected myth that black men have unusually large penises, which Fanon understands so well.[24] Even in the 'naturalized' realm of reproductive heterosexuality, white U.S. culture has the stereotype of non-whites as having huge families, displaying their inability to control their rate of reproduction, and, conversely, the legendary fear, held by figures such as Benjamin Franklin, that the white race will fade away, presumably because of its too-tight control on sexual desires. Rubin also writes about this explicit projecting of 'bestial sexuality' onto non-white races: "[In 1969,] the pamphlet *Pavlov's Children (They May Be Yours)* claims that UNESCO is in cahoots with SIECUS (Sex Information and Education Council of the United States) to undermine religious taboos, to promote the acceptance of abnormal sexual relations, to downgrade absolute moral standards, and to 'destroy racial cohesion,' by exposing white people (especially white women) to the alleged 'lower' sexual standards of black people" (1993, 8).

Dyer reads this projecting of sexual desires onto non-white races as a classic instance of disavowal. As he sees it, this projection provides "a means for whites to represent yet dissociate themselves from their own desires" (1997, 28). But it is exactly this slippage in the process of representation, this disavowal at the heart of representation, that can turn simple 'dissociation' into ugly bigotry and violence. As Dyer describes them, these "dark desires are part of the story of whiteness, but as what the whiteness of whiteness has to struggle against" (1997, 28). But this internal struggle, this struggle against parts of oneself that one categorically cannot embrace, is the site of an infinite self-hatred—the very sort of self-hatred that often fuels both racism and homophobia.

The relation of whiteness to heterosexuality is clearly neither comfortable nor stable. The problem is the problem of desire, the very law through which subjects emerge in late modernity. It seems that the only reason for a white body to give in to sexual desire is to ensure the pure reproduction of whiteness—to protect whiteness. It would seem, in fact, that celibacy is the most 'white' relation to sexuality (hence all the images of sexual purity as white in Christian imagery). Heterosexuality must construe desire as both natural to it and eminently controllable.[25] It does this through naturalizing sexuality as an instance of human nature—i.e., as an instance of utility, the hallmark of human nature that is more and more deeply sedimented as the Protestant work ethic drives more deeply into the psyche of late modernity. Sexual desire submits to a higher law, the command of reproduction. Subsequently, if the reproduction and protection of whiteness is the only acceptable motive for sexual relations, the projection of desire as dark, uncontrollable, and irrational is cast not only across non-white bodies, but also across any form of non-reproductive sexuality. Non-reproductive sexuality—particularly sexual desire that categorically precludes the possibility of reproduction—must also be dark, out-of-control, non-white.[26]

It seems then that same-sex desire, as the quintessential embodiment of non-reproductive sexuality, will always be read as a treason against whiteness. Subsequently, in a culture of phallicized whiteness that valorizes whiteness as the ideal toward which all races are striving, it will always also be read as a treason against one's race, whatever that race might be. And the problem is the problem of desire.

▼ ▼ ▼

But we are free to act on that desire. We are free, in the early twenty-first century in cultures of phallicized whiteness, to identify as gay, lesbian, or bisexual. We are free, assuming economic stability or willingness to ignore such concerns, to follow the law of desire to the abnormal and unnatural ends that it may lead some of us to.[27] We are free, despite the risks of physical and psychological violence that is still inflicted upon gays, lesbians, and bi-sexuals, to choose our desired objects of sexual exchange even if they are of the same sex as we are, foreclosing our actions from the greater law of utility.[28] Is this a freedom we should trust or celebrate?

I do not want to downplay the victories of gay and lesbian liberation movements. I know that I benefit from the struggles of thousands of men and women who precede me and that life in the post-Stonewall U.S. is much more free and easy. I do not want to sound like an ingrate or a youthful upstart without proper regard for history, although I inevitably will to some ears. To the contrary, it is precisely history that forces me to write. In that vein, I want to draw a distinction between my post-Stonewall life as an out lesbian and the life I am writing toward, a queer life. To identify as a lesbian may have nothing to do with being queer; and to be queer, one need not identify as a lesbian or gay person. To identify as a lesbian is to submit fully to the law of desire: it is to identify myself essentially through a reduction of my life to the kind of genital sex that I have, the site designated as the site of desire in phallicized whiteness's anxious relation to sexuality and the body. These are precisely the reductions that both heterosexism and phalli-cized whiteness demand, and incite.

They incite these reductions to concepts of desire and identity precisely through the oppositional logic and politics outlined above, with their col-lusion with the laws of prohibition. The argument runs this swiftly: white-ness in the world must remain white; for it to remain white, the reproduction of white bodies must be protected; to protect the reproduction of white bodies, heterosexism must control the domain of desire; for it to control the domain of desire, desire must heed the law of utility, which is also the paramount law of whiteness (since Locke, at least); for it to heed the law of utility, heterosexism prohibits any forms of desire that preclude reproduction; therefore, to be free in this system is to desire these prohibited forms of sexuality—i.e., to identify as a homosexual or bisexual. To identify as gay, lesbian, or bisexual is to enact the laws of phallicized whiteness and its henchman, heterosexism, doubly: it is to identify oneself essentially through the object of one's genitalized desire and it is to proclaim one's freedom through the transgression of a central prohibition, the prohibition against same-sex desire. To identify as gay, lesbian, or bisexual is to identify oneself clearly and distinctly, inscribing oneself with some prediscursive essence (written as a lack inscribed ontologically into one's desire) and presenting only the most contained forms of resistance against whiteness, heterosexism, and sexism. It is, finally, to resist in precisely the (oppositional) ways that phallicized whiteness and heterosexism desire, resulting in their further perpetuation.

The freedom achieved by gay and lesbian liberation movements is a difficult and dangerous one. Historically necessary, it cannot stand as the endpoint of all resistance. To identify as gay or lesbian in the early twenty-first century is to identify according to the very laws of desire and identity that underwrite the oppressive systems of heterosexism and white supremacist racism, as well as sexism, classism, and even Christianism.[29] It is to understand freedom as the liberation from social fields of power, the very conceptualization that frames classical liberalism and its ahistorical notion of the atomistic individual, which is ultimately free when it has transcended all material limits and prohibitions (a transcendence often achieved only in privacy, the domain that the law must protect). This is what leads Foucault to distinguish between liberation and freedom, particularly as he discusses dynamics involving sexuality. In a long passage worth quoting (often[30]) from an interview entitled "The Ethics of the Concern for Self as a Practice of Freedom," Foucault warns of reducing freedom to liberation:

> I have always been somewhat suspicious of the notion of liberation, because if it is not treated with precautions and within certain limits, one runs the risk of falling back on the idea that there exists a human nature or base that, as a consequence of certain historical, economic, and social processes, has been concealed, alienated, or imprisoned in and by mechanisms of repression. According

to this hypothesis, all that is required is to break these repressive deadlocks and man [*sic*] will be reconciled with himself, rediscover his nature or regain contact with his origin, and reestablish a full and positive relationship with himself. . . . I am not trying to say that liberation as such, or this or that form of liberation, does not exist: when a colonized people attempts to liberate itself from its colonizers, this is indeed a practice of liberation in the strict sense. But we know very well, and moreover in this specific case, that this practice of liberation is not in itself sufficient to define the practices of freedom that will still be needed if this people, this society, and these individuals are to be able to define admissible and acceptable forms of existence or political society. (1997, 282–83)

To liberate oneself is to remain within the conception of power as domination, the conception of power as prohibition. Historical and political domination are actual events. They wreak horrible violence in the lives of innumerable bodies all across the globe. They must be resisted. But particularly in cultures of phallicized whiteness in advanced capitalism, historical and political domination are not the only ways that power asserts itself in the socio-psychic field. And to fail to imagine these other ways is to fail to imagine different practices of freedom—it is to fail to become free. As Foucault asks specifically of the arena of sexuality, "does it make sense to say, 'Let's liberate our sexuality'? Isn't the problem rather that of defining the practices of freedom by which one could define what is sexual pleasure and erotic, amorous and passionate relationships with others?" (1997, 283)

This is not to say that liberation is unnecessary. Again, Foucault describes it as "pav[ing] the way for new power relationships, which must be controlled by practices of freedom" (1997, 283–84). If we find ourselves experiencing this complex phenomenon that we call 'same-sex desire,' we must identify as gay, lesbian, or bisexual if we are to break the bonds of domination that heterosexism, sexism, and phallicized whiteness hold over us. But the danger is precisely that we will think this is our final act, rather than our initial act. We must go further. We must follow out what these layered acts of 'outing' initiate. Seizing this freedom to be gay or lesbian or bisexual, we must push it much further, away from the dynamics of desire, identity, and freedom-through-prohibition. We must take this freedom to be gay, lesbian, or bisexual and transform it into the freedom to be queer. It may be through this bizarre site of signification, "queer," that we will create a more satisfying, sustainable, and different form of freedom. It may be through this site of "queer" that we can explore Foucault's provocation toward 'practices of freedom.'

Queer to Be Free

Despite my ignorance of such things in 1993, much ink has been spilled about the intersections of our intellectual and sexual predilections, particularly since the early 1990s. The advent of queer theory has generated an apparently endless stream of reflections on what these intersections might tell us about life in late modernity. And the ongoing domestication of that field of study by the academy, now codified as a full-fledged discipline unto itself, threatens to defuse any intellectual, erotic, or political edginess that such ink-spilling signified at one time. As numerous writers have documented, queer theory is a dangerous terrain that seems always to be in danger of losing its danger.[31] It is constantly in danger of being domesticated.

As a field of academic studies, queer theory is without doubt one of the most hotly contested, contentious, embattled, and even confused subdisciplines to emerge from the virtual implosion of disciplinary boundaries over the last fifteen years or so. This is a good thing, a good queer thing. It bespeaks the kinds of resistances to categorization and demarcation that constitute this site of signification, "queer." To be queer is not to assume a foregone identity. It is to enact, as David Halperin writes, "an identity without an essence" (1995, 61).

Queers have no proper identification papers, no passport.[32] As Gloria Anzaldúa writes, "I am all races because there is the queer of me in all races" (1987, 84).[33] Crossing, and literally double-crossing, all boundaries, queer confuses the very basis of kinship systems, leading us to resignify the meanings of "family" away from its biological moorings.[34] Queer strikes at the very heart of phallicized whiteness and its systems of domination, confusing the meaning of desire and its most precious child, subjectivity. To be queer is to not know exactly who or how one "is." It is to have confused the categories of identity so deeply that they no longer provide meaningful residence. It is to turn identity inside out, and identity politics on its head. To be queer is to 'verbify' the noun: to queer.[35]

Reviewing theorists' attempts to define this term, "queer," quickly becomes a humorous enterprise. The discourses run the gamut from a vague sense of a younger generation's dissatisfactions with the categories of gay and lesbian to the intentional toying with the gender-sex-sexuality nexus to the vexed attempts to define that which (categorically?) resists definition.[36] Michael Warner, adeptly avoiding the impossible issue of definition, describes the "preference for 'queer' [as] represent[ing], among other things, an aggressive impulse of generalization" (1993, xxvi). This lack of specificity becomes both the radical potential and the Achilles' heel of queer: it serves as both the resistance to domestication and the submissiveness to commodification. If queer is that which dare not be defined, we are immediately on some strange terrain in the very attempts to speak of it. We need to attune ourselves to the meanings and implications of this "aggressive impulse of generalization." We need to heed Bataille and learn to think generally.

Because, of course, speak of it we do. Queer has saturated the discourses not only of g/l/b/t lives, but of American urban culture more broadly: it appears easily in headlines of the *New York Times*.[37] As we speak of it, the problems attendant to any category, particularly those affiliated with the formation of identity, ensue. The term queer, despite the uses that twist and turn and undercut the always imminent threat of a rigidified, static meaning, nonetheless exercises a normative power over the fields in which it is deployed. Whether through class or race specificity, academic elitism, or market fetishization, the term queer has, despite its attempts not to do so, produced exclusionary effects in localized sites of its signification.[38] It has, in many arenas, become a site of privilege *par excellence*, positioning itself as the refusal of identity that only the most privileged can afford or achieve. This is an unavoidable effect of category delimitation, even when the category is one that attempts to erase itself upon its moment of utterance. It is, as Butler quotes Spivak, that "necessary error of identity" (1993, 229).

In the face of such difficulties, the attempt to speak of queer, and particularly its possible enactments of freedom, is daunting. But urgent. As a bizarre site of signification that speaks of "bodies and pleasures," not of identities and desires, it is a site toward which we are drawn—we, that is, who wish to resist.[39] Or, to put it in the first-person voice of queering that still seems imperative, it is the site toward which I am drawn. I approach it as a site, a space in which signification contests its own occurrence. I approach it as Foucault approaches Nietzsche's genealogy, or *Entstehungsherd*, of the concept of goodness.

▼ ▼ ▼

As I argued in the introduction, Foucault repeatedly nods toward spaces that appear to exist prior to, and also in the midst of, practices of signification. In his discussion of Borges that initiates *The Order of Things*, he confronts us with an impossible taxonomy of animals that our modern system of thought cannot think. The danger is the impossible narrowness separating the phantasms of the imagination from the materiality of the real. The simple and elegant power of the alphabetical series in Borges's text renders insufficient space between these categories. Consequently, the binary system of 'fantasy/real' no longer has sufficient purchase to capture the error at work. And so our modern thought reels back in terror, confronted by this primary anxiety of meaninglessness.

Later, in the 1970 lecture at the Collège de France that was published in English as "The Discourse on Language," the appendix to *The Archaeology of Knowledge*, Foucault again invokes this kind of disordered space that precedes the ordering of thought. Once again performing his own object of discourse, here the problem of beginnings, he attunes us particularly to the anxiety that this kind of space causes: "anxiety as to just what discourse is, when it is manifested materially, as a written or spoken object" (1972, 216). The anxiety is not about the object of discourse itself. We late moderns are all too comfortable with the givenness of discourse, the power and omnipresence of thought. It is the power of something other than thought, more specifically something other than reason (and often, more specifically still, instrumental reason), that disturbs us so deeply. The anxiety that Foucault invokes is caused by the very idea that discourse might not be a given, that there might be "conflicts, triumphs, injuries, dominations and enslavements that lie behind these words, even when long use has chipped away their rough edges" (1972, 216). His anxieties, which he always marks as modern anxieties from which he is not exempted, echo Nietzsche's provocations of a century earlier—that words function as coins whose violent multiplicities and arbitrariness are rubbed out over time.[40]

Finally, in "Nietzsche, Genealogy, History," Foucault turns to Nietzsche's influence in these passages explicitly. He reads Nietzsche's *Genealogy of Morals* as excavating a space wherein identities and concepts are formed, reorienting our focus from its habitual objects of identity toward the perpetual movement swirling within and about those (allegedly) static concepts. As Foucault writes,

> What Nietzsche calls the *Entstehungsherd* of the concept of goodness is not specifically the energy of the strong or the reaction of the weak, but precisely this *scene* where they are displayed superimposed or face-to-face. It is nothing but the *space* that divides them, the void through which they exchange their threatening gestures and speeches. (1977b, 150, my emphases)

It is not the clumsy nobles who fall to the clever intentions of the priests that draw Foucault to Nietzsche's text: it is this space in which "the endlessly repeated play of dominations" (1977b, 150) is staged. This is clearly not an Aristotelian space: "it is a 'non-place,' a pure distance" (1977b, 150). It undercuts any emergence of identities: "no one is responsible for an emergence; no one can glory in it, since it always occurs in the interstice" (1977b, 150). A space of endless contestation: if we approach queer as emerging from spaces such as these in Foucault's texts, queer is not and cannot become an identity—a verb, perhaps an adverb or adjective, never a noun.

My emphasis on Foucault here is meant to emphasize the historicity as well as the disordering effects of this discursive space, a space that I want to reconfigure as the space out of which queering emerges. This space is distanced considerably from the Derridean sense of *différance,* that other site of signification which simultaneously conditions and haunts any act of signification. The undecidability of Derridean (and DeManian) deconstructive practices expresses the uncertainty and instability endemic to discourse itself. A parasitic reading practice, as we saw in my readings of Irigaray, Derridean deconstruction orients us toward the trace, remainder, and supplement of language itself. *Différance* is both that which makes distinctions possible and the site of their undoing: it articulates the fundamental lack that drives discourse for Derrida, a lack not unlike that which drives desire for Hegel. It is what Richard Lee has called "an *archaic* lack" (2002, 6–7), whether expressed in the registers of discourse, experience, or self-consciousness. These effects of *différance* emerge posterior to discourse itself: it is only after entering the discursive space that Derridean *différance* surfaces, albeit with its decentering and vertiginous effects of endless differing and deferring.

To read the space of queering through these Foucaultian spaces distances us from this recurrent logic of lack (in its Hegelian or Derridean guise), driven as it is by the law of desire into the heart of late modern subjectivity. To emphasize the dynamic that scarcity and lack bring to this subjectivity compounds the difficulties of escaping identity politics. We are back in the projects of liberation, with their goals of freeing our desire to fulfill its lack. If a subject is necessarily a subject of desire, it conceives of itself as a discretely contained entity that is fundamentally driven by an ontological lack of that which would fulfill itself; political life subsequently must be understood in teleological terms. To read desire as driven by the dynamic of lack unleashes teleology. Lack demands an endpoint: we are what we want and we want what we do not have; therefore, we must pursue that which will fulfill us and we must be able to articulate clearly what that is. The thought that nothing might fulfill us, that we are ontologically lacking, will only drive us to desire more vehemently, to want more anxiously, and to become enmeshed more and more deeply in the bastion of identity—despite how far these desires and anxieties project us endlessly into the future. (The conflu-

137

ence of the logic of capitalism and heteronormative sexuality centers on this logic of scarcity.) This ability to clearly identify our desire is what makes us culturally legible, granting us the required agency of a political identity: we know what we want.

While Derridean *différance* expresses the impossibility of any such identity, by wreaking havoc with the metaphysics of presence that underwrites it, the undecidability of endless differing and deferring nevertheless operates within the same system of lack initiated by the Hegelian dialectics of desire and recognition. It troubles the system of identity and identity politics, but cannot offer any positive alternative. It always reads the gesture toward positing an alternative as necessarily bound to the metaphysics that it disrupts.[41]

But to queer is to create: we must heed bell hooks's admonitions (1992, 178) and decolonize our imaginations.

▼ ▼ ▼

The spaces of anxiety that Foucault invokes across his texts differ from this Derridean deconstructive practice of disrupting identity politics and the metaphysics of presence that underwrites it. Not a parasitic practice that surfaces posterior to discourses, the spaces that Foucault invokes orient us toward the emergence of discourses. This is not to fall nostalgically back into a prediscursive space. It is, rather, the site in which discourses shape themselves, a site of conflict, violence, disruption, discontinuity, struggle, contest, and endless movements. A site of powers. Agonistic forces. Excessive possibilities. To confront this space is to confront the arbitrariness of the cultural codes into which thinking is habituated: it is to confront both the excessive possibilities that are reduced to the order of the rational (where univocity still reigns as ideal) and the historicized character of what we take to be 'the order of things.' It is also to confront the ontology of order itself, an ontology without which we late moderns cannot think. Reading this space through Foucault allows me to emphasize both this excess prior to the codification of discourse and the historicity attendant to that codification.

If queer emerges from a space of endless contestation, it shifts and changes with historical contexts and their differential forces of power. To queer is to turn that historicity back upon itself, rendering order vulnerable to the excessive possibilities swarming in the site of its emergence. It is to reinvigorate the endless space of contestation that haunts any claims to stasis, or 'nature,' or identity. To queer is to emerge out of the fleeting space in which meanings are shaped before repetition rigidifies the excess possibilities beyond recuperation. This is not a moment in any Hegelian self-consciousness. This is the space prior to the emergence of that damning self-Other dyad: there is no self here and queer does not emerge against some Other. We cannot point to and identify 'that which is queer.' (It is not a noun!) We can only track down its reverberations in the socio-psychic fields of our experience. We can only attune ourselves to its effects, listening carefully for the interstice in which social signifiers are contested and excessive possibilities revisited or birthed for the first time. To queer things is to transform them, in ways we cannot anticipate: to queer is to foil anticipation and its temporality of a future-anterior.

If to queer is to speak and act from a space in which meanings are endlessly contested, this is not the space of reason. We late moderns constantly jump over this space, superseding it without even knowing we have done so. We habitually live in the space of assumed reason. Despite our alleged hedonism, we consistently grant privilege, and even a moral imperative, to the meaningful over the meaningless.[42] The meaningless causes anxiety, a restlessness that cannot function and is denied epistemological legibility. Rather than reducing it to the restful quietude and (alleged, apparent) stability of reason's control, to queer embraces this restlessness, antagonizing and exacerbating it. It causes anxiety in cultures of phallicized whiteness and their praise of reason. And it is this anxiety that takes on historicized forms, projected onto raced and sexed Others in cultures of phallicized whiteness, as we have seen over and over in these pages. This anxiety, expressed socially and psychically in the many forms of xenophobia, is bound tightly to the disavowal of meaninglessness, which we can only speak as a lack. Anxiety is the loss of reason, the beheading of reason, the entering of kinds and modes of experience where reason does not reign. To queer is to veer off the rails of reason, causing sheer anxiety in late modernity.

This is why we must learn to queer our pleasures: pleasures, or at least specific kinds of pleasures, answer anxieties. Not by laying them to rest through submission to an external law that only attempts to erase them or, more simply in advanced capitalism, by putting them to bed with a barrage of chemical sedatives.[43] Pleasures answer anxieties by taking their energy in more sustainable directions, in more pleasurable directions, in more free directions.

▼ ▼ ▼

If queer is this space of contesting historicized meanings, it will vary in its historicized emergences. That it has emerged in roughly the last two decades through domains of experience designated as 'sexuality' already indicates the sites of anxiety in cultures of phallicized whiteness. As we can see through specific examples of queering practices, however, to queer shifts and changes with the historicity of its own emergence. Therefore, in approaching queer as this Foucaultian space in which historicizing contestations of meaning and positions endlessly occur, I position queer along two primary axes that are necessary to its historicized emergence in contemporary cultures of phallicized whiteness, and its historical lack of specificity: its decentering of utility, through its degenitalizing of sexuality; and its orientation toward pleasures, not desire. I thereby distance it considerably from any conflation with the identity categories of gay, lesbian, or bisexual (and, yes, my consistent omission of transgendered is intentional) and their constitutive reliance on sexual object choice. To be queer may have as much to do with how one approaches one's sexual and erotic practices as with the practices themselves. And, given how the logic of desire locks us into concepts of the self as a discretely contained unit that projects itself into the future, it may, more than anything, have to do with how one lives out the modes of spatiality and temporality in the practices of freedom it creates.

Bataille's Eroticism: Queering Pleasures

Bataille historicizes this teleological orientation toward the meaningful as the mandate of utility in advanced capitalism. Reading it as the totalizing grasp of reason on experience in late modernity, he locates the utilitarian imperative through the logic of the limit. This logic provides western cultures with one of their fundamental tools to make social and psychological meaning of the world: the rule of prohibitions. Uselessness, excess, waste—these are prohibited, strictly so.

As he develops particularly in volume 2 of *The Accursed Share*, objects, subjects, and activities are eroticized via prohibitions. The exemplar for Bataille here, following and ultimately exceeding Lévi-Strauss, is incest. The prohibition of intergenerational sexual contact within biological families eroticizes the familial ties—and, most importantly, the marital tie—and thereby ensures the continued flow of erotic energy in this otherwise closed container. A primary function of limits in human communities is thus to prohibit and thereby eroticize particular realms of behavior. And the sporadic act of transgression, whether physical or psychological, becomes necessary to recathect those boundaries and the objects and subjects they constitute as valuable, as we have already seen in the example of sodomy.

Bataille thereby sees that the endless transgression of limits will never be a way to exceed those limits: limits are formed to be transgressed. As Foucault also shows, transgressing limits only reinstates their power, performing exactly as the logic of the limit expects and demands. Bataille therein sees the totalizing grasp of a limited Hegelian system, driven by the endless transgression of limits. He sees the impossibility of exceeding through transgression a consciousness primarily framed by limits, a consciousness primarily framed by lack. Writing this in the register of prohibition and eroticism, he sees that, as Derrida puts it, "the Hegelian Aufhebung belongs to restricted economy, and is the form of the passage from one prohibition to another, the circulation of prohibitions" (1978, 275). The Hegelian system is a system of prohibitions—of limits—that totalizes its grasp through ontologizing the logic of the limit. But its totality is and can only be a closed totality: it is "the world of the prohibition not perceived as such" (1978, 275). As a closed system, it cannot recognize that which falls outside of it and against which it thinks: the limitless.[44] Bataille sees that, if he is to exceed this closed system and articulate a different kind of limitlessness, he cannot do so through the route of transgressing prohibitions: we must refigure our practices of freedom from the normative and normalizing practices of liberation.

Referring to eroticism as the exemplary field of sovereignty and "the *accursed* domain par excellence" (1988–91, 2:18), Bataille turns to it as an experience that exceeds closed economies—i.e., that does not operate on the logic of the limit. Eroticism, for example, exceeds the field of sexuality. For Bataille, sexuality is the realm of human experience that is created through the ontological break with animality; that is, through the abhorrence of animality,[45] sexuality is humanized to distance it from simple animal sexuality. But as a field of experience grounded in 'contact with animality,' sexuality is haunted by the very abhorrence that originally produced it as a human field of experience. And this haunting is the realm of eroticism: eroticism is the persistent *attraction* to that which humans must—ontologically as humans— abhor. Whether animal sexuality, sacrificial deaths, or a squandering uselessness, eroticism enacts the human attraction to the very thing that humans, as humans, must abhor.

What incites this attraction varies across time and space, with a necessity that is only local to the closed economy in which it operates: religious taboos, economic codes, racial barriers, educational systems, and of course norms of sexuality all eroticize various acts, objects, and thoughts differently at different times and places. The erotic world is, as Bataille puts it, "imaginary in its form" (1988–91, 2:29); some aspect of culture is arbitrarily delimited as 'erotic.' Engaging Bataille's thought experiment and recalling that he was a medievalist, we can imagine rather easily an eroticized world in which sexuality is forbidden (see 1988–91, 2:29). What is sexual may be erotic; but what is erotic need not be sexual.

The erotic thus may be historically experienced primarily through the dynamics of prohibition and permission, but a *general* perspective shows that eroticism is not reducible to this sort of negation. Put differently, the logic of containment does not hold between the erotic and the sexual: the erotic does not 'give place' to the sexual, nor *vice versa*. A general view ushers us into the ways that eroticism uses arbitrarily defined prohibitions to historically reenact the ontological break from animality that ensures our very humanity, without reducing the erotic to the limitations (or containers) of the sexual. But a register of hauntingly Hegelian historicity surfaces here: eroticism is both what historicizes human sexuality (see Bataille 1988–91, 2:49) via its historical variety of forms, and also what gives it a transhistorical character as always operating through prohibitions. Looking dangerously like the cunning of Reason, eroticism becomes that which Bataille must 'push to its own limit' if he is to grasp the ways that it exceeds the laws of prohibition.

Bataille subsequently attempts to articulate the experience of the erotic without recourse to the historical forms of prohibition and transgression, of fetish and taboo. This is no easy task: the experience of the erotic enacts the site of our ontological break from animality—a site that resists delimitation. He writes this experience in many voices, struggling to find language that is not servile to reason and its dominant tool, conceptual (phallicized) language. Given that a language freighted with metaphysical concepts and the logic of the limit is the habitual plane of his late modern historical existence, the dilemmas facing Bataille are no different from those facing other twentieth-century European thinkers. But, as indicated above, his response differs substantially.

For example, here he distances himself considerably from the hyper-rational approaches of psychoanalysis, which would read the attraction to the horror of animality as a 'return of the repressed.' It seems that psychoanalysis has claimed the field of sexuality, the field of how drives and desires are structured symbolically, psychically, culturally, and individually, as its realm of investigation and analysis. Sexuality, not eroticism. Psychoanalysis has, from Bataille's general perspective, reduced eroticism to sexuality, which is reduced once more to the conceptual apparatuses of reason and its dominant logic of utility. If sexuality is the realm of experience created through the ontological break with animality, it is that which renders the experience in an acceptable form of 'contact with' animality. And it is this 'contact' that psychoanalysis has rendered reasonable, even if through negation—i.e., through mapping how the irrational functions in our human relations to sexuality. But for Bataille, this contact with animality is not one that can be fully reduced to either reason or reason's negation. Rather, the contact with animality in the field of sexuality is constant, haunting sexuality with the very abhorrence that originally produced it as a human field of experience— i.e., the abhorrence that originally drove it to distance itself from this contact. The abhorrence is ontologically necessary. And this is what eroticism enacts and expresses. Eroticism thereby exceeds sexuality, as well as the (rational) grasp of psychoanalysis that attempts to reduce it to the field of sexuality.

The excessive forms that eroticism can assume are precisely why I wish to configure this, too, as the space of queering. Bataille does not approach erotic experience as a transgression of limits or prohibitions, which give entrée to the voice of reason and meaning. Wishing to behead reason, he writes, for example, of the embrace between lovers. Listen to his phenomenological account:

> The moment comes when my attention in the embrace has as its object the animality of the being I embrace. I am then gripped with horror. . . . There is horror in being: this horror is repugnant animality, whose presence I discover at the very point where the totality of being takes form. But the horror I experience does not repel me, the disgust I feel does not nauseate me. . . . I may, on the contrary, *thirst for it* . . . (1988–91, 2:118)

This is not a moment constituted through transgressing a prohibition. Rather, it is the moment that renders transgressions erotic, but is never contained by those moments. The horror of repugnant animality surfaces in this moment as the totality that constitutes our very humanity. But it surfaces in a way that is not merely the tantalizing effect of (breaking) the taboo. It is in and of itself attractive: we thirst for the horror. We do not thirst to return to animality; this is not a cleverly disguised nostalgia for some romantic's version of a metaphysics of presence. Nor do we thirst to break the taboo that sets the animality at a distance from us: this is not a psychoanalytic 'return of the repressed.' We thirst for the repugnance and horror of animality. We thirst for the experiential return to the site of our ontological humanizing—and this site is horrific. Reason cannot contain it—reason has no 'place' here.

Eroticism is thus an example of general economy and sovereignty for Bataille primarily because it "cannot serve any purpose" (1988–91, 2:16). We cannot make meaning out of these experiences: there is no teleology to explain them to us. They are not experiences that we control or choose or desire. They are not useful. We do not work on them: they work on us, returning us to the horror that constitutes our very humanity. They bring us, in Bataille's words, to experience "the subject at its boiling point" (1988–91, 1:10). To boil the subject differs qualitatively from pricking and prodding the subject to see how far the grasp of reason reaches. To boil the subject is to behead reason, to rid the subject of its 'place' in the universe.

In "The Sacred Conspiracy," Bataille speaks in this sort of language. He speaks of human life as "exhausted from serving as the head of, or the reason for, the universe" (1985, 180). Kept from being absurd, barred from the meaningless, human existence has been "limited to utility" (1985, 179) in late modernity. Human existence and experience have been contained. Out of this fatigue, Bataille invokes a horrific image: André Masson's *Acéphale,* a headless man teeming with life. Alongside this, he writes, "Man has escaped from his head just as the condemned man has escaped from his prison. He has found beyond himself not God, who is the prohibition against crime, but a being who is unaware of prohibition" (1985, 181). *A being who is unaware of prohibition*—Not one who transgresses prohibitions or negates limits and thereby proclaims his 'place' as master of the universe, but one who has never been tantalized by prohibition itself—one who does not operate within the logic of the limit or the logic of lack that it enacts. And, consequently, one who may have no idea who or what one 'is.'

Very queer stuff.

▼ ▼ ▼

Bataille's sense of eroticism thereby exceeds both the conceptual schemas of sexuality and the grasp of conceptual reason itself. Foucault's spaces of heterotopia and *Entstehung* also call us to sites prior to the reign of reason: sites in which discourses are forged, in which the meanings of words are still violently conflicted and contested, in which excessive possibilities swarm prior to the reduction to univocity and meaning. To read these together brings us to some powerfully queer encounters.

First of all, through Bataille's texts, we can see more clearly how and why the category of 'queer' has emerged from the domain of sexuality.[46] This historical milieu of late modernity and phallicized whiteness, which we share with Bataille, has reduced eroticism to forms of sexuality. Bataille thus focuses primarily, although not exclusively, on how eroticism functions within forms of sexuality because these are the historical forms that present themselves to him, and to us. If we bring the discussions of Locke's nascent capitalism and the Protestant work ethic together with the collusion of heterosexism and white supremacist racism, we begin to see the powerful political, economic, and psychological effects of this social constellation of values.

Eroticism has been reduced to sexuality precisely because sexuality is the domain of experience in which instrumental reason can assert itself forcefully, driving so deeply into the social psyche that it shapes the very core of the modern self—namely, one's desire. Instrumental reason can demand that sexuality must be *useful*. As we have seen, it is from the installation of this fundamental value, utility, that white supremacism and homophobia collude to produce more general forms of xenophobia: if an act is not useful, it is not properly human; and if sexuality is not reproductive, it is perverse.

High modernity ushered the age of utility fully into being. For Locke, and for the hard-working, industrious, bourgeois cultures that are the phallicized cultures under excavation here, *the site of our humanizing is the abhorrence of all that is not useful.* Locke cannot read the Native Americans as *human* because they are not using the land on which they live: to be human is to be useful. Or, put in the language of Bataille's eroticism, to be human is to find the useless squandering of animal life abhorrent. Why must we, ontologically, distance ourselves from the contact with animality that is at the root of human sexuality? Because it is useless. To abhor squandering uselessness or, at the other end of production, to abhor excessive waste is to distance oneself from animality: it is to humanize one's self—and to give reason, particularly instrumentality, its fullest reign over our social and psychic lives.

This larger distancing movement from animality has itself been erased from late modernity's consciousness. Bataille argues that this distancing from animality functions as the primary criterion for separating humankind into social classes, races, tribes, groups—into differences. He writes, "And while it is true that wealth makes this observance [to distinguish men from one another] easier, it is not so much wealth—beyond physical strength, or the power to command—that *distinguishes,* that qualifies socially, as it is the greatest distance from animality" (1988–91, 2:69). But we late moderns cannot even recognize this originary moment of abhorrence. Not allowed to admit that any "*horror* can enter into consideration" (1985, 117), we can only recognize "the right to acquire, to conserve, and to consume rationally, but [we must] exclude in principle *nonproductive expenditure*" (1985, 117). We must jump over the possibility of uselessness, just as we always jump over the chaotic spaces of contested meanings prior to the reign of reason. Bataille's schemas of general economy, sovereignty, expenditure, and impossibility will further enrich our practices of freedom enacted in queering. But I want to focus for a moment on this fundamental logic of utility at the heart of sexuality and the ways that we might resist it by exceeding its limited notions of eroticism.

As Bataille brings the reduction of eroticism to sexuality into focus, he simultaneously demonstrates how sexuality functions as a closed economy. Provoking us to think generally, he shows over and over how eroticism is irreducible to sexuality, drawing on its many other possible expressions: religious sacrifice, spectacles, arts; competitive games, war, cults; flowers, jewels; the list goes on and on across his texts.[47] In the contemporary cultures of phallicized whiteness, the queering of sexual pleasures, along with the intense anxiety that it produces, enacts these excessive possibilities that eroticism harbors, exposing the arbitrariness of the historical forms it has assumed. If sexuality is the attempt to humanize sexual acts away from their abhorrent animality, queering sexuality returns us to that site of abhorrence. But, to invoke the Foucaultian spaces, it does so in a way that exposes the arbitrariness of that humanizing act and unleashes the excessive possibilities that the laws of reason have silenced.

The queering of sexual pleasures thereby exposes the arbitrariness of the law of utility through its enactment of excessive possibilities erased by that law. In the domain of sexuality, the law of utility demands that sexuality must be useful. This means that it must be reproductive: the fundamental principle of Catholic sexual ethics (with which both Bataille and Foucault were well acquainted) is that the sexual act must be *natural*. And the single criterion of that status is the openness of the act to the procreation of human beings. Sexual acts must not foreclose reproduction. They must be useful. That this criterion reduces the excessive possibilities to the singular act of heterosexual intercourse is only an obvious aside. This fastening on the utility of the sexual act then effectively reduces the domain of sexuality to genitals: sex is about genitals, about who does what with his or her genitals. This is the site of anxiety: this is what fuels homophobia, as the 2003 Supreme Court rulings on sodomy affirm.[48] Sexuality is about the proper *use* of genitals. And that is all. But the queering of sexual pleasures, as sex radicals and sex activists such as Annie Sprinkle, Kate Bornstein, and Pat Califia have shown for some time, decenters this coding of the sexual body, effectively decentering the grasp of utility as well.[49]

Queer pleasures may, in fact, not even be properly "sexual." Bataille's texts of erotic fiction are filled with eggs, eyeballs, fevers, milk, semen, sheets, wind, rain, illnesses, chalices, sunlight, blood, bicycles, and very bizarre physical positions. Genitalia, that which the law of utility deems the proper site of sexuality, are merely one more among this onslaught of objects; they are described with an odd matter-of-factness that contrasts sharply with the sumptuousness of eggs and milk.[50] To queer pleasure decenters us from the grip of reproductive sexuality and its heteronormative coding of the body. (Those "gay muscles" that David Halperin describes are gloriously useless![51]) To queer then is not necessarily to be involved in same-sex sex acts: it may not even occur in realms recognizable as 'sexual.' It may have nothing at all to do with sexual object choices or other transgressions of the prohibitive law of desire. To queer may mean to be involved in acts of pleasures that offer no return to the closed economies of societal meaning that are driven by utility and the mandate of closed, concise, clear endpoints.[52] It may mean to be involved in practices that expose the arbitrariness of this fundamental value, utility, and initiate more sustained acts of freedom.

Examples of queering therefore demand our imaginations. As experiences that enact the excessive possibilities silenced by this reduction of sexuality to genitalia and, more generally, of experience to utility, they may not be easily recognizable. The possibilities are themselves excessive. And to enact, perhaps even to imagine, them will bring considerable chaos into the social field of meaning.

▼ ▼ ▼

To get an idea of what it might mean to turn identity inside out, to have an "identity without an essence" or to live in the world through "bodies and pleasures" rather than identities and desires, one need merely read Bataille's *Story of the Eye* (1987). A hyper-performative text, it leads its readers directly to bodies, perhaps even giving their bodies to themselves in ways they have not previously experienced. The first chapter, "Cat's Eye," already puts one in a world of bodies and pleasures and fluids, and nothing more. Bataille elaborates the intricate acrobatics of these young bodies with great detail, inviting his readers to concoct some impossible physical positions.[53] And this, in addition to some cat's milk, eggs, and urine, is all we get. There are no characters in this piece of literature that Susan Sontag proclaimed, in a back-cover blurb, "the most accomplished artistically of all pornographic prose I've read." Yes, we get names and genders and ages, but there are no internal conversations or intercharacter dialogues that might give us some sense of 'what drives these people' or 'who these people are.' There is no narrative of desire, and consequently no character has an identity. Proper names function as placeholders for varieties of bodily fluids and physical positions. Rather, what Bataille gives us are the effects of their behaviors on their bodies: the text is filled with bizarre acts that seem to multiply possibilities endlessly.

To live in the world queerly is then to live in the world transformatively, with an eye always toward how relations of bodies and pleasures can be multiplied and intensified. If it is to veer off the rails of utility and reason, this veering may be some of the best indicators of queering's effects. To be intensely engaged in activities that are *going nowhere* may already be to be queering this culture: the slow, iterative time of intellectual work that never produces anything other than its own activity, and pleasure, comes to mind. Or to confuse the very question of genitalia beyond its registers of meaning would also be to queer this culture: trannies, both M-F and F-M, are twisting the question of sex as a question of genitals into hilarious contortions. To be as explicit as the law of desire demands: if a female-by-birth who identifies as a lesbian straps on a dildo to have anal sex with a male-to-female tranny who has both breasts and a penis, does this somehow make her straight? (Such an act would not have been criminalized under the recently outlawed anti-sodomy laws of Texas, which pertained only to same-sex couples.) Or, to speak in that first-person voice that queering apparently evokes, I surely have the queerest of relations with my flamboyantly gorgeous cat, with whom I am so intensely and erotically 'involved' that my lesbian lover often realizes she will always be second in my heart.

But I merely tease you with these simplistic examples here. Particularly amidst the commodifying powers of advanced capitalism and the nasty histories of elitism and exclusionary politics that are attaching themselves to "queer" as an identity and theory, to resist queerly must be more subtle, more complex . . .

If to be queer is to step off, even if only for a moment or a performance or an event, the rails of reason, it is also to step off the rails of spatiality and temporality that dominate and domesticate us now. We have already seen how spatiality functions in our cultures of phallicized whiteness, containing us in classed, racialized, and sexed selves that are to be read as discrete units working in the social world. Spatiality, functioning through the logic of the limit, contains us, leading us to conceive of freedom through the transgressions of prohibitions. It thereby enmeshes us in subjectivities of desire and politics of identities, where we conceive of ourselves as discrete units of private property that must overcome, perhaps even master, other discrete entities to answer our needs. We have not yet seen explicitly, however, how temporality functions in these cultures. If to queer is to step off these rails of spatiality and of temporality that dominate and domesticate us, we must explore temporality a bit before undergoing the queering of pleasures in the richest, most excessive, ways.

We must explore temporality before coming to those practices of freedom that have nothin' left to lose.

THE TEMPORALITY OF WHITENESS

Anticipating Pleasure (And Feeling Nothin' But Guilty)

5

The miraculous moment when anticipation dissolves into NOTHING, detaching us from the ground on which we were groveling, in the concatenation of useful activity.

—GEORGES BATAILLE,
The Accursed Share,
volume 3

The events of September 11, 2001, in New York City and Washington, D.C., seem to have acted as Althusser's cop calling us before the law: 'we'—the specific we of those living in material, political, and economic security in the United States—have been called to awaken to a reality that may jar us from our luxurious solipsism. The interpellation rings loudly, even if more and more sporadically, as we gain distance from the physical events of 9/11. Flags continue to wave—on t-shirts, hats, websites, backpacks, and even high-heeled shoes. The Patriot Act enters its second and third manifestations. Airport security checks continue with xenophobic zeal. "The American," "the all-American," "the Patriot" have all been called into existence with newly found legal vigor. And as the birth of categories and identities always does, this Althusserian cop of 9/11 has brought a renewed vigilance and policing of borders around these sacred identities—the identities that I cull together under the heading of 'phallicized whiteness.'

In this shared contemporary scene of

'post-9/11 U.S.,' Irigaray's plea to reconsider our entire problematic of space and time, the very mode of our embodiment and experience, seems an appropriate site for the slow work of intellectuals to inhabit. Moreover, given the first appellation coined for the U.S. strikes against Afghanistan in October 2001, the infamous "Operation Infinite Justice," it is right on the mark: conflicting modes of spatio-temporality may be most at stake in the waging of these wars. This name was haphazardly market-researched and quickly, if not sheepishly enough, withdrawn. An act of hegemonic hubris and blindness, it may sadly characterize the ongoing wars of the U.S. on behalf of 'freedom-loving people' and 'whiteness' itself. While the criticism of that phrase was focused on the kind of absolute justice it proclaimed, I heard only a temporality—a temporality that readily and comfortably invokes the infinite. An entire set of assumptions and subject positions are enacted in such a temporality, ones that constitute that still largely unnamed and unmarked entity, "whiteness." Pursuing Irigaray's provocative suggestion that to imagine ethical parity in our navigation of social power requires that we redeploy space and time, I suggest that the "war against terrorism" and its multiple invasions of other sovereign nations in which we in the U.S. are willingly or unwillingly implicated are, among so many other things, wars of temporalities.

▼ ▼ ▼

Temporality gives us away. A fundamental vector of social power written in our bodies, temporality is one of the basic lessons of childhood: timing is everything. We learn rather quickly not only which parent to ask for what, but more importantly when to ask for it and whether to dare ask for it at all. Whether we get $2, $5, $10, or $20 for the night's activities, whether we get to spend the night at Joni's or Joey's house, whether we get to go to the movies or the skating rink all hinge entirely on the fragile balance of timing. We learn to read the rhythms of the adult world with an unspoken precision. And this precision writes itself on our bodies with greater and greater force as we slowly enter that world of adult bodies.

The range of proper timing varies from place to place and community to community: urban time is certainly not what suburban time is, not to mention rural or small-town time; single time varies from coupled time; middle-class time differs from working-class and again from upper-class time; children's time seems infinitely longer than adult time; and "CPT" ("Colored Person's Time") and "QST" ("Queer Standard Time"), which are increasingly portrayed in popular culture,[1] differ considerably from the obsessive punctuality of white Protestant time. Nothing conscious, nothing intentional, and yet speaking more loudly than any of our professed values—temporality gives us away. It carves power into our bodies and into the world, telling where we came from and where we are placed in this world and its social map of power.

The configuring of race in this embodying of temporality surfaces easily across the transnational map. Historically, temporality has been a central tool of colonialism: the erecting of a clock in the center of a village in India, for example, signaled the arrival of the British and the dominance of a temporality of discrete, sequential time units, punctuality, and scheduling. More contemporarily, pharmaceutical companies work to convince the U.S. government that medicines for HIV and AIDS cannot work in Africa because Africans do not "understand western time"—i.e., they do not use clocks and cannot keep track of when to take their meds. (Acting out western hegemony, the companies never offer any self-reflection on their assumptions about temporality or more creative ways of explaining the temporality of western medicine to Africans.[2]) The widening economic gap between Asian and Latin American cultures could easily, if also reductively, be ascribed to their differing temporalities. Stereotypes tell us that the Latin siesta appears as a bizarre indulgence to the increasingly frantic pace of hyper-techno Asian cultures;[3] but both of these judgments assume Euro-U.S. time as the normative, operative criterion. And, finally, to return again to the U.S. war against Afghanistan, the U.S. government refused to stop bombing Afghanistan during Ramadan in a clear rejection of any holiday calendar other than the Christian one; moreover, this month-long holiday was simply "too long." Northern-western European and American temporality thus functions as the 'norm' against which other temporalities of the world are measured and judged. It functions as a regulative ideal—the regulative ideal of whiteness.

How exactly does it operate? I sketch two modes of this temporality of phallicized whiteness: the future anterior, which Lacan develops as a temporality of desire in phallicized symbolics; and the mode of anticipation, illuminated in the texts of Georges Bataille. These two modes collude to embed us, unconsciously, in two sets of socio-psychological values that ground cultures of phallicized whiteness: utility, and thereby capitalism with its concept of pleasure as satisfaction and convenience; and white guilt, with its enactment of the Protestant work ethic and the myth of Progress. But first I must locate the psychological horizon of desire in which these modes of temporality work, the horizon of the infinite.

The Infinite Desire of Disembodied Whiteness

As we have seen, whiteness gains its power through its basic posture as the universal and naturalized 'order of things.' In mutually grounding gestures, whiteness renders itself both invisible and ubiquitous. And at the core of this disavowal of race and of historical location *per se,* whiteness operates as the universal, unmarked signifier through its disavowal of embodiment itself. Echoing Lacan's phallus, it functions through remaining veiled. And a primary site of this veiling is its ontological denial of embodiment itself. This erasure of the body, as a primary erasure of the material particular, is a fundamental necessity for whiteness's claim to universality.

For phallicized whiteness, the appearance of bodies—both how they appear and that they are not 'real'—ensures its continued mastery of the symbolic field. The white straight Christian propertied male body appears as the 'normal' body—without marking, without distinction, and, consequently, in power. But it only appears this way through staking its ground as a universal subject in a space that transcends the body (and thus materiality itself, including history). The white straight Christian propertied male body claims its power through the idealizing of a disembodied state of being, perpetuating an ideal toward which all other bodies will continually aspire and which they will necessarily fail to achieve.

If phallicized whiteness is thus constituted by a fundamental disembodiment that renders the body an optical illusion, it locates universal subjectivity (i.e., the 'individual') in a realm that transcends the messiness of material vicissitudes. In the construction of the liberal individual, one must transcend dynamics such as history, the body, and desire to become a coherent, legible subject. It follows that all bodies signified as 'non-white' will be barred from full entrance to phallicized whiteness—and thus to subjectivity itself—fundamentally through their very embodiment. The significations of the 'non-white' may be complicated beyond simple racial ones to include signifiers of class, gender, sexuality, religion, and certainly nationality. However signified, these 'other' bodies are 'too real'—too fleshy to recognize that the field of bodily appearances, which is the field of social power, is a game of optics. They become objects or abjected others, never subjects.

We can trace this projection of *the body* by phallicized whiteness onto 'other' bodies in a number of ways: sports, music, dance, even cuisine and sexuality all offer areas of culture that have been coded to displace *the body* onto non-white cultures. Such a displacement cuts to the very core of 'whiteness,' particularly when it turns back toward and incites a kind of colonizing

153

yearning in whiteness itself. This yearning for *the body* is often coded in the desire for 'culture' and deployed as a lamentation through which whiteness disavows having any substance or power. (We can hear it in those pernicious claims that "whiteness has no culture" or "is not a color.") This yearning for the body ushers in one of the primary configurations of this disembodied whiteness—its infinite desire for a pleasure that is structurally impossible.

▼ ▼ ▼

A very brief and rather cartoonish look at the history of western metaphysics shows this infinite structure of desire. Since its birth in the garden of Aphrodite's party, *Eros,* this child of *Poros* and *Pena* (of abundance and lack), seems to have followed a trajectory of infinite deferral. The 'satisfaction' of desire seems largely not to be pleasure, but rather its own, endless self-perpetuation. The *telos* of *Eros* most often surfaces as an idealized form of respite from desire's endless cajolings. For example, several texts offer a variety of idealized spaces—the same sort of idealized space that phallicized whiteness claims for its 'true' self—that transcend the messiness of Eros: Plato offers us Forms; Augustine, God; Hegel, Reason; even Nietzsche gives us laughter. But these idealized places of rest, in their very act of idealizing, incite further desire, rather than quelling it.

For example, when Hegel describes the move to self-consciousness in the *Phenomenology* as the awakening of Reason, he thereby shapes desire into a more 'satisfactory' articulation: one that sets consciousness on an endless quest. Reason gives consciousness an impossible goal—namely, as Hegel puts it in the *Phenomenology,* "the point where knowledge no longer needs to go beyond itself" (1977, section 80). But it is the very structure of human consciousness, for Hegel, always to go beyond itself: the labor of the negative becomes an endless motor of knowing and desire in Hegel's texts. Accordingly, it seems that the only satisfaction of desire is the impossibility of its satisfaction. Ontologically severed from the messy materiality of the body, desire is conceptualized and performed across the history of western metaphysics—a history that offers a certain kind of history of 'whiteness'—as endless: desire is infinite. And the move to idealize its *teloi* only disguises desire's endless self-perpetuation.

As Irigaray develops in her early texts *Speculum of the Other Woman* and *This Sex Which Is Not One,* the machinations of idealization are grounded in the auto-eroticism of narcissism. To gloss rather crudely, the move to idealize the penis as the phallus in Lacanian psychoanalysis turns on the narcissistic cathexis of that organ in western (phallicized) cultures. Owning the most prized of values, visibility, the penis is granted its idealized status on this basis: Narcissus falls in love with his own *image,* not his own sound or smell or taste or touch. We have already seen how this register of visibility grounds systems of racism and their modes of space (and how idealization haunts even Irigaray's texts). I want to draw out the closed character of the economy of idealization further. Grounded in narcissism, idealization places the idealized object or value on a plane of specular adoration. Idealized objects and values draw us toward them, enticing us to gaze upon them with a particular longing—the longing that inspires mimesis. We long not to possess them, but to be like them, to shape ourselves in their images. *Deo imagio.*

As all closed economies must be, the closed economy of idealization is thus also a totalizing economy. If desire functions at an idealized level in western metaphysics and cultures of phallicized whiteness, it also functions as a closed, totalizing economy. As I argued regarding Hegel and Derrida, there is no outside to desire. Despite our impression that it operates teleologically, finding its satisfaction in pleasure, desire's idealization lands it in the space of endless perpetuation. It never finds its 'resting place,' to quote one of the western tradition's most passionate spokesmen for this dynamic, Augustine. Caught in this dynamic, we are forever snarled in a desire that seeks that which its own seeking already fulfills—namely, to keep seeking. We long for the ideal. And in a stunning example of performativity, our longing itself operates at an idealized—disembodied—plane of experience. Mimesis always falls short; but we always keep trying.

This is not to say that a concept of pleasure is impossible. To the contrary, conceptualizing pleasure may be one of Reason's best performances of idealization. As the ability to raise particulars to universals, to render apparent randomness logical, or, as Irigaray shows us, to turn those frightening and threatening fluids into invaluable solids, the concept may be the hallmark of western metaphysic's highest power, rationality. The act of conceptualizing is arguably the act of western metaphysics *par excellence.*[4] It is what enables Reason to perform some of its most valuable tasks: to make univocal sense of variegated, even chaotic, things; to vacate the present moment as nothing but a particular to be sublated into universalizing articulations; and to persuade desire of the fiction that the future anterior is reduced to a controlled possibility. Particularly as read through a Lacanian interpolation of Hegel, conceptual thinking (albeit historicized) is the exemplary enactment of phallic subjectivity—it is 'true' thinking, shaping experience into forms that can

distinguish, demarcate, centralize, evaluate, name, control, and make meaning out of objects and experiences in the world.

Our concepts of pleasure thereby only reensure the impossibility of experiencing it. In cultures of phallicized whiteness, we see this particularly in
the concepts of pleasure perpetuated under advanced capitalism. Advanced
capitalism celebrates itself as the triumph of pleasure. Whether in the voice
of moral disdain, coupled all too often with a naive nostalgia for Ward and
June Cleaver, or the voice of grand economic celebration, coupled all too
often with a rather boring Hollywood version of overconsumption, the reading of contemporary U.S. culture as a culture fundamentally driven by and
caught up in pleasure saturates our television screens, movie screens, news-
paper editorials, and church pulpits, and even some university boardrooms.
It seems to be our favorite reading of ourselves, our favorite register of self-
consciousness. Who are we, that famed or infamous United States? We are
either the grandest culture of the twenty-first century or the most decadent
one since that fabled ancient Rome; in either garb, we are a culture of
pleasure.

But as proclamations of self-consciousness often turn out, this one also
seems tainted by a limited reflection on the operative concept of pleasure.
What sorts of things are being proclaimed as experiences of pleasure in
advanced capitalism? The endless ownership of private property or the successful use of various tools (hammers, software, education, public policy,
religious ritual) to reduce the world to modes of convenience—these define
the dominant conceptions of pleasure. While they may have been sufficient
for Locke, these are, if anything, expressions of satisfaction, not pleasure.
They are derived from a logic that displaces the role of *Poros* in Aphrodite's
garden to one of merely fulfilling *Pena*.[5] Lack dominates this concept of
pleasure, intensifying its abstracted, idealized status and locking it into a
logic of teleology—of satisfaction. To conceive of pleasure through ideals of
satisfaction remains in the logic that frames pleasure as the *telos* of desire:
you desire an apple and you then indulge the pleasure of eating an apple.
But where is the space of excess in that linear causality? The logic of lack
and satisfaction impoverishes our conception of pleasure, reducing it to the
models of teleology and univocity that late modernity prizes so highly.

These exponential reductions—namely, of pleasure to satisfaction and,
increasingly, of satisfaction to convenience—have become hallmarks of advanced capitalism. Far from a historical accident, these are the outgrowths
of high modernity's reduction of rationality to instrumentality and the consequent reduction of the world to objects. (We appear to be trapped in

Locke's philosophical, political, and economic world.) Conceptual thinking allows reason to make things *useful*. It allows instrumental rationality to master the world, reducing that world to its use. Lost in the totalizing, closed economy of utility, we mistake the limited *teloi* of utility, satisfaction, and convenience for pleasure. Formless excess is displaced from the dynamism of *eros*, rendering the possibilities of queer difficult even to imagine.

These reductions and unconscious metamorphoses occur fundamentally, while not exclusively, through the temporalities of experience, those barely conscious rhythms of our lives, in cultures of advanced capitalist phallicized whiteness. While we who live in the material and solipsistic luxury of advanced capitalism may be maniacally obsessed with time and use it to carve our lives into the most useful units of efficiency, we seem to remain blinded to the effects of that time on the rhythms of our lives. This stands in stark contrast to those who labor in factories or live in the prison system, where the effects of time are ever-present in their explicit constraint. Blinded by privilege, we who live in the luxuries of phallicized whiteness remain unaware of the effects of that time on the very ways that we understand ourselves as desiring identities in the world of utility.

Temporal Modes of Mastery: The Future Anterior

As an abstracted ideal, phallicized whiteness functions through a strange sort of disembodied, never-present temporality. The absent-minded white male body is readily excused, and often acclaimed, for being lost in the intoxicating ether of intellectual work or political ideals—often so much so that it cannot care for its own basic functions of nourishment and hygiene. It is not *in* its body and thus is never in the present that such a body might inhabit. Again, the history of western metaphysics displays this over and over: texts ranging from Aristotle and Augustine to Husserl and Heidegger repeatedly reduce the present to a fleeting juncture between past and future that ontologically resists conception. Reading desire here, we find a desire that operates on a temporality which, while involved with the conditioning of the past in greater and lesser degrees, faces the future as if it is already beyond it. It faces the future from that strange place that Lacan calls the 'future anterior,' the temporality of the "will have been."

Perhaps, for example, I desire to travel to Venezuela—an example that, as many post-colonial and feminist theorists have shown, enacts one of the most persistent lingering impulses of colonialism in cultures of phallicized whiteness—namely, traveling.[6] If I were to desire to travel to Venezuela, both the desire and the very experience of traveling could not hold themselves in any present moment. The present is not, in phallicized whiteness's experience and conception of temporality, itself a 'place.' It is that fleeting, always already evaporating juncture between the future and the past that eludes language and conceptualization. We cannot speak it. It is in itself nothing, of no substance—only a transition from that which will be to that which has been. In this linear structuring of temporality, desire cannot locate itself in the present, future, or past: the present is 'no place'; the future passes immediately into the past; and the past only renders desire nostalgia.

Not in the present, future, or past, desire seems to locate itself beyond the future. "I desire to travel to Venezuela" implies that I desire to be the woman who has traveled to Venezuela—to become (future) the woman who has been in Venezuela (the act having already passed into the past). I desire that my act of traveling will become something that has occurred, that it "will have been." And I will likely provide such evidence of its 'having been' through taking innumerable photographs and buying various 'souvenirs' while I am traveling. In fact, these may constitute some of my primary activities while traveling—activities that already stand 'beyond the future' and structure the alleged 'present' as preparation for that anticipated future. That is, the 'present,' my traveling in Venezuela, becomes the gathering of proof for the future that it has occurred, that I have traveled to Venezuela. The temporality of my traveling is structured by becoming the woman who has traveled, just as my very desire to travel is also structured by this future anterior, this desire to become the woman who has traveled.

This strange space of the future anterior locates phallicized whiteness in a temporal space that transcends sequential moments of time (present, future, and past). In that temporal space, the subjectivity of phallicized whiteness transcends temporality just as it transcends the body. And this transcendence gives it power: from the space of the future anterior, phallicized whiteness positions itself as if it has already mastered each and every moment before that moment has occurred. Claiming a place once deemed appropriate only for deities, phallicized whiteness transcends the chronology of past-present-future and faces them as if it has already determined how that moment shall occur. It positions itself to appear as if it has achieved that ideal of the Steven Spielberg–Tom Cruise sci-fi futuristic flick *Minority Report:* "The guilty will be punished before the crime is committed." The phrase aptly describes the ideals of the current U.S. government in this 'war on terrorism' and the increasingly frightening instantiations of the Patriot Act: this temporality, and its power and dangers, are not fictional.

Anticipation, the Temporal Mode of Capitalism

Mastery thereby becomes the dominant mode of power in these configurations of temporality. The appearance of standing "beyond the future" becomes the appearance of having already mastered all moments leading toward it, effectively canceling any historicity at work in present or past moments. This posture of mastery is further bolstered through another tentacle of the temporality of phallicized whiteness, anticipation. In engaging the social field in a temporality of anticipation, phallicized whiteness guarantees that the temporality of experience is geared always toward the future—and thus implicitly always toward phallicized whiteness itself, which inhabits that space 'beyond the future.' Experience, if it is to be meaningful, must never face the past. History is dead, of no use, not important to whiteness, as we see in the liberal individual's (and its affirmative action debates') disavowal of it and the myths of the self-made western man in white guilt. Anticipation further sediments phallicized whiteness's idealized status.

A historical watershed in the discursive construction of phallicized whiteness helps us to see this—the Protestant work ethic. Emerging with capitalism and arguably phallicized whiteness's strongest contemporary tentacle, the Protestant work ethic codified two new regulative ideals of 'civilization': utility and the accumulation of private property. Through each of these, phallicized whiteness directs consciousness always toward the future, embedding it in a temporality of anticipation.

With the accumulation of private property, the public act of that private behavior Marx calls 'hoarding' in *Capital,* this temporal structure of anticipation is easy to see. Hoarding is "a mode of temporal deferral"—a mode that is then rendered abstract with the advent of capital. In an act that is exacerbated with the emergence of money, one hoards private property so that one can enjoy one's accumulated objects at a future time. But just as the experience of traveling is displaced endlessly into a future that never fully arrives, this promised enjoyment becomes that which hoarding forever defers. As Amy Wendling puts it, "The anticipated pleasure supplants the current one: hoarding leads to more hoarding and the temporal deferral becomes permanent" (2002). The culture subordinated to these practices finds itself locked in an infinity of deferred pleasure, an infinity of anticipation. The pleasure ultimately becomes anticipation itself, rather than the promise it holds, and we find ourselves once again in a perfectly closed economy of desire. Moreover, in advanced capitalism, we find ourselves in a perfectly closed economy of desire that incites us to work more and more furiously, more and more blindly.

We can see this endless anticipation in my example of traveling to Venezuela, an example that clearly assumes advanced capitalism and the particular type of traveling known as tourism.[7] The intense planning for such a trip blurs into the 'actual travel' and subsumes the object and experience of travel itself—the guide books, which we hoard and carry with us, instill an anticipation that ultimately displaces the sites to which we travel. Or, in a less superficial or self-indulgent example, we also see this at the core of the distinction between 'developed' and 'underdeveloped' countries—a binary I prefer to replace with Paul Gilroy's binary of 'overdeveloped' and 'underdeveloped' countries. The U.S., for example, can assert itself as a 'global power' because it has mastered its own future—concretely, it has hoarded enough oil not to be in danger of losing its own oil-based economy. (We have seen this in the Bush administration's rhetoric promoting drilling in Alaska because we do not want to 'use our reserves.') This ability to master one's future, to stand beyond one's future, becomes the benchmark for 'development.' It is connected, as Nietzsche tells us in his diagnoses of guilt, to the ability to make promises, where the master is the one with such rights. At the level of the individual, we see it easily in the increasing obsession with and anxiety over 401Ks and inheritance taxes in classes with such luxuries.

As hoarding feeds on itself exponentially and enmeshes us in the pleasure of anticipation, rather than the promised enjoyment it holds, those within this closed economy cannot see this endless deferral of anticipating pleasure. Particularly as this mode of desire is rendered more and more abstract with the advent of capital, we are blinded to its disembodied effects. Through its very promise—rather than actualization—of material enjoyment, the structure of the accumulation of private property and capital disembodies desire, immersing it in this closed infinity of anticipation. But such a disembodied desire of infinite deferral is quite at home in cultures of phallicized whiteness.

The Satisfying Certainty of Utility

Utility's enactment of the temporal structure of anticipation operates at a slightly more general level than hoarding and colludes with the future anterior to lodge us in phallicized whiteness's dominant register of experience in advanced capitalism. It assumes an intentionality that can control and master conditions necessary to achieve its desired end, usefulness. That is, it assumes an intentionality that transcends and can thereby control the present material conditions, just as phallicized whiteness does. The endpoint of one's activities in a utilitarian system is expected, anticipated, and awaited as the final judgment of all moments leading toward it. This is teleology at its strictest definition, in which the *telos* must manifest itself in clear and distinct—in useful—ways. Implying that these ends can be obtained, this temporality of anticipation also assumes that it will recognize its final achievement. Utility embeds us in a deep anticipation of satisfying certainty: it enacts the full substitution of satisfaction for pleasure. And in advanced capitalism, the mark of that satisfaction becomes convenience.

But utility's temporality of anticipation affects the present in ways that run at odds with this promised endpoint of satisfying certainty. Utility's temporality, in its demanding march toward its singular goals, performs some of the hallmarks of colonialism's 'divide and conquer' strategies. Each and every moment in a consciousness driven by utility is sequestered off into its individual role in the grand movement toward achievement. (And, in a performance of the prohibitions of waste that we have already encountered, one of these moments is likely to be the act of hoarding.) Utility divides our experience into separable, discretely contained moments that fall neatly into sequential lines, all leading toward—but perhaps never arriving at—the final point of use. The shirt is ironed so that the body will appear orderly so that the voice will be heard authoritatively so that the argument will persuade so that the position will be obtained so that the money will be earned so that the economy will flourish so that the citizens will buy more shirts to be ironed—and perhaps even travel to Venezuela. Again, such infinite circularity does not bother the closed economy of utility—or of desire.

With each moment divided discretely from the next, utility reduces the meaning of the present *qua* present to a nonsensical question. The present is judged, clearly and distinctly, by the role that it plays in the achievement of useful ends. The present is judged by the future, framed by the future anterior—i.e., the 'will have been'—that already reads each moment as if the future moment of utility has already been achieved.

Utility thereby totalizes its grasp, seeping into each discrete, sequential moment through the implicit judgment of that moment's usefulness. The very reduction of time to sequential, discrete units that are measured by precise tools further subordinates it to the closed economy of utility: we use tools to make time useful. The daily planner, the Palm Pilot, the endless list-making: we even schedule our emotions. But the judgment of whether each discrete moment is useful finally relies on an endpoint that transcends

161

the singular moment: the singular moment itself can never adequately account for its own *telos*.

Just as the infinite deferral of pleasure enacted in hoarding can never be seen by the one who is busily accumulating private property, so too does utility subordinate its practitioners in a circular infinity that a singular act can never grasp. We are trapped in Hegel's 'bad infinite.' Utility simply insists that it grounds itself—that it is self-evidently the *telos* of all acts. It thereby silences the more general question of what makes utility itself desirable. Each singular moment within the sequential march of utility is consequently prone to a judgment whose final criterion the singular moment can never provide. Such a criterion calls for more general principles, such as those invoked by Bataille's general economy, that necessarily supersede the singular moment.

Shutting each separate act off from the possibility of accounting for its orientation toward this (alleged) final *telos* of usefulness, utility thereby enacts phallicized whiteness's utopia—namely, the culture in which no singular moment *or person or race or class* can account for why phallicized whiteness and its trappings are desirable. No singular moment or person or race or class can account for the seduction of phallicized whiteness and its alleged freedom. Consequently, one cannot escape its grasp. To state it in a way that dangerously lacks subtlety: phallicized whiteness is the regulative ideal of U.S. culture and, consciously or unconsciously, that which we all desire and aspire toward—even, and perhaps particularly, when such a desire makes no sense or, worse still, when such a desire becomes violent, even self-violating. And yet we all, regardless of bodily signifiers or socio-economic standing, inevitably fail in this desire to "be" white—a desire that anticipates its pleasure infinitely. Just as no one 'has' the phallus or the enjoyment at the end of utility, so too no one is white; hence the perniciousness and violence of the endless attempt at the impossible, the pleasure of 'being white.' We kill ourselves in the endless asymptotic approach to the impossible.

Utility writes itself into our bodies in this culture of advanced capitalist phallicized whiteness in the very temporalities we inhabit. And the effects across the social map of power are abundant, expressing the distinct registers of oppression. When we hear that damning phrase "Make yourself useful!" the conscience of phallicized whiteness stings. We are judged nothing but guilty by this Protestant demand. There is nothing to do with that guilt, nowhere to go with it. And so we, the subjects of power in this culture of

phallicized whiteness, project that guilt across bodies of lesser power, changing the phrase accordingly: "Make yourself useful, *boyyy* . . ."

A southern twang, the mean trace of slavery's history, lingers in that
damning last word, which is always implied if not spoken in the command
itself. It pulls the command out of the sky of abstractions and slams it
squarely on the ground. This ain't about no lofty ideals—this is about bodies.
Bodies of control and bodies to be controlled. Bodies of discipline and bodies
in need of discipline. Bodies of power and bodies that obey. Bodies and
histories. That simple, far from innocent *"boyyy"* cuts the demand straight
into its fundamental register—the old but hauntingly familiar voice of the
patronizing white overseer that never seems to die. Whether spoken sternly
by a parent to a child, frankly by a boss to an employee, reprimandingly by
a teacher to a student, or jokingly by a friend to a companion, it is the same
voice speaking and the *"boyyy"* is at the end of every sentence. This command
of utility, whenever and however spoken, is about bodies—black, brown,
white, yellow; queer, female, trans, disabled, poor; Jewish, Catholic, Muslim,
Hindu. It is about bodies and the ways that utility seeps into them through
their social mappings of power.

The stories with bodies of color are all too easy to tell, bespeaking the
ways that racism lurks literally just beneath the skin in the United States.
Brown bodies are lazy, black bodies even lazier. White folks marvel at the
hard work of Mexican day laborers as they toil away in the white folks' yards
and bathrooms and garbage cans: *"that Mexican sure does work hard, don't
he?"* The surprise belies the expectation. Black bodies are seen only in crime
reports, drug zones, and welfare lines. Their usefulness all dried up post-
Emancipation, they are no longer even expected to work. And then the
yellow bodies, who have mistakenly taken the command of utility to the
other extreme—working much too hard, being far too useful, displaying their
zeal for success in extraordinarily bad taste. One must know how to appear
with just the right amount of usefulness to gain entrance to those cherished
boardrooms. To work too hard is not in good taste and, accordingly, not
highly valued, leaving the physical laborer with one of utility's most perverse
twists: it takes three jobs of hard, physical labor just to pay the bills. It is
not by accident that the bodies in those boardrooms all look alike, behave
properly, and display just the right amount of usefulness to ensure their lives
of luxury.

Sexualized bodies are disdained only slightly more subtly than racialized
ones: the queering of that *"boyyy"* as the effeminate one who cannot protect
himself has always echoed through its racialized tenor. (We hear this most

163

clearly in the contemporary voice of that white overseer, the white police officer poised on the brink of violently sodomizing his catch.) The perversion of queer bodies lies in their categorical refusal of the act that renders sexuality meaningful—the act that renders it useful. An affront to all 'natural' sensibilities, a sexuality that categorically precludes reproduction (the guise utility dons here) can be nothing but a breach of etiquette. The reverberations surface with humorously literal aberrations of taste: queens with cartoonish femininity on parade; gay men with 'too much' taste and a perfectionism that paralyzes; lesbians with bad haircuts and no taste at all. Again, the simple balance between too much and not enough is missed, but here it is biologically impossible: these sexual bodies cannot be useful. Granted, the categories are shifting as the lesbian baby-boom takes cultural root. But the lesbians in flannel shirts and combat boots have only been eclipsed by lipstick chic as the much promised polymorphous perversity has finally arrived: transsexual bodies will truly never be of any use at all.

Utility's gendering of bodies may seem old hat and obvious by now. Surely we know that masculine bodies are the ones that work hard (but not too hard) and produce useful commodities for the marketplaces—whether economic, intellectual, political, spiritual, or moral. Masculine bodies produce things. Conversely, feminine bodies, as idealized through phallicized whiteness, are put on their pedestals because they were never even made for working. As Bataille voices that which should perhaps remain unspoken (if the phallus is to remain veiled): "the prostitute[, as the perfection of femininity,] is the only being who logically should be idle"(1988–91, 2:146).[8] Feminine bodies perform their femininity perfectly when they behave as beautiful bodies untainted by even a trace of material servitude: only female bodies of the upper, non-working class can display 'true femininity.' In fact, it is through this pure inutility that female bodies become the 'natural' arbiters of good taste and the quintessential consumers, fixing the role of shopper as the subject position that bridges the gap between the 1950s ideal housewife and the contemporary sixteen-year-old female target of all marketing. How do women fit into the closed economy of utility? We shop 'til we drop. And yet are women not simultaneously the exemplary commodities exchanged? And is not the exchange value determined precisely by their disavowal of any role at all in the economy of utility? Following Irigaray here, we see that feminine bodies perform the merging of aesthetics and utility perfectly: it is in their beauty that feminine bodies are deemed valuable. It is in their complete disavowal of all crass utility that feminine bodies are judged useful to the (specular) economy.

Finally, we may see this reign of utility brutally at work in the realm of spiritual lives—or what we should properly call religion. Only those religious practices that issue into some moral statement about the world, some clear evaluation of behaviors, ideas, choices, or lifestyles, are worthy of the very name "religion." All others, whether meditative practices or pagan aesthetics, whether ritualized prayer or goddess festivals, only defame the concept of religion when they claim it for themselves. As the fount of all values, proper religion must exercise the power of a transcendent deity to master the world—to master the world and nature and all unruly desires. It is the place in which we learn the fundamental practices of discipline, spelled out before us in clear and distinct principles. And its rituals must be useful, whether through teaching a moral principle or offering the site for mercantile exchanges. ("Church" always offers the opportunity for fresh financial alliances: middle-class Protestant weddings, and even funerals, are business meetings as much as social gatherings. Or so I am told.)

These are, of course, cartoons. Cartoons intended to laugh at the arrogant voice that might actually speak them. But in that sad laughter we hear ugly truths. We hear the ways that racism, heterosexism, sexism, nationalism, and the hegemony of Protestant Christianity write themselves upon our bodies through the temporalities of utility. We hear the many forms that utility assumes: economic, reproductive, biological, moral—even aesthetic. Fundamentally, these forms write themselves upon our bodies through demanding that we become exactly the right sort of tool—the sort of (white) tool that labors without showing it, exploits the work of (black, brown, female) others while disavowing their abilities to work, supplies just the right amount of products (children), and declares itself pure and dedicated to clear, distinct principles of mastery and control (over nature, over others, over the world). It is the Enlightenment utopia. And it writes itself upon our bodies in the very ways we conduct ourselves from moment to moment, day to day, week to week. It writes itself upon our bodies in the kinds of tools that we become and the temporalities we inhabit.

White Guilt, White Confession

From its early religious roots to the secularized versions of the post-Enlightenment, guilt persists as one of the fundamental psychic dynamics functioning in and through western cultures. The tradition of western philosophy and literature is filled with meditations on guilt and its favorite child,

165

confession. From St. Paul, Augustine, and Shakespeare to Rousseau, Kant, and Freud, western culture speaks the language of guilt. It is unsurprising, therefore, that the discourse of "white guilt" has emerged as a lightning rod for discussions about race in the U.S. (For example, a Google search on the Internet for "white guilt" produces about 85,600 hits. Many of these include headlines from leading newspapers across the U.S.) Particularly since Bill Clinton apologized for slavery and the U.S. Congress began to consider a similar gesture, white guilt appears to be on the verge of becoming a state-sanctioned discourse.[9]

This discourse of white guilt may be one of the most pernicious psychic dynamics in anti-racist struggles. Usually framed as a recognition of the 'sins of my fathers,' white guilt poses as a quintessentially patriarchal act: the man who is morally 'big enough' graciously agrees to stand up for sins he did not commit. A benevolent patriarch, willing to take a hit to protect the future of his race. It enacts a dynamic that exacerbates the self-righteousness of those in power and thereby spills over into other forms of oppression, infecting the possibilities of resistance with complicated appearances of sympathy, compassion, and even apology. It can be a paralyzing emotion, freezing its subjects in states of guilty inertia. Simultaneously self-berating and self-edifying, the inertia becomes an end unto itself: on the one hand, guilty white subjects wallow in their guilt, paralyzed by its force and depth of judgment; on the other hand, the inertia becomes an edified stalling point, buoyed by the sheer recognition of racism and its historical and psychological depths. The recognition is enough. It is sufficient. Far from necessary, white guilt in this self-edified stance functions as a kind of gift—a gift of recognition, performed generously by the master in order to confess his own wrongdoings. What Hegel might have deemed a 'reconciliation.' Whether self-berating or self-edifying, white guilt becomes a horizon unto itself, a plane that sustains itself in a complicated enactment of phallicized whiteness's temporalities.

Many forms of guilt circulate in advanced capitalist, phallicized white U.S. culture. There is the quotidian cycle of generic guilt-and-apology that allows subjects in power to do as they please, and apologize later. The knowledge that an apology will follow, and the assumption that such an apology will be accepted, place these acts squarely in the nexus of temporalities shaped by the future anterior and anticipation. One stands in that place beyond the future that anticipates the accepted apology, reducing the present to nothing but the fulfillment of that predestined apologetic future. The anticipated apology erases the present. (Such a dynamic is often at work in U.S. foreign and environmental policies.) Guilt becomes an act of power here, a technique of pretension that deflects images of apathy regarding the disenfranchised: "of course we care; we apologize."

This quotidian cycle seems to function as a 'micro-guilt,' with its own micro-temporality, in the larger, more grandiose dynamic that has been named "white guilt." More complicated, white guilt operates at the boundaries of phallicized whiteness, threatening to expose dynamics that must remain hidden to maintain whiteness's power. White guilt enacts the fundamental exposure of race itself through a doubled racial identification: it both implicates the (liberal) individual with its race and, with even greater threat, forces that individual to take responsibility for its race, whiteness. White guilt both identifies whiteness as a race and identifies individuals as white. This doubled racial identification threatens to unveil the phallus: it exposes the 'natural order of things' as historical structures of power. The conception of history at work here is precisely the one that liberal individualism must disavow—namely, a historical materialism that exposes how material conditions affect that bastion of whiteness, the neutral individual. The transcendence of materiality that constitutes phallicized whiteness must be protected in this delicate posture of white guilt: those defenses come through a complex temporal mode that invokes infinity and eternity, once again, as the safe horizons of phallicized whiteness's subjectivity.

A Protestant Infinite: Progress

White guilt differs considerably from the manifestations of religious guilt that Nietzsche diagnoses in *The Genealogy of Morals*. But it seems to share some of the same temporal modes that he began to uncover. When Nietzsche diagnoses guilt as the most effective tool of priestly power, one that keeps slaves in place through the cruel twists of self-lacerating blame and responsibility, he distinguishes religious guilt from secular shame primarily through their differing temporal modes: religious guilt operates in the registers of the infinite and eternal. It is in fear of eternal damnation, the eternalized debt which comes from Creation, that guilt emerges as a dominant mode of social policing (Nietzsche 1967, second essay). While white guilt differs in the subjects of its practice—i.e., it is the priests, not the slaves, who submit to white guilt in this phallicized whiteness's slave morality—it nonetheless invokes the horizon of the eternal. And the rhetoric of responsibility that comes in guilt's wake saturates the ethics and politics of classical liberalism.

This is not to say that white guilt does not have a religious aspect; liberalism did not fully shed its religious roots. To the contrary, white guilt exposes phallicized whiteness's grounding not only in capitalism (arguably a religion unto itself[10]), but, more deeply, in Protestantism, particularly those brands deriving from Luther and Calvin and the development of the infamous work ethic. In this economic disposition, guilt derives primarily from a fear of non-productivity—of uselessness. As work becomes the indicator of the state of one's soul, the drive to work becomes an expression of both religious devotion and grace itself. The chosen are those who work well, work just the right amount and in the right ways—the very registers that usher white bodies into those cherished boardrooms of advanced capitalism. White guilt exacerbates the deep cultural anxieties about uselessness, expressed in moral disdain for laziness, in the temporal mode of that Protestant guilt: it invokes the infinite, even if the salvation of credit cards and the stock market displaces that of God.

This is again a serial infinite, the one deemed 'bad' or even pernicious by Hegel. The Protestant work ethic keeps guilt at bay through endless acts of labor. Labor is the act that guarantees one's state of grace. Given the ontological condition of fallenness, one must labor continuously to pay the debt of original sin, as Nietzsche might put it, or, with a slightly perverse twist, to prove one's grace. Acts of work thus pile one upon another infinitely: one works on one's job, one's home, one's car, one's yard, one's computer, one's relationships, even on one's self in the endless quest of New Age self-improvement. One works. Infinitely. But because this is a serial infinite, each act of work is sequestered clearly and distinctly from the next. Each act of work functions in relation to another act of work as a Kantian antinomy, frozen in its oppositional stance and intractable to any dialectical mediation.

But unlike what happens in the circular closed economy of utility, the invocation of the infinite and eternal in the Protestant work ethic renders this strict separation of each act of work from the next in a linear temporality. Each act faces forward toward a future that forever recedes, infinitely, and hovers before the act with the lure of an atemporal and ahistorical space, eternity. Eternity recedes infinitely; and we must relentlessly march forward toward it. (What's that old gospel song about "onward marching soldiers"?) The 'present' moment in which each act stands is consequently also atemporal and ahistorical, judged as it is by these standards and disconnected from any other act in the world. With no connections between any singular acts, there is no access to a temporality of abiding continuity, much less historicity. Just as thinking in Hegel's schema of the 'bad infinite' cannot think itself as a temporal phenomenon, so too work cannot come to any self-consciousness as a temporal or historicized phenomenon. There is no outside to this totalized linear economy of work. Bound tightly with the closed circular economy of utility, this linear infinite never closes back upon itself, rendering us yet more docile in the faith that its end will, finally, arrive. There is only the future, toward which each act of work is endlessly ambling. We cannot move beyond the Philosopher of the Understanding's metaphysics of external relations and atemporal formalism. We can only progress, infinitely.

Progress is, of course, one of the most treasured myths of western cultures. As a myth, both generally and particularly, it hovers outside of time. Klee's infamous *Angelus Novus* and Benjamin's beautiful riffs on it invert the temporal orientation of this myth. But Klee's angel is beholding the wrong scenes: facing the debris and wreckage of the past, it does not understand the freedom of Progress. Progress cannot face the past—and this is what sets us liberal individuals free. Progress is the mad rush toward the wild, wild west that Mike Davis chronicles in *City of Quartz*, a dash that cannot worry over the dangers or debris it leaves in its reckless past. Just as the temporality of the anticipated apology exonerates all present moments from any violences they might inflict, so too does the march of Progress blind us to any moment but the final one of salvation. The one to which we are destined, the one that frees us from our past. The one that never arrives.

Shaped by the combined temporalities of Protestant guilt and Progress, white guilt also faces the present from this strangely distant future that fails ever to exist in time. Phallicized white cultures are intensely responsible to these twin structures, the Protestant work ethic and Progress. The future standpoint toward which they orient experience functions as the standpoint of judgment. All acts are judged with reference to them. Rather than weakening their authority, the immateriality of this non-temporal, non-historical moment that never arrives grants these twin structures of phallicized whiteness their power of judgment. The future is invisible and ubiquitous—those same characteristics that empower whiteness. And the pursuit of it is unfailing, giving forth relentless judgment against any act that obstructs its (impossible) attainment. White guilt emerges from its responsibility to these myths and values of Progress and the Protestant work ethic. Whatever recognition of past violences that is at work in white guilt springs from these twin structures of authority, judging past acts—conceptualized discretely and safely from the present—as failures of whiteness's own standards, proper work ethics and progress. The guilt of white guilt, expressed in its acts of confession, emerges from a recognition that these values have been derailed, not from any deep engagement with the past. The guilt of white guilt speaks a deep fealty to utility.

As white guilt emerges from this cultural scene, it inhabits the same temporal postures. The serially and infinitely receding horizon drives whiteness to correct itself, to improve itself. But it cannot turn around and fully grasp the damages and debris in order to make "whole what has been smashed," as Benjamin writes of Klee's angel (Benjamin 1969). It cannot face, much less understand and conceptualize, the past. Like deer caught in the headlights, phallicized white culture is frozen in this dumbfounded facing toward the future. The guilt that it confesses must then come from that future, that never-arriving moment which judges all moments. The guilt cannot come from the past. The "1+1+1+1 . . ." character of this serial infinity lands phallicized white culture in a temporality that evacuates the present the moment it arrives, anticipating only that cherished future moment of how it will be.[11] To see the past through this perspective is then only to see it as it will appear in the future anterior—as it will have been. One can offer apologies for that briefly glimpsed past, as Bill Clinton did for slavery in 1998, but the very mention of "making things whole again" cannot even be heard: reparations will never become a serious conversation through the avenues of white guilt.

The Temporality of Confession: Narcissus Regained

What can a guilt of this sort of temporality mean in the world to which it addresses itself? It seems that the address itself, the confessional expression of guilt, performs its own meaning. Appearing as an act of cultural solipsism, the confession fulfills itself in the act of confession. It is its own *telos:* the act of verbalization fulfills itself, not pointing toward any further action or transformation. And, trapped by this temporal horizon of serial infinity, pursuing an endlessly receding eternity, white guilt locks into an obsessive repetition of these verbalizations. White guilt cannot stop proclaiming itself, over and over and over, 1+1+1 . . . (remember those 85,600 Google hits). Public and private, the guilt becomes its own horizon of existence. It confesses, endlessly; but to whom? And for what, exactly?

As Foucault tells us in the oft-quoted line from volume 1 of *The History of Sexuality,* "western man has become a confessing animal" (1978, 59). And as he traced in his final inquiries, the practices of confession reach back as far as the Delphic precept "know thyself" and the early Greek schools of philosophy, the Pythagoreans, Epicureans, and Stoics.[12] It seems that this mode of discourse dominates western subjectivity, albeit in varied practices and within varied instantiations of the subject. But the discourse of confession *per se* is one that reaches back into some of the deepest parts of phallicized whiteness's history (for it does have a history, despite its repetitive disavowals of it), and is thus an unsurprising tool for its power. The instantiation of the subject before us here, the neutral liberal individual that occupies the dominant subject position of cultures of phallicized whiteness, practices confession of its guilt *as white* in ways that strengthen its sociopolitical position, setting it apart from other practices of confession in the western tradition.

While confessions of the sort that we find in Augustine's classic *The Confessions* involve a practice that individualizes the subject, the confessions of white guilt resist this effect. Rather than intensifying the interiority of the subject as fraught with sinful desires and evil thoughts, the confessional practices of white guilt operate on the model of self-ownership that we found dominating the models of liberal individualism. The individual confessing white guilt owns the discovery of violent history with the distance and objectification that constitutes the economic ownership of private property and the psychic ownership of the Other. Just as the liberal individual owns differences as discrete properties accidental to its individuation, so too does the individual remain untouched by the nastiness of the history confessed. The temporalities of Protestant guilt and Progress function well here to leave the individual safe in its historical vacuum, facing the endlessly receding future: parts of history may be broken, but they do not affect the present or any other discrete moment. To confess the sins of the past amounts, simply, to an apology, a quick glue-it-back-together-Humpty-Dumpty-Band-Aid that allows whiteness to get back to its appropriate posture—the panicked deer-in-the-headlights gaze upon the future.

The registers of the confessions of white guilt thereby differ considerably from those of classical religious or modern epistemological-psychological confessions. The impetus driving the confession is not self-condemnation, nor condemnation of any sort at all. It does not center on the transformative force of the act of confession itself, as Foucault finds that early Christian monastic practices do, or on the discovery of a deeply hidden truth inside the subject, as he finds the practices of the modern subject do. Nor does it center on the redemption of one's sins, the other possibility Foucault sketches as the meaning of confession in the western world.[13] The confession of white guilt centers on the redemption of discrete moments located clearly and distinctly in history. And as we already know, such redemption, grounded in the materiality of history, does not affect the status of the neutral individual; in fact, it is unimaginable that the individual would really care about such a thing. To call this a plea for redemption may even be too strong: it is a plea for erasure. White guilt wishes to erase the sins of its past, not to do penance for them.

If it were interested in doing penance for them, a different sort of temporality would have to take hold. To do penance is to engage the suffering of the act for which one is condemned. It is to enter into and empathetically relate to acts that occurred in the past. It is to enter that space which I have deemed 'queer,' that conflictual space in which the meanings and powers of this world are still being contested. As that space rigidifies into a univocal discourse, the constriction attempts to silence, erase, even obliterate these excessive possibilities: it becomes a space of violence.

Placing the physical and psychological violence of slavery in this space, for example, we can understand these violences as the juncture in time during which Africans' meaning of freedom was being overcome by the meaning of freedom of whites in the U.S. This overcoming was violent: it involved the physical killing and 'seasoning' of bodies; the psychological terrors of rewriting histories, religions, communities, and identities; and the epistemological triumph of the western liberal narrative and its work ethic over any other conception of freedom. To do penance for that violence would be to reenter that space in which other possibilities might have occurred. It would be to engage a temporality that abides and connects us back to those 'lost pasts' deep in our collective histories. It would be, as Stephen Marshall puts it, "to talk about the ten million bodies at the bottom of the Atlantic Ocean."[14] It would be to find the courage and strength to excavate and listen to those "secrets [that] lie in the silted bottom of these waters," as M. Jacqui Alexander puts it so elegantly (2002, 82).[15]

Diagnosing U.S. culture as one "apparently bent on inculcating a national will to amnesia" (2002, 94), Alexander writes powerfully of the multiple erasures that cultures of phallicized whiteness rest upon. The eclipsing and supplanting of complex histories of colonialism by the more simple narratives of slavery, for example, lead to the erasures of identities. And this leads to a forgetting so deep we do not even know it is there to be retrieved: "Some blacks captured/sold from a geography so vast the details would daunt memory and produce a forgetting so deep we had forgotten that we had forgotten. Missing memory" (2002, 86). A forgetting so deep we have forgotten that we have forgotten. To retrieve these memories is not to track down facts and events, but to listen for the cracks and junctures of what we are not hearing. Again, Alexander explains that this would have "less to do with living in the past, invoking a past, or excising it, and more to do with our relationship to time and its purpose" (2002, 96). It may also have more to do with cultivating different and differing temporalities.

To do penance for these violences would be to engage this 'queer' space in which other possibilities still roam—for example, where the liberal narrative of freedom does not triumph—without a view toward the future meaning of such an engagement. It would be to engage this space of conflict and endless contestation without the habitual teleological guarantee that it will, finally, make sense. It is to suspend the comfort of some future reconciliation: it is to suspend the future altogether. To do penance for the violences of the past is to engage those lost pasts with no view toward the future, an act that is deeply transformative and decentering for the one engaging it. It is to refigure our meanings of hope toward a temporality that might dwell, courageously rather than sadly with resignation, in the multiple postures of what might have been.

The act of confession of white guilt, however, does not emerge from any deep interior regret that might transform the subject of its enunciation. And this is why it is so dangerous to struggles of resistance against phallicized whiteness's power. To the contrary, this odd confessional act, obsessively and increasingly repeated in contemporary U.S. culture by a variety of subjects in power, seems to emerge from an impulse of sheer magnanimity. Or so it pretends. It becomes an egregious act of power, an act that further substantiates and even increases whiteness's power. White guilt differs radically from the slavish, crippling guilt of Nietzsche's story. White guilt proclaims itself as further evidence of the magnanimity, generosity, and compassion of whiteness.

It is crucial to recall at this juncture that Protestants do not properly confess. The act of confession is a ritual that Protestants disavowed in their break from Catholicism. Accordingly, these confessionals of white guilt follow out a distinctly Protestant mode of discourse, the tradition of bearing witness. These acts of confession are located in a theater that is familiar to cultures of phallicized whiteness, the testimonial. Because these are public declarations wherein the declaration itself is the meaning of the act, the world is to behold these confessions of white guilt as acts of wonder in and of themselves. The world is to respond as one should properly respond to magnanimity—with gratitude. But ultimately the confessors, fully aware that magnanimity is the pose of power, are not concerned with how their acts are received. Ultimately, the act of confession is wrapped up in itself, performing its own assuaging of its conscience.[16] The familiar layers of self-assurance protect whiteness yet again here. The confession of wrongdoing in the past is a grand act of recognition that runs counter to everything that whiteness is based on and stands for—and that is enough. It is more than enough.

When Fanon tells us of his horrifying experiences with the young frightened white boy on the train, we should know that the white gaze will never behold anything other than itself—in the mirror, in the world, in the violences of its past, and certainly in its own utterances. Narcissism reigns over these confessional acts of white guilt, just as it reigns securely over cultures of phallicized whiteness. As in Lacan's mirror, there is only one reflection possible in Narcissus's pool, the image of whiteness. White guilt springs from phallicized whiteness's deep fealties to the Protestant work ethic, utility, and Progress—none of which allows for any deep or abiding engagement with transforming the past.

▼ ▼ ▼

As an arrogant act of self-indulgence, apologetic confessions of white guilt infect the possibilities of resistance to all forms of oppression perpetuated by phallicized whiteness. Sexism, heterosexism, Christian-normativity, classism, nationalism are all caught by this posture of the plea for forgiveness. The power reversals are classic acts of manipulation: it is the oppressed who are to have sympathy for and forgive the poor sinners, the oppressors. White guilt attempts to erase all forms of oppression in the singular acknowledgment of its *past* complicity, while conveniently distracting attention from its present sins. That acknowledgment, offered from the pedestal of magnanimity, should suffice to wipe the slate clean, and put us all on that mythical equal playing field of classical liberalism. In perfect Christian linear temporality, we move from the alpha of fealties to utility, the work ethic, and Progress to the omega of the destined return to the neutrality of the liberal individual. The cycle is complete, and the power of whiteness more secure than before. No one should trust an action grounded in white guilt.

Nietzsche, of course, tried to warn us about the illness of guilt, its weakening, crippling, and poisoning effects on the social body. As a reaction, it will never alter the terms that negotiate social power. And in the guise of white guilt, it will only perpetuate those structures of power, while pretending to alter them. To move toward resistance against these systems of oppression, we must imagine other possibilities, ones that will ground us in psychic dynamics of justice and passion and joy, not guilt or utility or progress.

And it is our temporalities, along with the spatialities they enact, that will signal to us the kind of dynamic underway.

THE FREEDOM OF
SOVEREIGNTY

Remembering Lost Pasts

6

If the world insists on blowing up, we may be the only ones to grant it the right to do so, while giving ourselves the right to have spoken in vain.

—GEORGES BATAILLE,
The Accursed Share,
volume 2

The Power of Mastery, the Freedom of Desire

In the worlds of liberal democracy and advanced capitalism, of white supremacism and advanced patriarchy, power operates fundamentally on a model of mastery and domination. To master our conditions is to set ourselves free. We measure our freedom by our ability to overcome limiting conditions, whether those are individuals, developed institutions, sovereign nations, or economic barriers, historical prejudices, personal hardships. We do this primarily through domination, reducing the Other to our own frame of reference, to the terms of our own narcissistic desire. To transcend and master the limitations upon our desire is to free ourselves: the more power we have, the more free we are to do as we please. To be free is to transcend, or transgress when necessary, any and all prohibitions on our desire. Freedom is the ability to do as we desire; and power is its necessary and apparently sufficient condition. Mastery, freedom, desire—

these are the ingredients of cultures of phallicized whiteness. We must understand the precise contours of their designated meanings if we are to survive in these cultures.

True to its Lockean roots, power is understood here as a tool that one owns. It is a particularly good and efficient tool, increasing its power through its repeated use. The more we wield power, the more power we will have. The more we master the world, the stronger we become. Power is understood as yet another unit of private property, perhaps even the fundamental one: the unit through which all other units are acquired. A sort of Ur-property, it belies the mythical status of the 'self-made man.' If we do not have power, the best we can do is work to get some small piece of it. Again true to the contract theories of classical liberalism, this power can be controlled, set down and picked up at will, transferred to others, put away with the briefcase and Palm Pilot that bear its public marks.

Because we cannot be free without it, power must be what we all most fundamentally want. This perfectly closed economy demands it of us. We thirst for power, desiring it more than all else precisely because it is that which will set our desires free. Power is what allows us to desire at all. It is our condition of possibility as desiring beings. This is how it sets us free, liberating us to act on our desires and liberating our desires to act on us.

If we are not free, we may not become the persons that we essentially are. Desires define the essence of who we are in this schema of the world. If to be free is to act on our desires, then it is also to bring our essential identity to fruition. Not to have the power to be free, to liberate our desires, consequently means not to become ourselves. And in this Lockean world the failure to develop our self, just like the failure to cultivate all forms of private property, finally means not to be fully human.

But, while necessary, power may turn out not to be the sufficient condition for this closed economy. There is another structure that both grounds this closed system and grounds itself, ensuring its own repetition: an economy of scarcity. In conceiving power as a unit of private property which we must have in order to dominate the social field and thereby liberate ourselves, we both assume and enact a fundamental dynamic of scarcity. To conceive of any entity as a unit of private property is to initiate an economy of scarcity. The dual functioning of the logic of the limit exposes this connection: to conceive of entities as contained units places them in a social field structured by the logic of prohibition, where the boundaries of one entity are what another entity must overcome, transgress, domesticate. To write this in the register of power, to conceive of power as a quantifiable mass of which we own greater and lesser portions leads us necessarily to conceive of another's power as a prohibitive boundary that we must overcome, transgress, or simply steal. With only limited amounts of power available, our freedom—and ultimately our ability to be fully human—depends on our ability to dominate others and possess their power. Not all beings can have power and the violent interplay that ensues becomes the defining characteristic of the social field, rendering us all aggressive and miserly. It is scarcity, not power, that serves as the necessary and sufficient condition for this closed system.

No wonder we are filled with such anxieties.

▼ ▼ ▼

Foucault warns us against these limited conceptions of power. Particularly in *Discipline and Punish* (1977a), part 5 of volume 1 of *The History of Sexuality* (1978), and lectures and interviews from the mid- and late '70s (1997), he writes toward that space in which the meanings of discourses are contested and forged to expose the arbitrariness of this late modern conception of power. To think that we can wield power as we wield a hammer is already to have been interpellated, shaped, and formed by numerous historical discourses—political, legal, medical, epistemological, religious, and others. For Foucault, it is never that this kind of power, which he calls sovereign power, does not exist, but that it is not the singular, natural, or given form in which power expresses itself.

He historicizes our notions of the sovereign, showing how modern concepts of liberal individualism and its discourse of rights operate structurally in the same manner as the pre- and early modern concepts of the king and his absolute rights over his subjects. And then he goes yet further, showing how this structure of power is being displaced in late modernity by what he calls, alternatively, disciplinary power or bio-power. Technological advances in surveillance, ranging from optical devices to state-sponsored demographic research to self-administered and self-monitoring confessionals in the guise of medical exams, introduce new kinds of power into the social field: normalization displaces domination, docility displaces the explicit violence of submission. And the model of power as a tool that we wield, the model of power as a finite and scarce quantity that we must steal from others and amass endlessly, itself begins to emerge as but one of many discourses interpellating us as subjects in these cultures of late modernity.

Foucault thereby historicizes the dominant model of power as a tool, as a piece of private property that we must own to be free. His critique, along with his genealogical style of thinking through which it is enacted, has had a profound impact on the ways that we understand power and freedom in the contemporary world: he exposes the sovereignty of freedom in late modernity as the sovereignty of mastery. Broadening our conceptions of power out from this instrumental model, his phenomenological descriptions operate at the level of history: they historicize our conceptions through exposing the arbitrariness of our assumed 'natural order of things.' This decenters us, pushing us back into that queer space in which discourses are forged and meanings contested. It is from this space that Bataille writes, speaking to the ontology that this historically dominant conception of power carries and enacts.[1] While Foucault describes both how this power operates and its historical arbitrariness, Bataille explains why it seduces us so deeply. He diagnoses why and how the model of power as an instrument to be owned and wielded, along with its restricted sense of freedom as mastery, continues to dominate our lives in cultures of phallicized whiteness. He explains both the sovereignty and seduction of freedom, while resignifying the possibilities of each—perhaps toward something more 'queer.'

Disgust with Servility

The dual function of the logic of the limit already leads us, through the dynamic that private property introduces into the social field, to see how an economy of scarcity conditions this conception of power and freedom as mastery. In Bataille's meditations on utility, particularly in the bourgeois worlds of advanced capitalism, this economy of scarcity assumes its ontological proportions as the inevitable, if disgusting, servility of the intellect to the world of instrumentality. As Bataille develops, upon the introduction of the tool into the social field, a development that ontologically precedes the emergence of private property, we undergo multiple reductions: we subordinate our experience to our intellect, our intellect to reason, and reason to instrumental reason. Experience comes to be judged by its utility. Waste is categorically prohibited. And the system is closed through the ontologizing of an economy of scarcity, the exclusion "in principle [of] *nonproductive expenditure*" (1985, 117).

Bataille sees very clearly that it is utility which ushers us into the restricted economies of advanced capitalism—and, in my view, of phallicized whiteness more broadly. Across the three volumes of *The Accursed Share* and in his essays of the 1930s, he diagnoses both how this occurs over and over in various guises across cultures and history, and how we might find ways to exceed its pernicious grasp on our politics, our erotics, our lives. For example, as he explains in "The Notion of Expenditure" in 1933, the world of bourgeois capitalism rests fundamentally within the closed system of utility. While human consumption bifurcates into productive, useful activities and non-productive, a-telic expenditure, bourgeois capitalism loses all sense of the latter. Severed from the social meanings of grandiose, spectacular waste and loss, bourgeois capitalism reduces its world wholly to the world of utility. "Luxury, mourning, war, cults, the construction of sumptuary monuments, games, spectacles, arts, perverse sexual activity (i.e., deflected from genital finality)—all these represent activities which, at least in primitive circumstances, have no end beyond themselves." (1985, 118) But they horrify us now. Having stripped them of the social role through which they bestow value, we disavow these activities. We find them absurd, without use or meaning. The idea that power should express itself through a willingness "to destroy or to lose" (1985, 121), rather than to accumulate and hoard, is confused at best, savage at worst, and just silly always.

Late modernity thereby cuts itself off from any model of power other than the one of utility. It reduces its world wholly to a world of tools. Such a reduction is always at work in human societies, but in advanced capitalism the reduction is totalizing. As Bataille explains toward the beginning of volume 3 of *The Accursed Share*, the initiation of an objective world requires the introduction of tools. To posit an object as such, he argues, humans must have required a tool; and this would always tempt us toward the totalizing lure of utility:

> The objective world is given in the practice introduced by the tool. But in this practice man, who makes use of the tool, becomes a tool himself, he becomes an object just as the tool is an object. (1988–91, 2:213)

To reduce ourselves to tools is therefore, in part, to be human. It is, to speak in the Hegelian vein in which Bataille locates his own discussion, necessary to the objectification of ourselves that is a constitutive stage of self-consciousness. But to reduce ourselves, our world, our relations, our values, and every moment of every experience to the judgment of utility is to pervert ourselves, to turn ourselves wholly into tools. It is to reduce ourselves to objects, severing us from the possibility of subjectivity.

When late modernity reduces its conception of power to instrumentality and its conception of freedom to mastery, it effectively withdraws from any economy but the closed system of utility. To view power and freedom as tools leads to a saturation of our lives by instrumental reason. There is no outlet for any other possibility. Reading our fundamental values as tools to wield, we reduce ourselves wholly to the order of things, the order of objects. We master our conditions because we view them and ourselves as nothing more than things: freedom is restricted to the order of objects. A totalizing servility to the order of utility lies at the heart of this (illusory) mastery.[2]

But that is precisely its point of slippage for Bataille. This servility to the order of utility that lies at the heart of our allegedly liberating mastery allows Bataille to read another ontology at work here. Humans are not necessarily servile to the order of instrumental reason. The reduction of humans to tools may be a necessary moment in positing the world and ourselves as objects, but it need not be a totalizing moment. And, in Bataille's view, it cannot become the totalizing moment that it promises in the name of Progress. There's a crack in the system. Not only does the alleged mastery operate on the basis of a more fundamental servility, but the actual modes of acquisition that this mastery portends are fundamentally subordinate to an absurd mode of expenditure. The ontology that situates us in the order of things is the product of a historical and primarily economic movement that finally cannot ground itself. Bataille's ontology of glorious exuberance, of non-productive expenditure, exceeds it.

He shows this through an analysis of the social role that expenditure plays in human societies and that persists, albeit through disavowal, in cultures of bourgeois capitalism. Drawing on Marcel Mauss's theories of 'potlatch' in the tribes of Northwestern American Indians, Bataille describes the rituals of religious sacrifice and communal festivity in a variety of ancient cultures to convey the social function of expenditure in societies where it is not disavowed: glorious, celebrated wastefulness and the spectacular destruction of wealth become agonistic practices through which power expresses itself with ever-increasing excess. The practices spill over into the entire society to bestow godliness and other-worldliness on the very means of power in the temporal closed order of things. In the opposite of acquisition and hoarding, these cultures function fundamentally "at the mercy of a need for limitless loss" (1985, 123). Not depending on the veracity of Mauss's observations, Bataille uses them as a point of departure to examine the muted, twisted roles that such practices of expenditure might still convey in our lives of late modernity, where the reign of utility seems complete but experiences of eroticism, passion, and joy still tease us.

In bourgeois capitalism, Bataille locates how the economy of scarcity infects our social psyches: he describes the capitalist as a stingy, miserly creature, with "a sordid face, a face so rapacious and lacking in nobility, so frighteningly small, that all human life, upon seeing it, seems degraded" (1985, 125). This sickening figure "is voluntarily the most far removed" (1988–91, 2:197–98) from sovereignty, the state of being which engages expenditure. The bourgeois capitalist seems filled with anxiety, the psychological register of phallicized whiteness. And Bataille locates that anxiety precisely in this disavowal of expenditure, a disavowal that can never be complete: it haunts us, making us anxious in the very practices of our market economy.

As Bataille writes, "at its *base*[,] exchange presents itself as a process of expenditure, over which a process of acquisition has developed" (1985, 121). Contrary to the economists of his time, Bataille argues that economies of acquisition emerged not to stabilize and secure one's wealth, but to allow greater and greater exhibitions of its destruction—to express one's power more spectacularly. But as bourgeois capitalism inherited and advanced these economies of acquisition, the scarcity that drives such economies gained the upper hand, transforming acquisition into an end in itself: hoarding became the hallmark of wealth, trapping us in the endless anticipation of enjoyment infinitely deferred. This leaves us late moderns in advanced capitalism with a doubly impoverished relation to expenditure: first, our economic ethic of acquisition remains haunted by its disavowal of expenditure, whose social function continues to surface despite this attempted erasure (e.g., the social function of the jewel that the groom-to-be cannot afford but nonetheless bestows upon his betrothed); but, second, because of this disavowal, such expressions of expenditure remain muted, thwarted by the bourgeois disdain for them, and we have nothing but stunted imaginings of the meaning or possibilities of expenditure.

We seem to point in two directions to find instances of expenditure: toward the wealthy classes' showy displays of glitter and glamour, and toward the ostentatious laziness and foolish squandering of limited funds by the poor. But both of these are judged as the two extremes of immoral and imprudent exhibition, even if with a tinge of jealousy. Severed from their agonistic roots, late modernity's attempts to display power through the expression of expenditure have been attenuated virtually beyond recognition. We no longer know how to express expenditure as it is tied not to utility, but to religious, erotic, or political drives—to fundamental social drives.

But the fundamental *need* for limitless loss does not go away. And it is insofar as Bataille writes from the space of that need that he also writes from the queer space in which discourses are contested and meanings are forged. He writes from the space in which the unquestioned reign of utility has not yet taken hold, in which a disgust for this sort of servility can still be voiced. He calls this the space of general economy and writes from such a space toward an existence that will not succumb to the subordination to utility—an existence he calls sovereignty.

To Die Like an Animal

For Bataille, the servility to utility is displayed particularly in the temporality of such a world—the temporality of anticipation. Returning again to the role of the tool, he writes,

> In efficacious activity man becomes the equivalent of a tool, which produces; he is like the thing the tool is, being itself a product. The implication of these facts is quite clear: the tool's meaning is given by the future, in what the tool will produce, in the future utilization of the product: like the tool, he who serves—who works—has the value of that which will be later, not of that which is. (1988–91, 2:218)

The reduction of our lives to the order of utility forces us to project ourselves endlessly into the future. Bataille writes of this as our anguished state, caused by this anticipation "that must be called anticipation of oneself. For he must apprehend himself in the future, through the anticipated results of his action" (1988–91, 2:218). This is why advanced capitalism and phallicized whiteness must ground themselves in a denial of death: death precludes the arrival of this future. It cuts us off from ourselves, severing us from the future self that is always our real and true self. Resisting the existential turn, however, Bataille refuses to read this denial of death as an ontological condition of humanity. For Bataille, this is a historical and economic denial, one in which only a culture grounded in the anticipation of the future must participate. He frames it primarily as a problem of the intellect.

In the reduction of the world to the order of utility, we have reduced our lives and experiences to the order of instrumental reason. This order necessarily operates in a sequential temporality, facing forward toward the time when the results will be achieved, the questions solved, the theorems proved—and also when political domination will be ended and ethical anguish quieted. As Bataille credits Hegel for seeing, "knowledge is never given to us except by *unfolding in time*" (1988–91, 2:202). It never appears to us except, finally, "as the result of a calculated effort, an operation useful to some end" (1988–91, 2:202)—and its utility, as we have seen, only drives it forward toward some future utility, endlessly. There are always new and future objects of thought to conquer and domesticate. Within this order of reason, death presents the cessation of the very practice of knowledge itself. Severing us from the future objects of thought and from our future selves, "death prevents man from attaining himself" (1988–91, 2:218). As Bataille explains, "the fear of death appears linked from the start to the projection of oneself into a future time, which [is] an effect of the positing of oneself as a thing" (1988–91, 2:218). The fear of death derives from the subordination to the order of utility and its dominant form of the intellect, instrumental reason.

While death is unarguably a part of the human condition, for Bataille the fear of death is a historically habituated response, one that grounds cultures of advanced capitalism and phallicized whiteness. In those frames of late modernity, death introduces an ontological scarcity into the very human condition: it represents finitude, the ultimate limit. We must distance ourselves from such threats, and we do so most often by projecting them onto sexualized, racialized, and classed bodies. But for Bataille, servility to the order of knowledge is as unnecessary as servility to the order of utility. To die humanly, he argues, is to accept "the subordination of the thing" (1988–91, 2:219), which places us in the schema that separates our present self from the future, desired, anticipated self: "to die humanly is to have of the future being, of the one who matters most in our eyes, the senseless idea that he is not" (1988–91, 2:219). But if we are not trapped in the endless anticipation of our future self as the index of meaning in our lives, we may not be anguished by this cessation: "If we live sovereignly, the representation of death is impossible, for the present is not subject to the demands of the future" (1988–91, 2:219).

To live sovereignly is not to escape death, which is ontologically impossible. But it is to refuse the fear, and subsequent attempts at disavowal, of death as the ontological condition that defines humanity. Rather than trying to transgress this ultimate limit and prohibition, the sovereign man "cannot die fleeing. He cannot let the threat of death deliver him over to the horror of a desperate yet impossible flight" (1988–91, 2:219). Living in a temporal mode in which "anticipation would dissolve into NOTHING" (1988–91, 2: 208), the sovereign man "lives and dies like an animal" (1988–91, 2:219). He lives and dies without the anxiety invoked by the forever unknown and forever encroaching anticipation of the future. As Bataille encourages us elsewhere, "Think of the voracity of animals, as against the composure of a cook" (1988–91, 2:83).

▼ ▼ ▼

Bataille writes of this sovereignty in multiple modes, styles, voices, with polyphonic and polyvalent subject positions. His calls to "nonknowledge" and "unknowing" are perhaps the clearest, if still bizarre, to our late modern rational ears. They initiate ways to avert, and perhaps even disrupt, the alleged mandate of utility. To get off the rails of knowledge, "not to derive a result that others anticipate" (1988–91, 2:208), is to engage that space in which knowing does not reign, in which anticipation has no purchase, in which utility means nothing more than any other value. For Bataille, "life *beyond utility* is the domain of sovereignty" (1988–91, 2:198) and "only unknowing is *sovereign*" (1988–91, 2:208). Given that the order of knowledge is driven by an economy of scarcity and its temporality of the future anterior, wherein "we know nothing beyond what is taught by action with a view to satisfying our needs" (1988–91, 2:201), these sovereign acts of unknowing derive from an economy of expenditure and abundance.

The difficulty, of course, is how to conceive of such acts from within the closed perspective of utility, scarcity, and anticipation that has reduced our world to a world of things. How to imagine a freedom that is not one of mastery, a desire that is not one of lack, a politics that is not one of future solutions, when the only gestures of thinking available to us are those of our deeply modern, capitalist habits of phallicized whiteness? Bataille puts this problem as the problem of moving from these closed economies to general ones: "It is not easy to realize one's own ends if one must, in trying to do so, carry out a movement that surpasses them" (1988–91, 1:21). What if the future that we, the quintessential desiring beings of late modernity and phallicized whiteness, most deeply and passionately desire cannot be desired? What if we must learn to think and live without a future?

Queering the "I": A Politics without a Future

To call for a politics without a future in this contemporary world of increasing imperialism and ongoing violence should strike all of us as odd or indulgent at best, perverse at worse. We already know a word for such a politics—nihilism. And writing from the material luxury of a white citizen of the U.S., I find such a call particularly noxious: what perspective but the most privileged and comfortable would gallantly proclaim the necessary disavowal of the future? But what if Bataille (and Benjamin, Adorno, Irigaray, Foucault, and many others along with him) is right? What if the only mode of hope open to us in advanced capitalism and phallicized whiteness is a strange disavowal of hope, particularly as it is tethered to discrete ends and useful goals?

Many writers have recently called for such kinds of approaches to ethics and politics. Theorists of gender, race, class, and sexuality have written toward a future that we cannot predict, one that we will not attempt to control and subjugate. They have emphasized this lack of predictability as the way to escape the modes of rationality that presently entrap us.[3] I am sympathetic to such attempts. But the lack of predictability, while necessary, seems insufficient to the kind of radical reorientation of our thinking and our lives that is required for any politics of resistance. It may be the concept of the future *per se* that we must relinquish.

To attempt to write concretely about such a politics of resistance consequently involves us in some strange contortions. Refusing the normative claim of "giving a prescriptive answer," I am nonetheless faced with the need to show how this kind of resistance might make sense in our everyday lives. To do this queerly, I hope to provoke you. Through a few sketches[4] of how we might approach various dilemmas of our historical present, I hope to push us into those queer spaces where we turn toward lost pasts, where meanings and discourses are contested and practices and pleasures are forged. Such work is genealogical through and through insofar as its details will shift and change as our historical presents shift and change: it can never be prescriptive. But it can be transformative as it challenges us to radically reconsider our assumptions, reorient our politics, refresh our perceptions of the familiar, and perhaps even reinvigorate our pleasures and freedoms.

In her introduction to her recent collection of essays, *Pilgrimages/Peregrinajes,* María Lugones writes of subject positions as they are abstracted and constructed by social maps of power. She invites us to engage in a thought experiment: "Visualize, remember, and sense a map that has been drawn by power in its many guises and directions and where there is a spot for you. All the roads and places are marked as places you may, must, or cannot occupy" (2003, 8). For Lugones, this map becomes the map of oppression and resistance, one that enables all of us "to become perspicacious in sensing/ understanding the spatiality of social fragmentation as it is lived by [each of us] in great detail" (2003, 16). She writes of the ways this map situates each of us in specific spatio-temporal locations that are constructed by power and reinforced by the desires, intentions, and alleged freedoms which that power produces in us. The most salient of those socio-historical structures of power in our contemporary worlds are race, sexual difference, gender, class, religion, nationality, and sexuality. These are the categories of identity through which our subject positions are fabricated and through which we must perceive ourselves, even if unconsciously, if we are to function legibly in cultures of phallicized whiteness; the normative spatial and temporal registers tend to linger underneath these identity categories, rarely surfacing to consciousness.

Lugones's map allows us to see at least two functions that open onto resistance to these structures of domination and oppression: 1) the map only functions at an abstract level; and 2) each of us inhabits multiple subject positions simultaneously, not all of which may easily overlap, reinforce, or coalesce with one another. To say that it functions abstractly is to call attention to the disjunction between the subject positions that we inhabit because of the social scriptings of our bodies and the move toward self-perception through those categories: the world may perceive me as a white middle-class Christian-heritage lesbian academic in the United States; but I may create myself as queerly as possible in ways that exceed and perhaps disrupt the grasp of those abstract categories. The map helps us to see how one might do this.

For example, if the map constructs this abstract 'me' that is told to go certain places, desire certain things, teach certain courses, write certain essays, love certain bodies, then one of the ways that I might resist the map is to act otherwise. Otherwise, not contrarily: the logic of prohibition and transgression may seduce us here, but this is not the only way to conceive resistance. To resist the map is not simply to refuse to do as I am told— e.g., either to go where I am told not to go (marriage is for heterosexuals only; therefore, as a lesbian, I should fight to get married) or not to go where I am told to go ("tour Venezuela and take lots of photos"; instead, I stay at home and watch TV). While these kinds of contrary acts may begin to call attention to the abstract social map of power, they will never overturn that map; these transgressions against the map's demands will only reassert the centralizing power of the map itself.

To act 'otherwise' will involve acts that are not thinkable on the map: pleasures irreducible to genital finality or to monogamy; traveling that exacts a decentering transformation; sustained activities that never produce for or consume from the market economy. The ability to imagine such acts may emerge from the disjunction between the map's script of my body and my self-perception of that mapping script. This disjunction yields an excess that is not mapped, offering possibilities and acts and pleasures that are unthinkable on the map. It gives us access to those queer spaces in which meanings are contested and discourses are forged. Out of a DuBoisian sort of double consciousness, we must cultivate our perceptual abilities to locate these disjunctions and cross through these cracks in the social map of power. While this will involve many kinds of perceptual acuities, it may be primarily through cultivating our memories that we begin to reclaim and imagine these excessive, queer possibilities.

▼ ▼ ▼

The map does not only express itself through identity categories; it also enacts specific modes of spatiality and temporality. As Lugones traces, spatio-temporal dynamics ground our identities, politics, desires, subjectivities. One of the ways to engage these queer imaginings, therefore, is to cultivate activities, experiences, and self-understandings that are not grounded in the spatio-temporality of phallicized whiteness—namely, that are not grounded in endless projections of our contained and delimited selves into the future.

Lugones's mapping exercise multiplies our allegedly discrete and singular selves: it exposes how we all simultaneously inhabit multiple locations. For example, to my white middle-class Christian-heritage Euro-American professional academic ears, the call not to project my life into the future is absurd: it threatens my secure economic and cultural place in the world and, because of that threat, I will prove that it does not and cannot make any sense. (I may even be tempted, in a perverse twist of self-delusion, to argue that this call to disavow the future is one that only a middle-class, materially secure position would encourage, thereby undercutting political resistance through a posture of alleged political self-critique.) But to my female, intellectual, lesbian ears, the call is more seductive, urging me toward spaces that I may already inhabit, even if unconsciously, and that may hold more sustainable and pleasurable freedom. The distinction between academic and intellectual work provides a simple example: the former set of ears cannot imagine securing one's academic life without projecting one's work constantly into the future; the latter set of ears experiences considerable relief and an opening toward exquisite ecstasy at the possibility of dwelling with intellectual complexities without the urgent and loud call of the future and its demands of utility. The call to suspend the future speaks differently to my different subject positions, leading me toward a critical moment of perception in any movement of resistance—namely, that the abstracted map of social power leaves fissures in our allegedly stable and stabilizing identities; as Lugones puts it, there is a fleshy concrete "I" that may not line up neatly alongside the abstracted "I" of the social map of power. And this misalignment can become a primary site of resistance.

But the map does not allow for this multiplicity of spatial locations or the impossible temporal simultaneity in which it stands. The script of liberalism, which dominates the social map of phallicized whiteness, demands static and demarcated locations, separable from others through clear and distinct boundaries. One is either the oppressor or the oppressed: it makes no sense to be both simultaneously. If one is going to claim both of these contradictory subject positions, one must at least claim them in a temporal succession. But the queering of the "I" speaks from both, and often from many, simultaneous subject positions on the map: the queer "I" does not suppress or repress this multiplicity, even when it yields contradictory and thereby strictly nonsensical utterances.

According to the map of power, for example, I should fight for the rights of gays and lesbians to be legally married. This right would produce material benefits in my own life, securing the rights and privileges of heterosexuality for my own relationship with my lover—e.g., the right to adopt children; the right to be insured through her employer or *vice versa;* the rights of tax deductions; the rights of joint property ownership without the economic and psychological cost of endless legal paperwork; and, perhaps most importantly, the right to hospital visitation. And yet I have argued against all of this. And I have done so without offering any clearly demarcated future alternative that might assure us of the wisdom of foregoing this fight. Foolishness? Or queer? As Michael Warner's thorough diatribe against the politics of normalization shows,[5] such may be the effects of a queering "I" that emerges through the cracks of the misaligned social map of power.

As Lugones points out, to perceive this misalignment requires acts of memory: the spatial disorientation of simultaneously occupying apparently contradictory positions is also expressed in the differing modes of temporality at work here. Bodies in power in the social map of liberalism deny their privilege and power through "a lapse, a forgetting, a not recognizing oneself in a description" (2003, 14) that may highlight differences within one's allegedly contained and cohesive self. Locked into a mode of fundamental self-deception, the oppressor cannot perceive the multiple subject positions in which the social map of power locates him/her: he/she is an individual, not a body with multiple subject positions scripted upon it. And subsequently, the body in power "does not remember across realities" (2003, 14).

This refusal of memory can occur at multiple levels of our social psyches—from disavowals of the deepest and longest histories to superficial and recent of lapses of recognition. Whether through a refusal to connect oneself to the slave-owning whites of the mid-nineteenth century and all of their violence or a mundane disavowal of the impact of one's masculinity in interactions with colleagues, the body in power *forgets* the multiplicity of his/

her subject positions and the multiply different experiences into which they lead him/her. The disavowal of the past, whether one long ago or as recent as thirty minutes prior, keeps the body in power intact. And facing the future obsessively, in turn, keeps this disavowal of the past intact.[6] The layers of denial multiply endlessly.[7] As Jacqui Alexander writes of the U.S. regarding the 2000 presidential elections, "We live in a country apparently bent on inculcating a national will to amnesia, to excise certain pasts, particularly when a great wrong has occurred" (2002, 94). Such amnesia plays itself out day to day and moment to moment in the social map of phallicized whiteness's power and its obsessive fixation on the future.

To call for a politics without a future, therefore, must also be to call for a politics of the pasts, the lost pasts that were silenced and erased by the forward march of univocal Progress. It is to frame experience through a temporality of "what might have been," rather than the dominant one of "what will have been." Such a call, if they/we can hear it at all, will render the masterful, free "I" of white bourgeois Christian subjectivity vulnerable to the violences of the pasts—those pasts suppressed by the ahistorical fortress of the liberal individual. It could also open possibilities of pleasure and freedom that are unthinkable to us now: we cannot possibly anticipate what might happen, how radically lives and ideas and worlds might change, if we were really to consider the ten million bodies at the bottom of the Atlantic Ocean. More strongly still, we cannot begin that dialogue and self-reflection without radically suspending the concept of the future that habitually structures our modes of thinking, tethering them to the demands of utility and its politics of domination.

Overcoming the Myth of Scarcity

The differing responses to a call to a politics without a future can be further mapped through the differing perceptions of one of advanced capitalism's most effective scripts, the myth of scarcity. In the advanced capitalism of cultures of phallicized whiteness, the perception of scarcity is a fundamental dynamic that differentiates subject positions on the social map of power. Capitalism and, more broadly, the modern subject of desire feed on economies of scarcity. An economy of scarcity is what drives the atomistic metaphysics at the heart of these systems, pitting discrete individual unit against discrete individual unit in the competition for limited goods. But, as Bataille exposes, this economy of limits is one which is historically laid upon an economy of excessive expenditure and abundance. Because late modernity relies upon a constitutive perception of scarcity, such expenditure is fundamentally disavowed, expunged from moral possibilities—forgotten.

But if we listen carefully to Bataille's ruminations on the persistent social roles of expenditure, the disavowal surfaces. For example, as continues to become more frighteningly explicit in U.S. foreign policy, the market economy of advanced capitalism requires, at its core, a war economy of excessive expenditure to sustain its need for infinite expansion, while simultaneously perpetuating the illusion of scarcity upon those within its (allegedly) closed grip.[8] Our locations on the social map of power affect the ways that we perceive this scarcity. For those most securely positioned, the scarcity is nothing but real, unarguably present, and one must direct all actions and desires toward protecting against future threats to what scarce goods one owns. But those with "nothin' left to lose" perceive this alleged scarcity of advanced capitalism as an illusion: the beggar, as Bataille tells us, is closer to sovereignty than the bourgeois capitalist ever will or can be—"The true luxury . . . of our times falls to the poverty-stricken, that is, to the individual who lies down and scoffs" (1988–91, 1:76).

bell hooks has suggested that one of the most lasting psychological damages wrought on persons living in poverty in the U.S., most often blacks, by this culture of capitalist white supremacism is the inability to think in the future.[9] Beaten down by the unrelenting impossibility of economic stability, poor blacks never develop the ability to project themselves into the future that is demanded for a bourgeois lifestyle. Whether taking the steps to prepare adequately for college, pursuing skills that will secure a more stable job, writing a budget to cover economic needs, or simply thinking about next week before purchasing goods beyond one's means, lives in poverty have never known any concept of the future—and consequently are not lived under its reign. While this fundamental disregard for the future apparently justifies social and even moral damnation by the dominant, white bourgeois class, it may also free those in poverty from the systems of domination—and their illusory freedom as mastery—that operate under this concept of the future and its attendant economy of scarcity.

There is clearly much more to be said and researched regarding such a claim. And I do not wish to perpetuate the pernicious legacy of white liberalism that romanticizes poverty. But I challenge the middle-class assumption that those in poverty necessarily experience their lives as impoverished and therefore wish to be in the middle class. This is not to say that lives of poverty are not materially burdensome, but rather to suggest that they may not live in the (fictional) states of fear that the myth of scarcity perpetrates upon middle-class lives.

While the service sector of the U.S. economy grows larger and the middle-class standard of living accordingly shrinks, "gated communities" are proliferating across cites and suburbs. Those who identify as middle-class seem to be living in greater and greater fear of losing that precious status, all the while not recognizing how their own consumption practices are slowly chipping away at any semblance of security: we hoard more and more goods to ward off the ever-present threat of scarcity. But lives of poverty often seem to scoff at such fear, just as they scoff at the mythical scarcity that drives it: the anxiety over the stock market's effect on a 401K or even the ability to make the new mortgage payment appears as nothing but absurd alongside the scramble to find the next meal or adequate school clothes for a child or reliable transportation to a minimum-wage job across town.

Moreover, lives of poverty also may not experience the flip side of that middle-class fear of scarcity—namely, the desire to move into the middle class. Despite the narcissistic middle-class assumption that everyone in poverty wants to be in the middle class, the iconography of advanced capitalist culture betrays no such trajectory. As the idolatry of sports and entertainment stars shows in this culture, those in poverty may direct their lives more by the wish to jump directly into the class of luxury, the other end of the spectrum that also disavows the concepts of the future and any economy of scarcity.

Bataille's point is that poverty and luxury sometimes inhabit the same psychic spaces. And yet the bourgeois values of advanced capitalist cultures reduce such luxury to its own narrow, sordid vision of the world. Our double standards are staggering: we pray at the altar of Donald Trump's wealth, while refusing to give a dollar to the homeless man on the corner if he's just going to go and buy another beer. But wouldn't he be foolish to do anything else with it? Should he really try to save all those coins and bills to buy a fresh shirt that will need to be ironed? The self-edifying moralism of the good ole Protestant work ethic lingering always just below the surface, we demand that those "below" us on the economic scale learn to spend money every bit as anxiously as we do.[10]

To expose the fictional status of this myth of scarcity in bourgeois consciousness thus may be a critical wedge in dislodging the systems of domination at work in cultures of advanced capitalism, patriarchy, and white supremacism. Insofar as it grounds the twin values of utility and the future, revealing this historical fiction may become one of the most queer political acts available to us in this historical present. And insofar as our practices of consumption have been eroticized as one of our most social expressions of desire, the dislodging of the myth of scarcity which drives that desire strikes at the heart of queering freedom. It can radically jolt us from our normalized spatio-temporal orientations, where we understand our lives and selves as discrete pieces of private property that we must protect and secure through constant projection into the future. While such work requires many kinds of transformations, it may most of all require a cultivation of memory.

Rather than assuming that the various objects of the market we consume on a daily basis were created *ex nihilo* for our particular needs or desires, we could undertake an archaeology of our own consumption practices.[11] Such a practice would expose the multiple histories buried in each of these objects and the interplays of scarcity and excess at work in their production. Take, for example, the rather bizarre ritual in the U.S. of mass frenzied shopping the day after Thanksgiving. Ironically following the day devoted to excess and abundance, when good citizens of the U.S. celebrate our history by grossly overeating (and the cooks worry anxiously over whether they have prepared enough food), masses of people in the U.S. awaken early to storm all kinds of stores for their infamous sales. Images of these crazed shoppers, jamming through the doors of retailers as they open at oddly early hours, fill our televisions and newspapers: the ritual has become a nationwide, communal frenzy of combating scarcity.

But if we undertake a brief archaeology of our consumption, we are faced with the fiction of this alleged scarcity. Let's say we burst through the doors of Best Buy, a 'big box' electronics retailer in the U.S., at 6 A.M. the day after Thanksgiving. We want to get that RCA 27" television for its record sale price of $140, and we know there are not many of them to be had. We must have it: we live in the country that ranks second in the world for number of televisions owned, and we must do our part to make the U.S.A. #1 in all things![12] So we arrive at Best Buy well before dawn and we get it: scarcity vanquished, at least for us and our little individual piece of the pie. But if we trace the making of that television, we learn it was constructed in Thailand, whose gross domestic product per capita is $7,400 (#85 or #97 in the world), as compared to $37,800 (#2 or #3 in the world) in the U.S.[13] Thirty-one percent of exports from Thailand are electronics products, and the U.S. is the largest market for Thailand's total exports; meanwhile, citizens of Thailand own enough of those television sets they produce that Thailand is #17 in the world in number of televisions owned.[14] And if we dig a bit deeper, we will likely find that there are human rights violations charged against the sweatshops that employ the laborers, underpaid and uninsured day-laborers transporting the televisions across oceans and lands, and perhaps even non-unionized workers stocking them at Best Buy.

The scarcity at work in the production of our cheap consumer goods is not the scarcity of the middle class in the U.S. The United States is not a country of scarcity, but of a remarkably lopsided distribution of immense wealth.[15] The excess that drives our market economy perpetuates inhuman scarcity in the lives that produce its goods. To excavate these lost pasts erased from our consuming consciousness opens middle-class consciousness onto the actual scarcities at work in the fictional scarcity of our consumption practices. To cultivate these 'memories' opens onto a queer consciousness of how desire perpetuates systems of domination. It can also open onto possibilities that things could be otherwise: we could consume differently, buying and growing and exchanging locally; we could even enjoy our lives without the onslaught of cheap consumer goods that increasingly keep most of the world's population trapped in economic dependency and political subordination, while also locking us into the endless cycle of anxious consumption and future satiety. And we could recognize that the alleged scarcity of goods that sends us into buying frenzies and their promise of a more secure future is nothing but another marketing tool, one that depends on our not remembering how or where or why or for whom these objects are made.

Our senses of power and freedom change when we begin to think and act in these queer ways. Power is not about one class wielding economic and political power over another; it is about a web of interlocking values that perpetuate the domination of the most privileged at the expense of all other lives, most often through the narrative of desire and its myth of scarcity. And freedom is not to own as much as we desire; it is not to gain an illusory and impossible security in George W. Bush's "Ownership Society." Freedom is to recognize the lost pasts embedded in our everyday practices and to cultivate pleasures that do not perpetuate these violences. It is to stop ignoring and erasing these lost pasts in our idolatry of the (market's) future, and thereby open onto different kinds of pleasures.

These snapshots of different subject positions' responses to living life without a concept of the future give us some sense of how cultures of phallicized whiteness perceive a call to a politics without a future. To halt the temporality of the future anterior as the dominant mode in which we live our lives is to resist these cultures and their values. It presents a way of interrupting and disrupting the domination of phallicized whiteness, decentering its grip on us. At the same time, to halt the temporality of the future calls us to risk radical uncertainty in the politics and erotics of our lives, to open ourselves to not-knowing and unknowing as viable modes of experience. For bodies in power, such a call to risk will likely affront our deepest senses of our selves and worlds: it will likely fall on deaf ears. For oppressed and dominated bodies, this may already be how we are living and to embrace it consciously may be experienced as a call to joy and creativity or, at a minimum, a profound relief. (I use "we" on both sides of this division to express the multiple subject positions I hold on the social map of power.) The call to a politics without a future strikes us in varying ways; it can be decentering, or even a relief, hilarious, and a sense of grounding for movements already underway, giving voice and a space in which to cultivate unimaginable pleasures. How we respond may tell us much about how queerly multiple our "I" of identity can become.

From Anxiety to Joy: Remembering AIDS

David Wojnarowicz, an artist who resisted the commodification of his work and of the world more broadly, wrote of his life as one that is begging to be freed from the future. As a travelin' man who grew up in New York City and spent a good deal of time on the highways of Mexico and the southwest United States, Wojnarowicz expressed, in virtually every visual and written medium available to him, the intensity of a life consumed by the queering of its pleasures. Coming of age in the '70s and dying of AIDS in 1993, he lived in a period of intense governmental and religious surveillance of 'private' sexual lives. As a man turned on by the sight of another man's tanned arm hanging out the cab of an eighteen-wheel rig, Wojnarowicz knowingly lived his life under the law's microscope and telescope. His life was never a private life. Nor did he experience it as a life of intense internal desire played out on the horizon of the future.

His book *Close to the Knives: A Memoir of Disintegration* (1991) chronicles his body's endless pleasures: gazing upon tanned, muscled male bodies working on a defunct swimming pool in a rundown highway motel; shutting his eyes while driving on desolate highways in the desert, awaiting the 'bump' of a cactus to jar them open; seducing a man out of the danger of the rest stop's bathroom onto a dusty side road, where steaming sex can at least see the law before it arrives; witnessing the rage of a lost youth against "the preinvented world," a youth who uses his Camaro as a weapon of death against anyone in his path. The heat of the desert simmers off the pages of this text. You cannot read and understand this book; you can only feel its heat and pleasures, and follow it into the maddening, dizzying desert.

With his own death and the death of so many others around him always imminent in the age of AIDS, Wojnarowicz does not write or create with any concept of the future. There is no future in this text. And this, more than anything, is what Wojnarowicz finds to be freeing: no point of arrival. As he writes,

> Transition is always a relief. Destination means death to me. If I could figure out a way to remain forever in transition, in the disconnected and unfamiliar, I could remain in a state of perpetual freedom. (1991, 62)

Living in some of the most oppressed—and watched—intersections of that social map of power, Wojnarowicz has got nothin' to lose. And his life is excessively filled with pleasures, envisioning other worlds and other freedoms constantly.

It is not coincidental that David Wojnarowicz died of AIDS. This epidemic, which has been sexualized, racialized, nationalized, and classed more vehemently than any prior to it,[16] brings together these multiple strands of sovereign, queer politics and their reworking of our spaces, times, selves, and pleasures. Having undergone several interpellations since its emergence, AIDS continues to haunt the social psyche of the overdeveloped world as "the gay disease," that horrible blight upon homosexual men for the sins of their perversions. Because its recognition was economically conditioned, the disease entering medical discourses only after communities of middle-class gay men began contracting it,[17] AIDS remains a highly sexualized disease: it is the disease that infected our most intense pleasures—our sex lives. And it infected them in such a mysterious and forceful way that it had to be morally expunged, while still not medically cured. AIDS brought together the ultimate taboos of western, advanced capitalist, white supremacist cultures: sex and death. And no one but a pervert could do such a thing.

Attaching itself to the practices of sexuality that undermined the utilitarian mandate, AIDS was always already a queer virus. But as the epidemic has allegedly departed the shores of the U.S., we white citizens of that country seem to have done what we are trained so well to do: we have forgotten all about it.[18] Out of sight, out of mind—and out of existence, both past and present. As a "tropical" model displaces once again the "epidemiological" model that intermittently dominated AIDS discourse in the first two decades of the disease's emergence, the normative space-time of colonialism has taken hold once more: 'savage' lands are again displaying their inherent inability to enter civilization, and we must remain securely separated from them—physically, economically, politically, and, most of all, psychologically.[19] We must protect our own future, and the necessary condition for such security is the complete disavowal of those lives and pasts lost to AIDS: we must forget AIDS ever happened in our own lands.

This forgetting is fraught for queer politics in several ways. It erases the explicit stigmatization of gay lives in the 1980s that now invigorates the only slightly more subtle politics of homophobia in the U.S. in the early twenty-first century; and in so doing, it severs us from the radically transformative practices not only of sexuality, but of sexual acts as they are conjoined to a different disposition toward death. AIDS forced queer communities to reconfigure our sexual practices—and, because we were doing so in the face of death, it forced us to face death differently.

Among the many radically innovative forms of political activism that emerged as a response to the AIDS epidemic in the 1980s,[20] the work of the Gay Men's Health Crisis (GMHC), one of the oldest activist organization focused on AIDS in the world, continues to radically transform sexual and political practices. Emerging in 1981, the same year that the Center for Disease Control first issued a warning about a strange form of pneumonia, which it later diagnosed as "gay cancer" and which eventually became AIDS, in young gay men in Los Angeles, GMHC queered sexual politics in the midst of the outbreak of the AIDS epidemic. Working in various communities, spanning sexual, gender, racial, class, and drug-use differences, it enacted (and continues to enact[21]) a coalitional politics that involved gay men, lesbians, and straight women working in its ranks (straight men were conspicuously absent from these ranks, and from the AIDS movement more broadly). GMHC recognized that a rhetoric of fear, the preferred mode of phallicized whiteness and unsurprisingly of federal, state, and local governments during the AIDS crisis, would never alter the complex psychic dynamics implicated in desire and its expression in sexual practices. To the contrary, GMHC developed safe-sex education that was as hot as the practices it performed. Ranging from comic strips in pamphlets to community screenings of erotic films, GMHC showed how safe sex could actually *be* hot sex and not just a slogan. It also saved lives.

In taking this route against the ravages of the AIDS virus, GMHC queered sexual and political discourses in the U.S. The infamous promiscuity of gay men suddenly became a route to health, rather than a moral scourge and death sentence. As Douglas Crimp, drawing on Cindy Patton's work, explains,

> Gay people invented safe sex. We knew that alternatives—monogamy and abstinence—were *unsafe,* unsafe in the latter case because people do not abstain from sex, and if you only tell them just say no, they will have unsafe sex. We were able to invent safe sex because we have always known that sex is not, in an epidemic or not, limited to penetrative sex. Our promiscuity taught us many things, not only about the pleasures of sex, but about the great multiplicity of those pleasures. It is that psychic preparation, that experimentation, that conscious work on our own sexualities that has allowed many of us to change our sexual behaviors . . . very quickly and very dramatically. (1987, 252–53)

GMHC reclaims the histories of sexual practices and pleasures irreducible to the utility mandate of reproductive heterosexuality and its normative act of penetration. Out of those excessive possibilities, it creates new kinds of sexual pleasures that dramatically reduce exposure to HIV: in 1982, 21 percent of the uninfected gay population in the U.S. had developed antibodies to HIV (indicating they had been exposed to the virus); in 1983, when public health education programs directed at gay men began, that number plummeted to only 2 percent and it was down to 0.8 percent by 1986 (Crimp 1987, 264 n. 29). Promiscuity, and the whole-hearted embracing of its variations and pleasures, saved lives.[22]

But the federal government, led by the infamous Jesse Helms, cut federal funding of GMHC's safe-sex erotica.[23] (It is now a non-profit organization that continues to produce an array of educational materials, funded through private donations.) And since the 1980s, we have witnessed the rapid displacement of safe-sex education by abstinence-only campaigns in our middle and high school curricula, paired with the often mean-spirited disavowal of promiscuity and celebration of monogamy in the gay/lesbian movement's championing of same-sex marriage.[24] Moreover, to complete the triumvirate of this general attack on pleasure, President Clinton refused in 1998 to lift the federal ban on needle-exchange programs, despite proof that such programs do not encourage drug use, and the United States continues to refuse to decriminalize prostitution and other sex work, despite the World Health Organization's repeated recommendation that it do so.[25] Pleasure has been under attack for some time, and along with it are the sexual, racial, class minorities who practice such queer acts.[26]

Occurring at the precise juncture of sex and death, AIDS confronted western, bourgeois, patriarchal, white supremacist culture with the ultimate challenge to its sacred value of utility. Faced with death, the queer politics of safe sex undermined the authority of the future over its lives through valorizing pleasures that give no entrée to reproductive utility. Disavowing utility doubly, the queer (and safe) pleasures of sex that we find in Wojnarowicz undermine not only heterosexism, but death as well: he knows he is going to die, and in response to such knowledge he transforms his life into one that relishes never arriving at any destination and is filled with sexual, erotic pleasures that may be as intense as gazing upon a tanned arm hanging out the window of an eighteen-wheel rig.

If we forget AIDS, we forget these pleasures.

If we forget AIDS, we perpetuate the domination that silences all sexual, racial, class, and religious minorities. If we are to queer our lives, we must reclaim these lost pasts, lost lives, and lost pleasures. We must return to these sites of creativity when sexual practice itself was being radically reoriented from the genital-centered practices of reproductive heterosexism—and when the very notion of "self" was subsequently reoriented as a figure with no clear boundaries.[27] We must return to these periods in history in which viral infections became the vehicles of xenophobic rage—sexualized as perverted, racialized and classed as the effect of drug use and/or ignorance, and finally nationalized as the mark of savagery. We must return to these periods when discourses were being forged that now silence all possibility of a celebratory promiscuity or a safe and hot erotica, when practices were being transformed toward pleasures that foreclose the future and its mandate of utility. In the present pandemics ravaging Africa and Asia, and rapidly spreading to Eurasia and more of South Asia, we must return to these lost pasts not out of guilt, but out of political commitment to open our practices of pleasure onto more sustainable practices of freedom.

▼ ▼ ▼

To suspend the future, radically, may be to enter a kind of freedom that we do not readily know or even *want* to know in these cultures of phallicized whiteness. To do so requires courage and risk from some; from others, persistence and the simple strength to go on. It means to be involved in experiences and pleasures that offer no return to the closed economies of societal meaning, driven by utility and the mandate of concise, clear endpoints. It means to queer our worlds. And to queer is not to respond to the law of desire or its illusion of scarcity: it is to have no fixed idea of who or what you are or might become, and to find this an extraordinary pleasure.

At the end of his short preface to *The Accursed Share*, Bataille turns

Gay and Lesbian Task Force, the Lambda Legal Defense and Education Fund) perpetuated the racist trends of the gay/lesbian movement and marketed gay and lesbian life to mainstream U.S. as upper-class and white; on the other side, playing to the other pole of racist imagery (the asexual savior of whites), the religious right—despite its longtime racism—forged alliances with black ministers and pastors against the same-sex marriage movement. The same-sex marriage movement has thereby repeated the errors of all too many allegedly 'progressive' political movements in the U.S.: it has perpetuated racist images and toyed with racist pasts so that white middle- and upper-class people can fight over who gets which piece of the pie—and how secure that piece will be well into the cherished future.

Despite work by the two leading national gay/lesbian organizations, HRC and NGLTF, to appear more racially diverse, the same-sex marriage movement is a white movement. For example, NGLTF released an article on October 6, 2004, that proclaimed, "Black Couples Have Most at Stake in The Same Sex Marriage Debate" (NGLTF 2004). Matt Foreman, the Task Force's executive director, used the census data on income, employment, home ownership, residential patterns, and family structures to expose the hypocrisy of the Bush administration's "aggressive attempts to deprive same sex couples [of] equal marriage rights while touting its multimillion dollar 'African-American Healthy Marriage Initiative' as a way to strengthen the African American family" (NGLTF 2004).[4] Using the fact that three in five black female same-sex households (61%) are composed of mothers raising children, putting lesbian couples at nearly the same rate of parenting as black married opposite-sex couples (69%), the article argues that banning same-sex marriage poses "a disproportionate threat to Black same-sex couples and their children" (NGLTF 2004). NGLTF thereby poses as the champion of anti-racist politics. But is marriage really going to solve the fundamental inequalities suffered by couples that earn $20,000 less per year than white same-sex couples and are less likely to own their own homes (as the article also notes)? Or is it only going to force these non-traditional and non-white home structures into more and more homogenized models, as many critics argue and predict?

Historically, black communities have found great strength to survive in the white supremacist U.S. through their various forms of "family": the word "parent" had a wide range of meanings and connotations in many black communities (and poor ones as well), potentially encompassing one's biological grandmother, aunt, cousin, or sibling; or one's longtime family friend, neighbor, schoolteacher, or pastor. Biology, with its political roots in sexist and racist domination, has not determined what it is to be a "family." But the same-sex marriage debate is erasing all such alternatives, thereby undervaluing non-white kinship systems and simultaneously disallowing one of the most promising sources for broad, coalitional resistance—namely, the reconfiguration of "the traditional family" from its patriarchal, white, bourgeois roots. This radical reconfiguration of the family is precisely what many same-sex parents have understood themselves to be doing (and offers one of the most compelling arguments for same-sex marriage: parental rights). But the same-sex marriage debate is threatening to flatten and erase any such possibilities. Rather than fighting for this kind of broad-based, race-inclusive, class-inclusive, and gender-inclusive redefinition of "family," the leading organizations advocating same-sex marriage have circulated innumerable images of "the perfect nuclear family": two (mostly white, clearly middle-class) parents and children, perhaps even a dog. These images enact racism, patriarchy, and bourgeois classism all at once: they erase historically non-traditional families, while simultaneously abandoning the possibility that same-sex parents might join with those historically non-traditional families to reconfigure the fundamental social unit of phallicized whiteness, the family.

The second major strand of argument against same-sex marriage emerges through the view of various transgender communities in the U.S. Despite the largely gratuitous addition of the "t" to l/g/b/t movements and organizations, the needs or desires of trans individuals in the U.S. are not at all considered in this same-sex marriage movement. The kinds of problems facing transgender individuals in the U.S. range from basic access to health care, social services, and housing, to overcoming discrimination in employment, education, and the justice system.[5] Transgender individuals are likely to spend inordinate amounts of time, energy, and already-scarce money to negotiate the Kafkaesque bureaucratic machinations involved in documenting a change in gender identification. Without such legal documentation, which often involves the near-impossible (particularly in the post–Patriot Act U.S.) alignment of all identification documents (birth certificate, social security card, driver's license), transgender individuals are denied access to many of the major services and institutions most of us take for granted: health care, education, employment, fair housing, and of course, voting. Without access to those basic goods and rights, transgender persons quickly slide down the slippery slope toward the three major institutions that warehouse such 'non-functioning' members of this society: homeless shelters, mental health institutions, and incarceration. With cruel irony, these spaces in turn become intensely violent for transgender persons: they are sex-segregated.[6]

Not only will the legalization of same-sex marriage not solve any of these problems, but it will likely exacerbate the surveillance of transgender lives. If same-sex marriage invites the state into queer lives, transgender persons will likely suffer most from heightened state surveillance of same-sex and same-gender relationships. For example, those transgender persons presently parenting children with a person of the opposite gender will likely no longer pass as straight under such heightened state surveillance.

Moreover, let us not forget that g/l/b communities have not been a steadfast source of support, strength, or coalition for trans communities. G/l/b communities still suffer from intense transphobia, as we see all too easily in the increasing tendency of popular culture, including gay culture, to frame transgender persons as the scapegoats that make jokes funny.[7] It seems that the socio-political world of most gay/lesbian/bisexual communities is still haunted by a subtle kind of biologism, wherein only those with a clearly and distinctly defined sex can participate in the extension of liberalism's rights. Transgender persons thereby become the necessary Other against which these communities continue to form their liberal identities: g/l/b communities still have a long way to go on this ugly form of discrimination, transphobia.

But both the racializing and trans-exclusive politics of the same-sex marriage movement coalesce in a yet deeper blind spot that drives the movement: class. As Craig Willse reframes the 1,049 "denied rights," perhaps these are actually benefits that still function to exclude major sectors of society, while perpetuating advanced capitalism's myth of scarcity. As he puts it, "I think that we will see that gay marriage will primarily benefit the same people that straight marriage benefits—those [with] property to protect and economic entitlements to share. . . . I worry that we are justifying the gains of racially and economically privileged people at the costs of a broad spectrum [of] poor people, people of color, immigrants and their political struggles" (Willse 2004). Still operating on the fundamental conflation of rights and property, the same-sex marriage movement will only extend ownership of goods and rights to those who can already afford them, thereby making the myth of scarcity more and more real to those who cannot. As Willse points out, "a working class gay person who has a job without health coverage will not be able to extend their nonexistent benefits to their new gay spouse" (2004).[8] Extending marriage to same-sex couples will only enable those already projecting their lives into the future to continue to do so, with the increased illusion of actually controlling it.

Why are the national gay/lesbian organizations not fighting for universal health care, rather than for participation in an elitist health care system that increasingly insures and hospitalizes only the richest and most secure? Why not fight for a living wage and broad socio-economic justice, rather than for tax breaks and inheritance laws that benefit only the richest and most secure? Why not fight against the Patriot Act, rather than for the rights of those few immigrants who are actually welcomed into the U.S. as healthy economic participants? Why not fight for women's access to all reproductive rights, for broad reconfiguration of the welfare system, and against the global economic structures that have created markets for child-trafficking, rather than for the exclusive rights of custody on behalf of those wealthy enough to secure them? Framed as a white-identified, patriarchal, Christian-centric middle-class movement from the beginning, the same-sex marriage movement functions squarely within the myth of scarcity that I have traced across these pages. Consequently, it works on the same politics of fear that many of us find so abhorrent in the national political parties of the U.S. If we are to queer these politics, we must find our ways out of these myths of liberalism and scarcity, and transform our resistances from ones of fear to ones of joy.

Some activist groups are already well underway in this queering transformation. The work of the Sylvia Rivera Law Project, for example, focuses directly on the struggles facing the low-income people of color who are transgender, intersex, or gender non-conforming. It is founded on two fundamental principles: "that gender self-determination is inextricably intertwined with racial, social and economic justice," and "that justice does not trickle down, and that those who face the most severe consequences of violence and discrimination should be the priority of movements against discrimination." Consequently, its agenda focuses on those "who face multiple vectors of state and institutional violence: people of color, incarcerated people, people with disabilities, people with HIV/AIDS, immigrants, homeless people, youth, and people trying to access public benefits" (SRLP 2005, mission statement). They work constantly with other activist groups focusing on prisoners' rights, immigration laws, mental health practices, police brutality, social services, and so on.

Recognizing the interlocking systems of domination, the vision of the Sylvia Rivera Law Project is inspiring: to resist domination through broad-based coalitional work that does not labor under liberalism's identity politics or advanced capitalism's myth of scarcity. It both challenges the gay/lesbian political agenda that galvanizes the desires of the racially and economically privileged and steps beyond the myth of scarcity that demands our allegiance. When I heard Dean Spade, the founder of SRLP, talk in Austin, he closed his remarks with the incredible joy and hope he finds in his daily work with the Sylvia Rivera Law Project: such is the hallmark of stepping beyond the anxieties of domination and toward the queering of freedom.

NOTES

INTRODUCTION

1. Foucault writes of "the historical *a priori*" in *The Archaeology of Knowledge* (1972), part 3, chapter 5. This theme echoes across virtually all of his writing, and is most explicit in his distancing himself from Kantian transcendental idealism.

2. See Borges 1968, "The Analytical Language of John Wilkins."

3. Frankenberg argues that whiteness is unmarked only in those specific historical periods in which it is stabilized (1997a, 5). This leads not only to a heuristic device for reading anxiety in history, but also to the political strategy of exposing whiteness with the hope of thereby destabilizing it.

4. For this reason, I continue to be deeply suspicious of and resistant to any formation of a disciplinary field that might call itself "whiteness studies," just as I am resistant to any disciplinary field called "masculinity studies"—or, what I have not yet heard of but will undoubtedly emerge, "straight studies."

5. As Frankenberg writes, "if focusing on white identity and culture displaces attention to whiteness as a site of racialized privilege, its effectiveness as antiracism becomes limited" (1997a, 17).

6. See Chanter (1995, 45), who argues that the valorization of gender over sex in Anglo-American feminism also, through inattention to the body, feeds blindness to race, particularly blindness to the pernicious effects of the alleged neutrality of whiteness.

7. See Gilroy 2000, 15–20.

8. See Echols 1989; Giddings 1984.

9. There were clearly exceptions to this kind of agonistic pitting of sexism against racism. For example, consider the remarks of two early feminists who moved from the Civil Rights Movement to the Women's Rights Movement. Drawing on their experiences as civil rights workers, Casey Hayden and Mary King, two field secretaries for the Student Non-violent Coordinating Committee, tentatively voiced comparisons between their situation and that of southern blacks, thereby attempting some brand of coalitional politics. Writing in 1966, Hayden and King argued that, just like blacks, "women seem to be caught up in a common-law caste system that operates, sometimes subtly, forcing them to work around or outside hierarchical structures of power which exclude them. Women seem to be placed in the same position of assumed subordination in personal situations too" (1966, 36). I am grateful to Eric Selbin for bringing this example to my attention. (See also the Chicago Women's Liberation Union's Historical Archive, at http://cwluherstory.com/CWLUArchive/archive.html.) From a different angle, Kelly Oliver has argued that the early dismissal of "French" feminists (Luce Irigaray is Belgian, Julia

Kristeva Bulgarian, and Hélène Cixous Algerian) may have been an effort on the part of Anglo-American feminists to deflect the criticism launched by feminists of color (bell hooks [1981, 1984], Angela Davis [1981], and Gloria Anzaldúa and Cherríe Moraga [1983]) of essentializing gender over race. For Oliver, the relation of Anglo-American feminists to French feminist theory is not only a matter of Francophilia and Francophobia, but also a question of how white feminist theory in the U.S. has negotiated the vexing dynamics of race and racism. See Oliver 1993, 163–68.

10. As Tina Chanter develops in her problematizing of the sex/gender distinction and the essentialist/constructionist binary that it spawned in the late '80s and early '90s, "It is worth noting that among the (perhaps unintended) results of feminists emphasizing gender over sex there has been a fostering not only of sex-blindness, but also of color-blindness. . . . Despite the ostensibly neutral discourse of gender, the standards of patriarchy have remained more or less in place, just as the privileges enjoyed by whites over blacks have gone largely unchallenged" (1995, 45). As I will develop at length below, ostensible neutrality has become one of the most forceful masks that white supremacist racism dons. It seems to be one of the masks that the sex/gender distinction cannot fully shed.

11. To offer an incomplete and fairly arbitrary list, the works of bell hooks, Luce Irigaray, Gloria Anzaldúa, Rosi Braidotti, Elizabeth Grosz, Cherríe Moraga, Judith Butler, Drucilla Cornell, and Donna Haraway have all troubled the possibility of reading the body or its more general mode, materiality, outside of historical discourses through which it is deployed. Some may be surprised by, or even want to contest, my inclusion of Anzaldúa and Moraga in this list of post-structuralist feminists. I argue that their work, while not drawing explicitly on these European texts, nonetheless works to historicize materiality and decenter subjectivity in ways that intersect with that of others in this list. It is in that vein, in addition to contesting the latent racism that may lurk in a desire to exclude them, that I list them here. By no means do I intend to suggest that any of these feminists are reducible to some law of the Same: they are all working out different problematics in different ways and voices.

12. Foucault 1977b, "Nietzsche, Genealogy, History."

13. See *Gender Trouble* (1989) and *Bodies That Matter* (1993). The works of Monique Wittig (1981) and Christine Delphy (1993) also problematize the ways that the sex/gender distinction operates on a fundamental logic of heteronormativity.

14. Given the cultural taboos around 'coming out' as an intersexed person by birth, statistics on such surgeries are rather difficult to track. For information on these surgeries and the emergent movement around reclaiming intersexuality in more healthy ways, see the website of the Intersex Society of North America at http://www.isna.org. ISNA describes itself as "an advocacy and policy group for people with atypical genital and reproductive anatomies" and it offers advice to medical doctors on its website.

15. See, for example, the work of Alphonso Lingis (1994, 2000), Elizabeth Grosz (1989b), and Ladelle McWhorter (1999) for a sampling of these kinds of arguments and phenomenologies. I turn to these questions of desire, pleasure, bodies, and politics explicitly in chapter 4.

16. For a particularly incisive historical study showing this, see Rubin 1993.

17. See particularly essays in hooks 1990 and 1992.

18. The ironies here expand beyond just our historical narrative. As I will argue in chapters 2 and 3, Irigaray's work struggles, with debatable success, not to valorize sexual difference over all other differences, particularly racial difference. In analyzing racial dif-

ference through this concept of morphology, I am also problematizing the primacy of sexual difference in the fields of psychoanalysis and feminist theories following from it.

19. See Chanter 1995, esp. chapter 1, and Whitford 1991 on Irigaray's development of the category of sexual difference along these lines. For a more orthodox reading of this category in Lacanian psychoanalysis, see Seshadri-Crooks 2000, esp. 2, 35–48. For a discussion of how sexual difference differs from the categories of sex and gender in Anglophone feminist theory, see Sheperdson 2000, 2.

20. This is a serious critique, and one I continue to largely agree with. See Deutscher 2002 for arguments against it. I turn to this explicitly in chapter 3.

21. See, for example, Appiah 1992, Zack 1997, Hall 1996b, Gilroy 2000, and Eze 2001.

22. Anti-racist theorists from perspectives as widespread as those of Lewis Gordon, Kalpana Seshadri-Crooks, Chris Cuomo, and Kim Hall have all argued that social constructionism ultimately begs its own political question; namely, who/what is doing the social constructing? And how, exactly and historically, is it being done? Gordon, arguing from an existentialist perspective, insists that social constructionism cannot answer the first of these questions (1997, 47–48). Arguing from a psychoanalytic perspective and following David Roediger, Michael Omi, and Howard Winant, Seshadri-Crooks shows how race as socially constructed "can translate rapidly into more-digestible claims that race is false consciousness, falling easily into the conservative rhetoric of 'voluntarism,' wherein one 'chooses' to be raced" (1998, 354). (To draw connections that will become more intrinsic in this reading of phallicized whiteness that I am offering here, this suggestion of 'voluntarism' interestingly echoes conservative rhetoric regarding queer sexuality.) Finally, the socio-politically oriented Cuomo and Hall argue that the widespread acceptance of race as socially constructed easily leads to a conservative resignation to and quietism about race and racism—i.e., "we're all socially constructed, so there's nothing to be done about it" (1999, 2).

23. In *Desiring Whiteness: A Lacanian Analysis of Race*, Seshadri-Crooks offers a compelling reading of whiteness operating as a master signifier through just these sorts of processes of inclusion and exclusion. While she also focuses on the critical role of visibility and the fantasy of wholeness in these symbolic organizations of difference, my work departs considerably from her Lacanian perspective in my attempts to read sexual difference as historicized along with, while also differently from, racial difference. For Seshadri-Crooks's Lacanian perspective, sexual difference operates at the level of the Real, while racial difference serves as a symbolic offering of excess to compensate for the lack at the heart of sexual difference. Whiteness thus functions with power in the symbolic field because it promises the wholeness that sexual difference desires but can never provide. Rather than reading this fantasy of wholeness as a necessary fantasy of human psychic life, however, I am attempting to historicize its very emergence as our dominant fantasy through this investigation of the logic of the limit. This consequently means I am attempting to historicize our dominant senses of sexual difference itself, a suggestion that is anathema to Seshadri-Crooks's Lacanian perspective.

My work is similar to Seshadri-Crooks's in at least three ways: we both frame whiteness as a master signifier in which the body plays a critical role; we both focus on visibility in the machinations of difference; and for both of us wholeness plays a critical role in the ways that bodies and difference itself are constituted. But our critical differences can be framed as differing approaches to both Foucaultian and Lacanian analyses. Seshadri-Crooks dismisses Foucaultian analyses almost completely, including feminist

(2000, 6) and anti-racist (2000, 13–14) work grounded therein. This leaves her text with a diminished sense of power, consistently reading power as ideology. As will become clear particularly in chapters 2 and 4, I ultimately wish not to dismiss either Foucaultian or Lacanian theoretical fields.

24. I am arguing that 'whiteness' functions as an effect of these discourses and practices in much the same way that Judith Butler, following Foucault, argues that 'sex' is an effect of discourses and practices. See Butler 1989 and 1993.

25. Language becomes a critical site of such marking, particularly when we must choose whether to speak of bodies as "black/white," "raced/raceless," or "white/non-white." I have chosen in this text to use the term "raced" to refer to all bodies that are not white; I refuse the term "non-white," as it continues to reinscribe whiteness as the privileged and determinate signifier. When referring to white bodies, however, I have chosen to use the term "white" in an attempt to color these bodies—to race them, to mark them, to render them visible and thereby interrupt their power.

26. Seshadri-Crooks describes race as "a practice of visibility" (2000, 2).

27. Alexandra Chasin and Lisa Duggan argue that the social categories of identity and identity politics are the explicit tools of liberalism, in its traditional seventeenth-century form (Chasin), its nineteenth-century development (Duggan), and its twentieth-century instantiation of neo-liberalism (Duggan), which infects both feminist and gay/lesbian political movements (Chasin, Duggan). See Chasin 2000 and Duggan 2004. I develop the connections between liberalism and phallicized whiteness in chapter 1.

28. I am grateful to Michael Bray for this phrase, which he coined, inspired by both Benjamin and Adorno. Private conversation, July 1, 2003.

1. Liberalism's Neutral Individual

1. While I cannot offer a comprehensive bibliography of this work, some of the following texts have been particularly influential in reconceiving liberalism's alleged neutrality: on class, MacPherson 1962; on sexual difference or gender, Brown 1995, Pateman 1988, Okin 1989, Hirschmann 1992, Hartsock 1983, MacKinnon 1989; on race, Mills 1997; on race and gender, Zack 1996; on class, race, and gender, Williams 1991.

2. For an account of how these traditional values of liberalism, particularly individualism and its identity politics, have developed into contemporary forms of neo-liberalism in the U.S., which in turn have infected both feminist and gay/lesbian political movements, see Duggan 2004; for an account that focuses on the impact of liberalism in contemporary gay/lesbian political movements, see Chasin 2000.

3. For Locke this concept of enclosure emerges as historically and politically salient because of the critical role it played in the politics of seventeenth-century agricultural capitalism, where the ability to enclose and thereby restrict use of previously "common" land played a critical role in the transformation from feudal agriculture to one of competing rentiers. See Hill 1980 and Holstun 2000. I will return to this question of Locke's own historical conditioning, and his philosophical/epistemological dismissal of its import, below. I am grateful to Michael Bray for bringing this point to my attention and, more broadly, for sharpening my general understanding of Locke.

4. Parts of one's identity are thereby traits that one possesses. Elaborating her argument regarding the foundation of liberalism for the gay/lesbian political movement, Chasin explains how the movement conceives of sexuality as a "possession" and thus a

"right": "the movement held at a premium the right of individuals to possess a (homo)sexuality. Whether conceived as an identity feature or a behavior, (homo)sexuality is always conceptually located in the body. Because the body is private property, as long as it properly contains its sexuality within a domestic sphere, what is at stake, according to liberal logic, is the right to privacy" (2000, 15). I will return to these dynamics in the context of queer pleasures in chapter 4.

5. As I show in the following section, such a lack of historical consciousness functions as a necessary and constitutive blind spot in the structures of phallicized whiteness. Furthermore, to foreshadow the language of chapter 4, Locke's *de facto* approach sets him squarely outside the conceptual schemas of genealogical thinking, a thinking that attunes itself to questions of historical and discursive origins, and one which I will eventually signify as a 'queer' kind of resistant thinking.

6. MacPherson's argument centers on the introduction of money into the state of nature, which divides the state of nature into pre- and post-monetary stages of development. He shows how this transition effects a shift, for Locke, in the essence of rational behavior: the mark of "full rationality" moves from industrious appropriation, via one's labor, toward unlimited accumulation, via the capital of money and land. To be a capitalist is then to be fully rational—i.e., fully human. See MacPherson 1962, 232–47. Naomi Zack argues that this introduction of money in Locke's theory can help to account for the ideal of white masculinity as "entrepreneurial" and the eventual sexualization of race during slavery in the U.S. via the monetarization of race—i.e., the 'breeding of livestock' as the justification for the rape of slaves; see Zack 1997.

7. MacPherson notes that this line was added to the third edition of the *Treatise*, indicating Locke's apparent need for a more direct argument for this critical justification of cultivation (MacPherson 1962, 211).

8. Again, as we saw in his discussion of the move to the state of society, Locke writes of the invention of money from a perspective of its *de facto* development, rather than offering a genetic account of why it must develop. He is, once more, not a genealogical thinker.

9. This argument about the role of money in Locke's thinking is central to MacPherson's reading; I have only sketched a condensed version of it here. See MacPherson 1962, 203–38, for the full argument.

10. This sense of time runs through Descartes's reflections on experience. For example, see Meditation III: "For a lifespan can be divided into countless parts, each completely independent from the other, so that it does not follow from the fact that I existed a little while ago that I must exist now" (Descartes 1964, 105). I am grateful to Michael Bray for bringing this to my attention.

11. This is Cynthia Willett's helpful phrase, which distinguishes the legacy of modernity (in figures such as Locke, Descartes, Hume, and Kant) that continues to affect our social attitudes and institutions from that more complicated, nuanced period of philosophy known as 'modernity,' which could include figures such as Pascal, Hobbes, Spinoza, Leibniz, Diderot, and Rousseau. See Willett 2001.

12. For a much fuller development of the damages and dangers of such a self-contained, sovereign self, see Oliver 2001. I am grateful for the provocation this text offered to my thinking, particularly about these sections on the individual. I also develop the self-Other dynamics more explicitly in chapter 2 through a discussion of Lacan and Fanon, and again in chapter 4 in a discussion of Hegel and Kant.

13. As we will continue to see, this shifting of categories of difference complicates the subjectivity of phallicized whiteness, granting it Richard Dyer's "semiotic flexibility," which makes it difficult to pin down and too slippery to resist.

14. I leave the category of sexuality in parentheses here because it seems not yet to have emerged as a matter of identity, power, or freedom in the seventeenth century. See note 19 for further elaboration.

15. We can see this dynamic at work in the kinds of crimes and activities that dominate the contemporary culture of the mainstream U.S. Debates about things such as abortion, rape, birth control, sodomy, and even terrorism all turn around how sexed, raced, classed, and sexualized bodies are not in control of themselves—and thus become subject to the 'neutral' law of the state. I elaborate further below when I turn to 'kinds' of bodies as opposed to the neutral individual who is not affected or bound by its bodily comportment.

16. For the full argument about how difference will always be read as 'unequal' within the logic of liberalism, see Brown 1995, chapter 6.

17. We will see how color-blindness functions as a shared assumption on all sides of the affirmative action debates below. For an incisive argument about the ways that color-blindness functions as a hysterical symptom, thereby displaying the fundamental anxiety around race in contemporary western cultures, see Oliver 2001, chapter 7.

18. As feminist work has shown extensively, the nexus of sexuality and gender in western cultures is impossible to unravel. In referring to the sexualizing of racial difference, I invoke the category of "sexual difference," which refers to both gender and the inevitable sexualizing of that social index in a way that avoids the obstacles of the sex/gender distinction. I thus refer to the racializing of both gender and sexuality simultaneously and, *vice versa*, to the gendering and sexualizing of race. See the introduction for discussion of this category and the epistemological, political, and historical problems of the sex/gender distinction.

19. I will attempt to clarify the awkward, difficult, political, and philosophical complexity of listing the categories of difference that obtain to the subject position of phallicized whiteness. I have chosen to attempt to mark the historical emergence of these categories diacritically: I will leave categories that have yet to emerge in parentheses and list all other categories that have already been codified or are in the process of being codified. In this present listing, then, the categories of Christianity and property ownership are assumed as codified categories of this subject position, as our discussion of Locke clearly indicates. The categories of whiteness and maleness are, as I am arguing in this section, emergent in this period of the post-bellum U.S. But the category of sexuality remains parenthetical, because the category of sexuality as a matter of 'orientation,' as we call it these days in the U.S., was still in its nascent stages of formation in the post-bellum United States, a period that served as a sort of cauldron of race, class, religion, and gender in which sexuality was fired. The category did not emerge explicitly until the end of the nineteenth century, as the work of Gayle Rubin (1993), David Halperin (1990), Michel Foucault (1978), and others has shown. Once these categories are fully codified, I will shift to the shorthand of 'phallicized whiteness,' which I use to include the categories of property ownership, Protestant (or culturally Protestant) Christianity, maleness, whiteness, and heterosexuality.

20. The works of James Baldwin, Ralph Ellison, Zora Neale Hurston, Toni Morrison, and Richard Wright all easily come to mind here. For further discussion of these dynamics, see Winnubst 2003.

21. For these historical arguments, see Williams 1944 and Patterson 1982.

22. In her account of the development of nineteenth-century liberalism into late-twentieth-century neo-liberalism, Lisa Duggan shows historically how these two identity categories emerged: "During the first decades of the nineteenth century, as property qualifications for voting were eliminated in state after state in the U.S., requirements for full citizenship shifted from a complex array of economic, racial, gender, religious, or genealogical characteristics to the simpler identity markers: *whiteness* or *maleness*" (2004, 5).

23. See Nietzsche 1967 and Foucault 1978 for the most concise of these arguments about power.

24. While Locke did ground his epistemology in empiricism, I argue that this still reduces the role of the body to that of a servant of rationality, its master and the seat of all value. The body is, as Descartes codifies, still viewed as a machine that must be tightly controlled and regulated if it is not to deceive reason. Embodiment as it has been taken up in the twentieth century is not a philosophical or political category for high modernity.

25. Contemporary U.S. culture is filled with easy, recent examples of this. I cite only two: 1) Kevin Spacey's character in *American Beauty*, a film that enjoyed huge popularity in the United States, is tormented by his desire for a young girl but ultimately transcends it and thus emerges as the (tragic?) hero; and 2) the infamous sex scandals of Bill Clinton's presidency were largely displaced onto the shoulders of Monica Lewinsky. Simple stereotypes also convey this sense of disembodiment: the epithets hurled at women for sexual promiscuity are too numerous to list; there are comparatively few for men, who are rarely judged for promiscuity or for any of its effects. (If judged, men are rarely judged on the basis of their maleness; judgments against men as "lechers" are made on the basis of their age, not their maleness.) I appreciate the comments of Walt Herbert that pushed me to elaborate this point.

26. For an example of a conservative argument that insists on the individual as the fundamental social unit protected in the U.S. Constitution, see Welch 1996. Welch directly connects individualism with protection against "the prevailing political winds" (159)—or, in the language I have developed here, he uses individualism to maintain an ahistorical space for the law and for white privilege. For a broader view of how this logic works, and its connections to questions about historicity in the law, see Young 1990.

27. Wendy Brown notes that Locke and other theorists of liberalism understand social violence exclusively through the category of property ownership (Brown 1995, 150). For these theorists who are arguing from the alleged neutrality of the individual, where no bodily difference matters, it is only private ownership that becomes a source of social conflict. Perhaps the legacy of affirmative action in the twentieth century and the erasure of the social category of class from the U.S. cultural psyche indicate a growing threat to that subject position protected by liberalism's alleged neutrality; that is, perhaps the increased emphasis on differences that *do* matter indicates a loosening of the difference/sameness logic of liberalism. The question I am raising here, however, is whether such a shift in conceptual schemas is possible within the logic dominating debates around affirmative action.

28. See Mills 1994, 5–7, for a fuller discussion of these political machinations and their effect on Title VII. I have gathered these brief historical sketches from Belz 1991 and Mills 1994.

29. As noted above, see Oliver 2001, chapter 7, for the argument that color-blindness functions as a hysterical symptom. For a fascinating take on the chaos and violence that such blindness might unleash, see José Saramago's brilliant *Blindness*.

30. Nicolaus Mills captures this sort of sentiment when he explains how conservative opponents of affirmative action argue that "the white college student hurt by an affirmative action admissions policy is someone too young to be held responsible for educational racism" (Mills 1994, 31). Concepts of history and responsibility displace recognition of race, class, gender, and religious differences in such arguments. And we return, once more, to the ahistorical space of the neutral individual as the space that the law is called upon to protect.

31. I am sympathetic to and grateful for Young's work here. But I wonder if she is not still trying to save the project of classical liberalism, a project that I am arguing is ontologically connected to cultures of phallicized whiteness. Young assumes a feminist model of empowerment in her solution of offering all perspectives a voice in decision making. While this is certainly a step in the direction of diffusing the centralized power of the dominant subject position of phallicized whiteness, it operates on the liberal model of power as a tool that an individual owns and wields, consciously and intentionally. An instrumental view of power hovers beneath her models of "democratic decisionmaking." Freedom is thereby understood as the expression of this willful power and, while different subject positions will presumably wield power differently, the basic unit of enfranchisement remains the neutral individual.

2. Is the Mirror Racist?

1. An exciting and burgeoning line of inquiry has clearly emerged along this intersection since, roughly, the early 1990s. A sampling of such work includes Abel, Christian, and Moglen 1997, Fuss 1995, Gilman 1993, Johnson 1998, Lane 1998, Pellegrini 1997, Seshadri-Crooks 2000, Spillers 1996, and Walton 1995.

2. Psychoanalytic theory gives us tools to answer that which these social constructionist approaches always assume but never account for: how race attaches to individual bodies and psyches (the imaginary), while simultaneously operating through a trans-social logic (the symbolic). It allows us to articulate both how race is historically and socially constructed and how it is individually embodied. In short, if it is through the embodiment of race that racism works, then the belief that race is socially constructed is, in its inability to articulate the complex processes of embodiment, insufficient to diagnose the mechanisms and structures of racism. As Hortense Spillers frames this issue, the signifier 'race' constantly traverses the boundaries of the 'private' and the 'public' (Spillers 1996, 78–88)—and psychoanalytic theory also attempts to cross these boundaries and account for such crossings (through accounting for the delineation of such boundaries). See particularly Seshadri-Crooks 1998, for an incisive argument that mere social constructionism actually lends itself all too easily to conservative views of voluntarism. See also Gordon 1997, 47–48, for a discussion from an existentialist-phenomenological perspective of the inadequacies of social construction to account for any agency.

3. Arguing "that neurosis is not a basic element of human reality," Fanon writes, "Like it or not, the Oedipus complex is far from coming into being among Negroes" (1967, 151–52). A robust dialogue has developed around Fanon's texts in the last several years. Both Spillers 1996 and Vergès 1997 disagree with this claim and argue that it exposes inconsistencies and conflicts in Fanon's own subject position as a 'French Negro' who wants to posit a clear separation between 'white' and 'black' culture. For more sympathetic readings of Fanon's deployments of psychoanalytic discourse to disrupt colonial dynamics, see Bhabha 1990, Fuss 1995, chapter 5, and Hall 1996a. See also Bergner

1995 for the argument that Fanon's ambivalent relation to white culture may be a function of his ambivalent relation to white masculinity and the phallus, rather than simply to whiteness; I return to this issue of the phallus as white later in this chapter. Generally, while Fanon is focusing on the colonial context, I am importing some of his observations on race and psychic development into the multiracial settings of contemporary northern and western Europe and North America, where, I am arguing, a white, racist symbolic dominates the conceptual and intersubjective universe—and thus all subject-formations within it.

4. As were the majority of European intellectuals in the early twentieth century, Lacan was influenced by Surrealism, and particularly Dali, early in his career. See Roudinesco 1997 for a detailed account of this relation. Roudinesco also offers the odd biographical detail that Lacan gave his daughter Caroline, born in 1937 while he was writing the lecture that would come to be "The Mirror Stage," the (officially noted) nickname "Image" (137).

5. For a provocative discussion of race signifiers as grounded in the visual from a Lacanian perspective, see Seshadri-Crooks 2000.

6. More specifically, Spillers argues that, in yet another twist of racist logic, Freud disavows any 'cultural uniqueness' of his theories to evade the anti-Semitic impulses of his era.

7. A sampling of this recent work on the difficult questions of historicity and psychoanalysis includes Copjec 1994, Lane 1998, Sheperdson 2000, and Žižek 1989.

8. Interrogation of psychoanalysis's claims to universality has been a central site for several theorists attempting to both use and limit psychoanalysis for discussions of racialized subjectivity. The questions emerge in several ways. On the one hand, several theorists have troubled the unquestioned reliance on sexual difference as a fundamental principle structuring subject-formation—both separate from and ontologically prior to racial and other differences. More broadly, theorists have also argued, as I do, that the central hesitancy of psychoanalysis to turn toward racial difference is itself an instance of its historico-cultural specificity and has produced "a hegemonic silence on the issue of race" (Walton 1995, 780). For both of these, see Seshadri-Crooks 1998 and 2000 and Walton 1995. Walton gives a brief historical genealogy of the reluctance to turn to race within psychoanalytic theory, tracing it all the way back to the conflict between Bronislaw Malinowski and Ernest Jones in 1928.

9. Boswell actually argues that race operates in Lacan's text of "The Agency of the Letter" at the margin of the symbolic, thereby providing a productive site of interrogation. While her argument, which relies on a reading of Toni Morrison's *Sula*, is persuasive for the function of materiality in Lacan's accounts of signification (her focus), it does not—despite several references to mirror images—problematize the role of the visual in this racializing symbolic.

10. Contemporary scholarship already offers us many examples of race functioning in these ways. Charles Mills argues in *The Racial Contract* (1997) that classic social contract theory (from Hobbes and Locke to Rousseau and Kant) operates through the disavowal of its racialized and racist conceptions of equality, thus allowing the social contract to function, through the guise of an unbiased, democratic ideal, as a primary tool for cultural imperialism, economic exploitation, and racial genocide. Similarly, Paul Gilroy argues in *The Black Atlantic* (1993a) and *Small Acts* (1993b) that race functions as a disavowed but steadfastly necessary condition for British cultural and economic imperialism. For similar approaches, from very different directions, see also Dyer 1997, Gold-

berg 1993, Gordon 1997, Oliver 2001, and Willett 1995, among other works. Finally, Walton 1995 argues that white feminists have reenacted this blind spot of psychoanalysis in their resistance to theorize the racial domain as white (see Walton 1995, 799–804).

11. Oliver continues her work on vision in Lacan to argue that his understanding of the subject as ontologically aggressive hinges on this assumption that space is empty, an assumption she challenges. As she writes, "the *sight* of the other incites aggression because sight only serves to remind us of the abyss separating us from others" (2001, 189). See her chapter 8, particularly 183–90, for her entire discussion.

12. As the work of Braidotti (1991), Grosz (1990), and Irigaray (1985a) shows, Lacan gives an account of the ego-formation of a male infant—despite, or perhaps in step with, his claims to universality.

13. Certainly, much ink has already been spilled on the ways that this self-splitting in the mirror stage ushers the infant into the intersubjective field of desire and aggression. For insightful discussions, with various emphases, of these processes of development, see the following: on self-splitting and the social ego, Grosz 1990, 28–49; Ferrell 1996, 67–72; and Oliver 1993, 37; on the missed role of the caregiver, Willett 1995, 63–68; on the connections between narcissism and aggression, Brennan 1993, 39–49. See Oliver 2001, chapter 8, for a recent account that takes up the role of race in this process of self-splitting and ego-formation and questions the notion, functioning within it, that vision operates in empty space.

14. It is of course crucial to distinguish between the other (small o), who is embodied by a living person, and the Other (capital O), whom this other is always representing. As Elizabeth Grosz explains, "the Other is not a person but a place, the locus of law, language, and the symbolic" (1990, 67). Aggression against the other emerges primarily out of the frustrated desire for the Other that can never be sated by a human relation to the other. This dynamic suggests that this forming ego is ontologically aggressive.

15. See Lacan's essay "Aggressivity in Psychoanalysis" (in Lacan 1977) for further elaboration of the connections between narcissism and aggression and the ontological status that both assume within his theory.

16. As I discuss in chapter 3, Irigaray, in *An Ethics of Sexual Difference* (1993a), reads western, phallic conceptions of space, and their subsequent erasure of sexual difference, as trapped in precisely this logic of containment, which she locates in Aristotle's *Physics*.

17. To put this differently, sight is always already interpellated by speech for Lacan.

18. See Gilroy 1993a for the wonderful deployment of this term to refer to industrialized nations and thereby destabilize the common rhetoric of referring to non-European nations as "underdeveloped."

19. I am grateful to Casey Bledsoe for much of the following discussion of the space of discrete bodies bound by skin. See Bledsoe 1997.

20. Distance is a necessary condition and dynamic for the very functioning of the symbolic. See Žižek 1998 for an incisive discussion of the ways that the symbolic functions only through its distance from the fantasmatic frame, which in turn provides the distance from the Other that is necessary to incur violence against it. See also Oliver 2001, chapter 8.

21. Not all cultures operate on this conception of embodiment grounded in bodies bound by skin. In grossly general terms, South Asian and Chinese cultures, along with

growing practices of 'alternative healing' in the U.S. and Great Britain, conceive of the body in dynamics of energy, rather than containment.

22. Structured by such a space, the aggressive ego spawned by the sight of his own image now finds its proper home in this space of containment, distance, power—and mastery. While Lacan interestingly develops the role that space plays in aggression in his essay "Aggressivity in Psychoanalysis," he never theorizes it in terms of a social mapping of that space. Recognizing that "the individual's relation to a particular spatial field is, in certain species, mapped socially" (1977, 27), he does not read the developmental space of the mirror stage as interpellated by any such social mapping.

23. As the work of Irigaray shows, our phallocentric symbolic cannot tolerate 'messy' bodies (Irigaray 1985a, 1985b). For a provocative reading of the ways that this demand for tightly sealed bodies affects masculinity and its sexuality, see "Sexed Bodies" in Grosz 1989b.

24. See Lacan 1977, "The Signification of the Phallus." The phallus and the visual do not seem to be ontologically connected: although the phallus works itself out in the visual, the visual need not be dominated by the phallus. However, if sight is always already interpellated by speech, as the 1953–54 Seminar suggests (Lacan 1988), then it does seem that the visual field must always be phallicized.

25. For a much closer, more detailed reading of Lacan's interpolation of Hegelian metaphysics through the figure of the phallus and the central role of the visual, see Winnubst 1999.

26. For compelling readings of the intersections of racial and sexual difference, see Bergner 1995, Boswell 1999, and Dyer 1997.

27. As this essay is itself arguing, the two seem to be mutually constitutive.

28. This remains a controversial and much debated claim. For a concise argument, see Gordon 1997, 5. For a more prolonged discussion of the ways that whiteness functions as a master signifier and thereby structures racial differentiation through a white-black polarity, see Seshadri-Crooks 2000.

29. In addition to the works enumerated below, see Bhabha 1990, Hall 1996b, Mills 1997, Oliver 2001, and Wright 1966 for readings of race as primarily registered through sensibilities of vision.

30. The semiotic flexibility of race plays differently across different bodies. Thus, for example, it might be racist stereotypes such as 'the Jewish nose' or 'Latina hair' or 'Asian eyes' that signify race differently from sheer skin color. The argument here, however, is that visual markers continue to signify race and are grounded in the white-black duality, and where one falls in that spectrum determines the kind of racism one may experience.

31. The dynamics of visibility play across the essays in Williams's *The Alchemy of Race and Rights,* but see particularly "Teleology on the Rocks."

32. For a compelling account of the ways that Lacan's texts account for this position of "being interpellated into the system, not as a people, but as things (slaves), animals," see Boswell 1999, 121.

33. I am relying on Judith Butler's work on cultural legibility and the practices of repetitive iteration for subject-formation here. See Butler 1989 and 1993.

34. For an excellent study of the ways our "imaginary bodies" constitute, rather than reflect, social relations, see Gatens 1996, especially chapter 5.

35. Parenting thus becomes one of the primary sites through which images—and

thus realities—of authority are transmitted. Interracial parenting, as an enactment of authority that differs racially (both from the larger cultural images of authority and within the family itself), becomes a possible site of disruption of white authority.

36. For an incisive discussion of disembodiment as the figuration of the phallicized male body, see Butler 1993, 48–49.

3. The Place of Sexual Difference

1. In what one might call her more 'political' writings, Irigaray does take up problematics of rights and duties in more traditional manners; see such texts as *Je, tu, nous: Toward a Culture of Difference* and *Thinking the Difference: For a Peaceful Revolution*. See also Deutscher 2002 for a comprehensive account of both Irigaray's political undertakings and how her texts are used in politics, particularly by Italian feminists.

2. See Burke 1994 for a broad discussion of the periods and foci of Irigaray's work to that date. For Burke's particular discussion of *An Ethics of Sexual Difference* and Irigaray's emergent focus on ethics, see 252, note 8, and 256–67.

3. I have developed these two styles of reading Irigaray in the context of her work "about" language and her work "in" language in Winnubst 1999, 23–28.

4. See Butler 1993, 36–39; Grosz 1989a, 132; Schwab 1994, 371.

5. See Butler 1993, 37–39. Seshadri-Crooks 2000 makes just this argument regarding whiteness as a 'master signifier' that totalizes the field of racial signification, structuring it as a black-white dynamic.

6. The reverberations of this polarity in gender differentiation are also evident at the institutional and political register of academic disciplinary boundaries: philosophy continues to be dominated by men in North America and northern and western Europe. As a woman in philosophy, I was introduced to this polarity early, when an undergraduate professor encouraged me to consider English for graduate study because it seems like a more 'feminine' field of study.

7. *The Use of Pleasure,* the second volume of Foucault's *History of Sexuality,* argues that texts of ancient Greece leading up to the Platonic-Socratic dialogues were concerned with pleasure and had no real concept of 'desire.'

8. Despite much attention to the strong voice of Lacan in virtually all of Irigaray's texts, there has ironically been no attention to it specifically in her reading of Aristotle. Tina Chanter gives an excellent discussion from the direction of Heidegger, but offers virtually no mention of or concern with Lacan or Freud (Chanter 1995, 151–59). Lorraine is very clear on Lacan in precise places (Lorraine 1999, 24, 31). For broader readings of Irigaray's work that consider the role of psychoanalysis, see Braidotti 1991, Butler 1993, Cornell 1992, Deutscher 2002, Grosz 1989b, Whitford 1991, Willett 2001.

9. Generally, Irigaray is much more explicitly in conversation with Freud than with Lacan or any other psychoanalytic theorist. The essay that discusses Lacan most explicitly is "The Mechanics of Fluids" in *This Sex Which Is Not One.*

10. Irigaray's later texts increasingly idealize the heterosexual couple as the fundamental unit of sociality. I develop this dynamic and what it tells us about the limits of her project, and of western metaphysics more broadly, at the end of this chapter. Meanwhile, as I offer a detailed exegesis of her essay on Aristotle's *Physics* and a few other texts, I will also note, however clumsily in these footnotes, various places in her texts where this latent heterosexism also surfaces.

11. I put this directly in the hypothetical because this location of desire in the

crossing of the interval seems to me to be operating on an assumption that desire emerges out of lack. As we will see, the figure of the interval becomes a central connection in our larger discussion here. The questions of desire and lack will increasingly become the focus of this text as we head into the final three chapters.

12. Irigaray conspicuously does not place her discussion of the *Physics* in any larger context of Aristotle's work. As we will see, this affects her reading of the fundamental *aporia* in Aristotelian logic as the gap between physics and metaphysics. For a sustained and subtle argument that Aristotle breaks from the Platonic heritage of conceiving of first principles mathematically and moves toward conceiving of them physically—i.e., primarily as movers or things that induce movement—see Gadamer 1986.

13. I am using translations worked out in collaboration with Phil Hopkins, to whom I am very grateful both for the translations and for the philosophical conversations about Aristotle's Greek.

14. Given that Aristotle's texts, which are largely 'notes' compiled as texts, are by no means the same sort of 'texts' that twentieth-century hermeneutics demands, this sort of reading for diacritical, textual marks is not as effective when reading Aristotle. The subtleties of Aristotle's Greek are carried in his grammar.

15. Briefly, in the psychoanalytic terms that inform Irigaray's texts, morphology implies that cultural coding of physical bodies which is ontologically present. It provides a conceptual framework in which metaphysical and physical concepts can be read as mutually constituting one another. As I develop at greater length below, it calls into question the very division between discussions of "physics" and "metaphysics"—a division that may be more ambiguous in Aristotle's texts than Irigaray diagnoses.

16. See Halperin 1990 and Foucault 1990a. Judith Butler also warns against this reduction, while nonetheless arguing that "the exclusive allocation of penetration to the form, and penetrability to a feminized materiality" occurs in Plato's *Timaeus* (Butler 1993, 49–53). I return to the persistent problem of heteronormativity in Irigaray's later work at the end of the chapter.

17. The meaning and role of this pesky preposition "in" is the focus of my discussion below, following a full exploration of Irigaray's texts, when I return to the meaning of the interval in Aristotle's texts.

18. For Bataille, this contrast between homogeneity and heterogeneity marks the division between meaningful and meaningless experiences for western cultures, and often also for fascism. It is intriguing to note here how Aristotle conceives the heterogeneous as "in place." For Bataille's most explicit discussion of these dynamics, see "Psychological Structure of Fascism" in *Visions of Excess*.

19. There is an inkling of an infinite regress in this parenthetical comment—the infinite regress that gets called "God" in Irigaray's eyes. For discussion of this dynamic, see note 24 below.

20. In general psychoanalytic terms, sublimation and repression act on different dynamics of the psyche—i.e., on drives and external events, respectively. For example, sublimation, as the deep burial of an aggressive drive, may allow the memory of a violent external act to be repressed and transformed into a memory of lesser violence, or even lost altogether. Conversely, the external act initiates the dynamics of sublimation, which become essential to the process of 'finding one's place in the world,' as I develop below. While working on different parts of the psyche, the two dynamics work in concert to transform experiences, drives, and memories into events that can be incorporated into the psyche, keeping the ego functional.

21. To reduce this to a singular act, one might suggest that it is ultimately the Oedipal drive/desire to 'have' one's mother that is cathected in all acts of sublimation and repression. Such a reduction requires discussion far beyond the scope of this essay, but the suggestion is nonetheless provocative for the larger discussions of 'place' and its morphological register, the womb.

22. Freud's case of Little Ernst and his *fort-da* game is another instance of the ways that the male child learns to exercise mastery over the absence of his mother as a key to subjectivity. For Irigaray's reading of this game as an exemplary act of the *méconnaissance* at the heart of patriarchal belief and a reading of it through the figuration of the womb, see "Belief Itself" in *Sexes and Genealogies.*

23. Irigaray concludes her essay on Aristotle and place with this section of "On the Great Longing" in *Thus Spoke Zarathustra.*

24. As we will see, how to rejoin these becomes one of her final questions (1993a, 55). She also reads this disjunction as the disjunction between, as Tina Chanter puts it, "the first and the last place, the place provided by the mother, and the quest for the infinity of God" (1995, 158). I take up the question of kinds of infinity in cultures of phallicized whiteness in chapter 5.

25. Irigaray argues in *Speculum* that Freud falls prey to an unexamined assumption of analogy between the body and the psyche, which then functions as a similar blind spot in his lectures on femininity. Her style of deconstructive mimicry then leads her to take up the approach of analogical reason and take it to its limit, where the erasure of sexual difference surfaces as the dynamic driving the impulse toward analogy.

26. I do not mean to suggest that the psychoanalytic divide between the symbolic and the imaginary can be mapped onto the Aristotelian divide between metaphysics and physics. There are innumerable, subtle differences that far outstrip the scope of my discussion here. The concept of morphology, however, contests any clear demarcation of the physical from the conceptual or linguistic, a demarcation that undergirds both the psychoanalytic (where it is turned upon itself) and Aristotelian schematics.

27. While Irigaray's early work, particularly essays in *This Sex Which Is Not One,* flirt with disrupting the normativity of heterosexuality, her later work seems to have only fallen more deeply into this dynamic. See Deutscher 2002, 77–78 and 137–39 for a careful discussion of this increased emphasis on heterosexuality in Irigaray's later work. I return to this dynamic and these textual questions at the end of this chapter.

28. I want to be clear and subtle in this crucial point. It is not that Aristotle claims for his own texts a firm, airtight foundation on which he then builds a system; I do not think any text from the history of western metaphysics actually operates with this sort of hubris. However, we late moderns have very often read such a singular foundation back into these texts—either to claim them as the cornerstone for our own metaphysical/ethical/political investments or to debunk them, again, on the way to making our own point. Irigaray is not only more subtle, but also highly vigilant about such teleological system-building.

29. For a compelling and thorough reading of Irigaray's corpus of texts as writing toward an "impossible difference," see Deutscher 2002.

30. Her discussion of this myth in "Belief Itself" (1993c) articulates the problems of a closed interval more clearly than her discussion of it toward the end of "Place, Interval" in *An Ethics of Sexual Difference.* It also serves as an example of her heteronormativity: Aristophanes' myth does not open a space between her and her or him and him, but Irigaray does not heed these possible configurations.

31. I develop this style of Irigaray's as "imaginative" toward the end of the chapter; she also writes in a style of interpolative, deconstructive mimicry that Butler diagnoses as "penetrative" (1993, 45). In these imaginative texts, Irigaray writes in a style that opens toward a reimagining of sexual difference, a style that Deutscher reads as writing toward an impossible "anticipatory difference" (2002, 6), one that differs and defers. This sort of textual style cannot be teleological in form, which is what Butler ultimately suggests in reading Irigaray's style as penetrative. When she is at her best, Irigaray writes toward an open, unpredictable future, not one that is already determined by the phallicized conceptual apparatuses at hand. However, as I develop at the end of the chapter, I finally agree with Butler both about the limits of Irigaray's project and about the disjuncture between her early and later texts. And as I suggest in note 35 below and develop more fully in chapters 5 and 6, the specter of the future may already be a tool of domination subtly at work here.

32. See particularly 212a12–14, where Aristotle brings several possibilities into play and does not side with any of them. Thus, here we have an "interval," connected somehow with "air, which is thought to be incorporeal," that is regarded—although not necessarily by Aristotle—as empty. For the connections to air, the forgetting of air, and the central roles these play in Heidegger's reading of Aristotle, as well as Irigaray's reading of Heidegger, see Chanter 1995, chapter 4, particularly 164.

33. The experiences of reading these texts (particularly orally) in classrooms, where both male and female bodies seem to tingle with various invitations, speak loudly here.

34. In addition to Grosz and Lorraine, whom I discuss here, see Willett 1995, 2001, and Whitford 1991 for further discussions of these dynamics of touch in Irigaray's work.

35. Lorraine proceeds to read this shift in spatiality largely through the registers of predictability and anticipation—i.e., we cannot anticipate where the relation of touch might take us, but we can predict where the distanced relation of vision will. Both Deutscher 2002 and Ziarek 2001 also underline the lack of predictability as a strength of these anticipatory politics. I am sympathetic to these undertakings, but also worry that the temporality of anticipation functions as a temporality of phallicized whiteness, an argument I develop in chapter 5.

36. See particularly Lorraine's discussion of Irigaray's readings of Freud's Little Ernst and his *fort-da* game in contrast with a little girl's "whirling around" for another example of touch as reorienting spatiality and thus grounding a different symbolic field (1999, 31). As Lorraine develops, a girl's play of 'whirling around' enacts contiguous contact with the world; subsequently, her relation to her mother, her site of birth, and her own body are configured not through a subject-object split that is the effect of distanced, external relations between contained bodies (and which, as we saw with the Lacanian space of the mirror, ushers in aggressive mastery and control), but through a sense of space as self-generating of the play. As Lorraine describes, "She swirls in space to feel the living vitality of her own body which is in complete contact with the world around her. And yet, through identification with the mother she is also able to retain some sense of self in this twirling. She makes her world in this twirling, and so makes herself" (1999, 31). For a more critical discussion of Irigaray's differentiation between the boy's *fort-da* game and the girl's circle dance as lacking sufficient attention to the roles of power, see Willett 2001, 136–44. I agree with Willett and develop this fundamental critique further below.

37. In these early texts, Irigaray often hints at lesbian separatism; but she never

names it explicitly and never recognizes that such kinds of movements are alive in the U.S. at the time she is writing. In short, she does not historicize her own thinking. The contrast of these early texts with later ones highlights her move toward increasing heterosexism, which we see already in *An Ethics of Sexual Difference* and has come to full fruition since *I Love to You* (1996) and onward. I continue to develop these intertwining dynamics, of both historicity and heterosexism, below.

38. This follows Willett's fundamental critique of Irigaray, which argues that Irigaray finally leans toward a cosmic sort of spiritualism that does not pay sufficient attention to historical power struggles and therefore cannot ground a resistant politics. For Willett, the exemplar is Irigaray's configuration of the placenta as a virginal, unscarred place, rather than as a site affected by the dynamics of power or history; see Willett 2001, 152–53.

39. Irigaray argues that belief is central to patriarchal systems, because one must believe the fiction and fantasy of patriarchy that is fundamentally not true. As she develops, this is what makes belief and religious imagery, such as angels, fundamental sites of phallocentric values. As she writes of belief in phallocentric symbolics, "what deceives some people and destroys others about belief is the way it makes us forget the real. . . . Belief is safe only if that in which or in whom the assembly communes or communicates is subject to concealment. . . . Therefore, I shall term the preliminary to the question of sexual difference: belief itself" (1993c, 27). See 1993c, 26–27, and 30–33 for further discussion.

40. It is all too easy to read these first four characteristics as carrying racial overtones.

41. See, for example, his discussions of intentionality and finitude in *Cartesian Meditations* (Husserl 1977).

42. As I have mentioned and will develop in the remaining three chapters, the effort to transgress limits only reasserts the power of the limit. This helps to explain why Irigaray's figures of lips, touch, mucus, and angels may finally fall back into and reinscribe the logic of containment.

43. Again, these are the Derridean terms in which Deutscher develops Irigaray's central project. See note 31 above.

44. For the earliest assessment of Irigaray's readings of heterosexuality and homosexuality, see Grosz 1994. First published in 1987, this essay argues against an interpretation of Irigaray that sees her as advocating lesbian separatism, a position that is not often held in 2005. Grosz argues that Irigaray attempts to disrupt all models of sexuality, whether homosexual or heterosexual, insofar as they participate in the definitional models and restrictions of being "conceived in phallic terms" (1994, 348). The problem, as Grosz frames it, is one of identity and binary choices. But Grosz nevertheless leaves some of Irigaray's basic assumptions intact—e.g., the conflation of auto-eroticism with homosexuality (1994, 338), which inscribes them both in economies of sameness; and the fundamental teleology of heterosexuality in Irigaray's texts: "Strategic, perhaps even therapeutic, relations to women are prerequisite to viable, ongoing relations between the two sexes." I am sympathetic to Grosz's readings of Irigaray's attempts to disrupt the conceptual schemas through which we identify discrete forms of sexuality within phallocentrism. But her essay seems both dated and overly generous to Irigaray, particularly in the dynamics of historicity she grants Irigaray's texts, as I develop below.

45. Deutscher is, of course, well aware of the thorny discussions of essentialism and addresses them comprehensively. She avoids this term in her critiques of Irigaray's heteronormativity; I use it here not to invoke the debate yet again, but because the gesture

toward erasing the historical enacts a kind of essentialism here. For the most concise laying to rest of the essentialism/constructionism debate *per se* and particularly in Irigaray's texts, see Chanter 1995, preface and chapter 1. See also Fuss 1989 for one of the first and most incisive critiques of this false dichotomy.

46. Deutscher follows Grosz here, arguing that Irigaray is responding to historical conditions and changes in her positing of lesbianism as a provisional and temporary stage through which femininity might be conceived. See Grosz 1994, 338–39.

47. Irigaray has been read as advocating lesbian separatism in these texts, because of her call for "tactical strikes, [wherein women would] keep themselves apart from men long enough to learn to defend their desire" (1985b, 33). But as I indicated above in the mentions of "Boston marriages" and 1970s lesbianism, the models of this lesbian eroticism are hardly erotic: this is political lesbianism at its worst, a call for lesbian relations merely as the apt vehicle for political and philosophical ends, leaving desire aside.

48. It is interesting to note here the proliferation of images of angels across mainstream culture of the U.S. in the early '90s. From a political point of view, this coincided with the full reemergence of the religious right, the sort of political movement that often perpetuates a location in the transcendent ahistorical, a location that cannot offer resistant politics.

4. FREE TO BE QUEER

1. One might readily suggest that the connections between these two experiences are all too obvious: I, like so many lesbians and gay men, had been "liberated" by volume 1 of Foucault's *History of Sexuality*. However, not only is this a gross misreading of Foucault's text, which argues against such narratives of liberation, but I was also far from reading that text as a transformative account of my sense of my own identity. Focusing on abstract questions about method, ethics, and the politics of genealogy, I was not "undergoing' " Foucault's texts in the radical ways that Ladelle McWhorter has so nicely developed (McWhorter 1999, xviii). That would only come after my actual liberation from "Straight College, Pennsylvania," a departure that made many kinds of transformations possible.

2. I am playing with David Halperin's lovely suggestion that gay male body-building creates a specific set of "gay muscles" that circulate only in economies of desire, not utility. See Halperin 1995, 115–19. This will become central to my arguments about the signifier 'queer.'

3. Dynamics of identification become extremely thorny for 'queer politics,' particularly for its attempts to avoid the essentialism involved in traditional narratives of 'coming out' and the consequent exclusionary politics of identity politics. However, queer theorists continue to write in the first-person autobiographical mode, implying a self-identification at work in the text. Eve Sedgwick has suggested that queer can only be auto-descriptive, a move that "dramatises the difference between what you call yourself and what other people call you" (quoted in Jagose 1996, 97) and thereby performs the kind of destabilizing that I will develop below. I also suggest that this first-person narrative voice links queer theorists to the legacies of feminist theory and its persistent attempts to write of dynamics that are simultaneously abstract, political, and personal.

4. I explore this work in greater detail below. See note 9 for a brief bibliography.

5. This argument is implicit in chapters 2 and 3, as will become clearer in this discussion of Hegel. I have argued it more explicitly in Winnubst 1999.

6. I prefer to use the German *Aufhebung* because of the rich, and crucial, senses of both cancellation and elevation that it enacts; these are lost in the English "sublation."

7. See hooks 1992, "Eating the Other." While not explicitly about Hegel, her argument that difference is fetishized as an Other to be commodified, objectified, and then eaten as "a little spice" on the Wonder Bread sandwich of phallicized whiteness pertains nonetheless.

8. Lisa Duggan (Duggan and Hunter 1995, Duggan 2004) and Michael Warner (1999) argue that this logic of liberal tolerance has domesticated gay/lesbian political movements and rendered them the playgrounds of white, elite gays and lesbians. See Warner for a thorough account of both the roots of liberalism in early gay/lesbian politics and the corporatization of that movement across the 1990s. See Duggan 2004 for a thorough account of the emergence of neo-liberalism in the U.S. in the late twentieth century in both mainstream politics and gay/lesbian politics. In the epilogue and in my discussions of queer pleasures below, I hope to augment these arguments for a different kind of queer politics.

9. A sampling of work in ethics of alterity, from a variety of positions, includes Anzaldúa 1987; Butler 2004; Chanter 1995; Deutscher 2002; hooks 1990; Lingis 1994, 2000; Moraga and Anzaldúa 1983; Guha and Spivak 1988; and Ziarek 2001.

10. For a discussion of how I understand the category of subjectivity as a product of high modernity, see chapter 3.

11. Age is, interestingly, one of the ways that straight white males' behavior is regulated in cultures of phallicized whiteness. We have already seen this in the ways that the label of "lecher" can attach to such bodies after a certain age. In light of the discussions to come, Jagose interestingly suggests that age functions as a regulatory index for gay male communities; see Jagose 1996, 70–71.

12. As I will develop below, contemporary U.S. culture has a narrow conception of desire as reducible to sexuality, which is reduced in turn to genitalia. The signification of queer troubles all these reductions.

13. In the summer of 2003, the Supreme Court handed down its historic 6-3 ruling in *Lawrence v. Texas,* thereby abolishing the sodomy laws of the state of Texas and thirteen other states. I return to this ruling and its revalorization of the reduction of sexuality to genitalia below; see note 48.

14. See also Cornell 1992, 19, for discussion of Adorno's reading the ways that the Hegelian system eats its own tail in not allowing an outside, and thus not allowing the very mediation with otherness that is constitutive of identity.

15. The dynamics under discussion here can be articulated in a variety of registers. As I have implied, the dynamics of narcissism and recognition provide another way to articulate the domesticating grasp of desire in Hegel's text. For a thorough critique of any politics of recognition, particularly those developed under the aegis of 'multiculturalism' by Charles Taylor, see Oliver 2001. For a subtle reading that defends the dynamics of narcissism in Derrida and suggests that his sense of difference as differing/deferring could accentuate Irigarayan ethics, see Deutscher 2002, 131–40. I offer a counter-reading to Deutscher's below, see note 41.

16. See Duggan and Hunter 1995, 167; Halperin 1995, 15–16; and McWhorter 1999, xv–xvi, for overviews of these relations.

17. This argument is now taken as a point of departure for queer theorists. Butler 1989 was the first text to argue this circularity between heterosexuality and binary systems of gender. For a humorous reading of this dynamic as it is at work in Carl Sagan's

illustrations for use on NASA's *Pioneer 10* in the early 1970s, see Warner 1993, xxi–xxiii. Finally, I am arguing that phallicized systems work primarily through closed economies, a notion that I implied through Bataille's texts in chapter 1.

18. For one of the earliest arguments about the historical emergence of the category of heterosexuality, see Katz 1990; for a critique of this article from a Foucaultian perspective, arguing that Katz insufficiently historicizes his own epistemic position, see McWhorter 1999, 36–41. For a thorough overview of arguments about the historical emergence of the category of homosexuality, see Jagose 1996, 10–16.

19. Drawing from a quintessentially patriarchal attempt to protect young white girls from prostitution, laws establishing legal ages of consent in the late nineteenth century in both England and the U.S. slowly extended across a wide range of sexual acts, including male homosexuality. For example, in the U.S., the Mann Act, a federal anti-prostitution law passed in 1910, also became known as the White Slave Traffic Act, making explicit that the focus of anxiety was specifically on white female bodies. Rubin goes on to argue that this 'sexual panic' about the activities of young white female bodies grew into the 1950s obsession with 'the homosexual menace' (e.g., the McCarthy hearings' conflation of Communism and homosexuality as the arch-sins against the nation) and 'sex offenders,' which became code for homosexuals. As she writes, "In its bureaucratic, medical, and popular versions, the sex offender discourse tended to blur distinctions between violent sexual assault and illegal but consensual acts such as sodomy" (1993, 5), thus giving ample fuel to the policing and persecuting of homosexuals as sexual deviants and dangers to, of course, those beloved and infantilized white female bodies.

20. Duggan and Jagose also describe the "ethnic model" of identity politics assumed in gay/lesbian liberation movements; see Duggan and Hunter 1995, essay 12; and Jagose 1996, chapter 6, for discussions of problematics endemic to the identity politics model for gay liberation. See also Chasin 2000 and Duggan 2004 on the limitations of identity politics and their neo-liberal frameworks in gay/lesbian political movements.

21. William Turner begins his text on queer theory with exactly this suggestion, noting not only the three highly publicized deaths of 1999—James Byrd, Matthew Shepard, and Billie Jack Gaither—but also the ongoing violence against gays and lesbians (Turner 2000, 1–2).

22. I thereby disagree with Michael Warner's suggestion in his introduction to *Fear of a Queer Planet* that connections between racism, sexism, and homophobia, "whatever [they] might be locally, are not necessary or definitive for any of these antagonisms" (1993, xix). I think we need to continue to push toward the interdependencies in these dynamics, while also preserving their analytic distinction.

23. On March 29, 2001, newspapers in California announced that, according to the 2000 census, this shift has already occurred in California. I delivered a first version of this chapter in San Francisco on March 31, 2001, making my argument rather easy to support.

24. For one of the most well known reflections on the myth of large black penises, see Fanon's *Black Skin, White Masks* (1967).

25. In his excellent articulation of queer politics and ethics, Michael Warner argues in *The Trouble with Normal* (1999) that sexuality fundamentally carries a stigma with it in western cultures, which in turn fuels moralist attempts to control both sexuality itself and, failing to do so, others' sexualities. Warner goes on to argue that this fundamental anxiety or shame about sex itself has also infected gay/lesbian political movements from their beginnings, inserting a contradiction regarding identity and sexual practices at the

very heart of those movements. Describing this contradiction as the tension between "stigmaphile and stigmaphobe" movements, Warner argues that this dynamic will ultimately domesticate those movements, urging them toward "normal," stigmaphobic values of heterosexist cultures—e.g., marriage—and thereby render the movements uninhabitable for queer persons, who may respond differently to the stigma and shame of sexual pleasures. Warner is attuned to the dynamics of race, class, and age in the changing face of who those queer persons are, but never systematizes those dynamics. I am hoping to offer a more synthetic account of how these "normal" values are those of phallicized whiteness and its expression in numerous categories of identity.

26. This disavowal of any "non-useful" energy is surely connected not only to homophobia, but also to racist stereotypes of non-white races as alternatively lazy or hyperefficient. I will return to the social effects of the value of utility in chapter 5.

27. Sexual orientation remains an unprotected category in the federal laws of the United States. As of September 2004, the Employment Non-discrimination Act is still a bill pending full sponsorship in Congress: on October 4, 2002, HR 2692 had 194 cosponsors in the House of Representatives and S.1284 had 45 cosponsors in the Senate. Only fourteen states and the District of Columbia presently have laws prohibiting discrimination on the basis of sexual orientation. For further information, including "scorecards" for members of Congress, see the website of the Human Rights Campaign at http://www.hrc.org.

28. The National Coalition of Anti-Violence Programs reports that there were 2,052 cases of physical violence reported against lesbians, gays, bisexuals, and transgender people (both male-to-female and female-to-male) in 2003 (http://www.avp.org/publications/reports/2003NCAVP_HV_Report.pdf, accessed April 4, 2005). In addition to these, considerable psychological damage continues to be caused by alienation from biological families, religious supports, and other networks of kinship that are assumed by heterosexuals in U.S. culture.

29. Queer theorists have been aware of these pitfalls for a long time. For a historical overview of the shifts from homophile to gay liberation to lesbian feminism to queer theory/politics, see Jagose 1996 and Warner 1999; for the dangers and epistemological impossibilities involved in narratives of coming out, see Sedgwick 1993; for a particularly self-conscious rumination on the ways that discourses of coming out threaten to locate the person doing so in a matrix of medical and political normalization, see McWhorter 1999; and for the argument that "*any* gay politics based on the primacy of sexual identity defined as unitary and 'essential' . . . ultimately represents the view from the subject position 'twentieth-century, Western, white, gay male,' " see Duggan and Hunter 1995, 162.

30. This passage is a favorite of queer theorists working with Foucault. See Halperin 1995, 193–94, note 9; and McWhorter 1999, 223.

31. For a comprehensive overview of such positions, see Jagose 1996. See also Abelove, Barale, and Halperin 1993, Halperin 1995, Warner 1993.

32. On the critical role of identification papers to one's subjectivity, see Fuss 1995; on this as specifically a queer phenomenon, see Halperin 1995; and on the material difficulties and dangers presented to transnational g/l/b/t relationships, see Miller 2002.

33. Anzaldúa uses the categories of sexuality interchangeably: queer, gay, lesbian, homosexual all signify in similar ways in her texts. She constantly connects sexuality and race, the intersections in which she lived her life. She writes of the evolutionary purpose of the queer and mestizo at this point in history: "Being the supreme crossers of cultures, homosexuals have strong bonds with the queer white, Black, Asian, Native American,

Latino, and with the queer in Italy, Australia and the rest of the planet. We come from all colors, all classes, all races, all time periods. Our role is to link people with each other—the Blacks with Jews with Indians with Asians with whites with extraterrestrials" (1987, 84–85).

34. On confusing kinship systems, see Haraway 1997 and Winnubst 2003. On the reworking of family in the "house-system" of *Paris is Burning*, despite the reidealizing of heterosexuality and whiteness, see Butler 1993, Essay 4. And, of course, there is the slang in which g/l/b/t communities refer to themselves and their members as 'family,' a code word that only grows more and more clever as the rhetoric of family values increases from the religious right.

35. As my students will readily attest, I am the daughter of a grammar snob. My disdain for this seemingly endless 'verbification' of nouns in the English of the U.S. runs deep. To call for the redeployment of this alleged noun always in its verbal form is therefore also to laugh at myself rather heartily. But queer has called to me as a verb and not a noun from my first encounters with it: my favorite slogan for those pride marches in central Pennsylvania in 1993 was "Queerify Straight College."

36. Jagose argues that "queer" is a category that cannot be delimited (1996, 7–9) and remains hopeful that this lack of specificity can result in non-exclusionary politics (76). She also quotes Hennesy as characterizing queer as "anti-assimilationist and anti-separatist" (99). Duggan offers a great snapshot of the "various contradictory definitions [of 'queer' that often] coexist—in a single group, or in an individual's mind" (Duggan and Hunter 1995, 165–67). Halperin also reads queer as signifying both a fundamental refusal of identity and resistance to the 'liberation' of identity politics: "Those who knowingly occupy such a marginal location, who assume a de-essentialized identity that is purely positional in character, are properly speaking not gay but *queer*" (1995, 62). I return to the nasty problems of exclusionary politics below and in note 38.

37. My own sense of American culture gives itself away here, clearly. As national elections increasingly indicate, the U.S. is becoming two nations: urban and rural.

38. On the difficulties of exclusion endemic to identity politics and on the specific racial exclusions of queer as a white-centered identification, see Butler 1993, 226–30, and Chasin 2000, 225–29; on the way the term queer gives a false impression of inclusiveness that once again erases differences within 'queer communities' and provides "a means of de-gaying gayness," see Halperin 1995, 64–67; and for hopes that queer's non-specificity could still render it non-exclusive, see Jagose 1996, 76. Again, on the marketability of 'queer,' one need merely pay attention to the headlines of the *New York Times* and, beginning in 2003, witness the phenomenon of television's biological essentialism on parade in *Queer Eye for a Straight Guy*, where gay men are both signified as 'queer' and presented as harboring some essential disposition toward style. For a critical analysis of this series and other recent television representations of g/l/b/t lives, see Straayer and Waugh 2005. See also Chasin 2000 on the ways that market consumption and identity politics mutually implicate one another, and on the ways they perpetuate white supremacist racism within gay/lesbian markets and politics (e.g., 48–49, 224).

39. Diagnosing the schematic of subjectivity grounded in desire as a mechanism of domination, Foucault concludes volume 1 of *The History of Sexuality* with a provocation: "The rallying point for the counterattack against the deployment of sexuality ought not to be sexual desire, but bodies and pleasures" (1978, 157). McWhorter grounds her 1999 text in this dynamic, entitling it *Bodies and Pleasures*.

40. "On Truth and Lying" (1872), in Nietzsche 1989.

41. I hereby disagree explicitly with Deutscher's arguments regarding Derridean and Irigarayan ethics and will turn toward Bataille both later in this chapter and in chapter 6 to explore a position that grounds itself in an excess of possibilities, rather than this lack of the logic of desire. We can also hear echoes of these disagreements in the role that the future plays as the endlessly pursued horizon of satisfaction that lack never achieves; the future cannot be the temporality of queering, as I develop in chapters 5 and 6.

42. We can see this easily in Hegel's texts, where that which is meaningful is that which Hegel assumes all human rationality seeks. We can also see it in both Hegel's and Aristotle's language: particularly in the forms used, Aristotle's *periechontos* and Hegel's *begreifen* and *Begriff* connote not only the physical senses to surround, encompass, embrace, handle, and grasp, but also the mental acts of understanding, conceiving, realizing, and comprehending. For both Hegel and Aristotle, to be delimited or 'in place' means to be thinking well and grasping experience fully, displaying a predilection toward that which is "meaningful" as the telos of human consciousness.

43. I want to emphasize that I do not write this as a mere abstraction. The writing of this book has brought with it various forms of anxiety, and many, many people in the U.S. suffer from anxiety in such debilitating ways that they would not be able to function without chemical relief. In my experience with such maladies, however, no one would prefer those chemicals to a transformation of energy that would allow the energy burned in anxiety to be rechanneled into more sustaining forms of psychic life. It is toward that transformation that I am arguing the queering of our pleasures might take us.

44. Hegel's discussion of the 'good' and 'bad' infinites in the *Science of Logic* reads ('good') infinity as the very horizon on which identity is formed. He argues that, as finite beings, we unfold on an infinite plane of relation. Infinity thus may appear to transcend the finite, but the finite is "in no sense acted on by an alien force" (1969, 138). Infinity is not the mere negation of what is finite, but the true realization by the finite of finitude's ground of being: infinity is what 'gives finitude place.' This effectively keeps Hegel from conceiving of an infinite that is not oriented always toward the finite, toward a 'place.'

45. Bataille reads this as the ontological ground of the practices of sacrifice. See *Theory of Religion* (1992) for more details; and volume 2 of *The Accursed Share* (1988–91, 2:51–56).

46. As I have already noted, a good deal of queer theory has drawn on volume 1 of Foucault's *History of Sexuality* to argue for the emergence of queer politics out of the realm of sexuality. I hope to augment those discussions with this emphasis on Bataille, a writer who influenced Foucault's thinking and often offers a more ontological account for Foucault's historical arguments. I return to these connections between these two thinkers in the first section of chapter 6.

47. See particularly "The Notion of Expenditure" and "The Language of Flowers" in *Visions of Excess* (1985) as well as volume 1 of *The Accursed Share* (1988–91).

48. On June 26, 2003, in *Lawrence v. Texas*, the Supreme Court struck down the sodomy laws of Texas, effectively erasing all remaining anti-sodomy laws in the U.S. This is a historical breakthrough for the rights of g/l/b/t communities, and its reverberations may be far-reaching: it is a historical moment of liberation. But, in keeping with my prior questioning of liberation, I emphasize that this case continues the explicit reduction of sexuality to genitals. It is not only about sodomy, a very specific act of genitals, but more particularly about what the genitals of men may and may not do with other men's

genitals. It reduces g/l/b/t lives to genitals, marking them out as once again the problematized arena. To queer is to exceed such a reduction.

49. See Sprinkle 2001, Bornstein 1994, and Califia 2000.

50. I have Story of the Eye (1987) and Blue of Noon (1986) particularly in mind here.

51. See note 2 above.

52. In his lamentation over "the geography of shame . . . being mapped for New York City" under Mayor Giuliani, Michael Warner turns to Henry Lefebvre's accounts of urban space, where people "need to accumulate energies and to spend them, even waste them in play" (1999, 191). Connecting queer lives and pleasures to this disavowal of utility, Warner sees in Lefebvre's accounts the recognition "that the worldliness of the city is inseparable from the possibilities of waste, play, and sex—in other words, from its more or less queer appropriations" (1999, 192). In this context, we may be losing not only queer values, but also the very existence of urban space, in the U.S.: doesn't Times Square feel like a suburban mall?

53. I had great fun one evening attempting to map out whether some of these positions are humanly possible with a group of ten (slightly—but only very slightly—stunned) undergraduate students in the Seminar on Bataille at Southwestern University in the fall of 2001. I am grateful to all the students in that wonderful, if sometimes trying, seminar for their energy and indulgence.

5. The Temporality of Whiteness

1. The films of Spike Lee, for example, talk about "CPT."

2. Report on All Things Considered, National Public Radio, July 2001. This same 'logic' has also been used for countries in Latin America, where it has been argued that combinations of anti-viral drugs (a.k.a. "cocktails") should not be prescribed because inhabitants of poorer countries are unable to follow a complicated medication timetable. On July 15, 2003, Jim Lehrer's NewsHour refuted such claims with the report that persons with HIV in Brazil now take their HIV meds more regularly than persons in Baltimore, and at about the same rate of regularity as those in London. The narrative at work here is what Cindy Patton diagnoses as the "tropical model" of AIDS discourse, wherein colonialism reasserts itself; see Patton 2002 and chapter 6 for further discussion.

3. See James Gleick's Faster (1999) for a quick tour through "the acceleration of just about everything" (its subtitle). Gleick catalogs the various ways that lives in the late twentieth century have become increasingly accelerated and talks explicitly about Asian cultures in this regard, while not noting the stereotypes such descriptions may perpetuate. I am grateful to K. D. Winnubst for letting me steal this book from her collection.

4. See Winnubst 1999 for both this argument about western metaphysics and a more detailed account of the Lacanian interpolation of this Hegelian metaphysics.

5. While aptly translated as "excess" or "abundance," poros carries a connotation of a limited sort of abundance, one that is always oriented teleologically. Insofar as desire has developed into a mechanism dominated by lack rather than excess, this more limited notion of abundance may be a more accurate rendering of Plato's Greek.

6. There is a great deal of interesting and provocative work on traveling, particularly as an imperialist impulse and strategy of domination. A brief sampling of this work includes Clifford 1989, Grewal and Kaplan 1994, hooks 1990, Kaplan 1996, Kincaid

1988, Lugones 2003. For an essay that traces the specific imperialist structures of white gay travel, see Alexander 1998; and for speculative work on the possibilities of a "queer" tourism that might resist these imperialist structures, see Puar 2002.

7. There are, we can hope, different kinds of travel, in which travelers engage the culture to which they are traveling and may even be transformed by it. One salient way to distinguish types of travel is to investigate their temporal modes.

8. For another discussion of the sleight of hand always at work in feminine work, which must never appear as work in order to protect this ideal of idleness, see McClintock 1995. I thank Amy Wendling for this latter point.

9. Clinton offered an apology for slavery on his trip to Uganda in March 1998. The U.S. Congress rejected a resolution for such an apology in 2000, but another resolution was reintroduced on June 19, 2003. As I note below, George W. Bush side-stepped the issue of apology during his visit to Africa in July 2003.

10. For a concise argument that capitalism is a religion, see Loy 1997. I am grateful to Laura Hobgood-Oster for bringing this field of study to my attention. See also Walter Benjamin's provocative essay "Capitalism as Religion" (Benjamin 1996).

11. Of course, this $1 + 1 + 1 \ldots$ formulation invokes Irigaray's use of it to depict the inability of phallocentrism to count to two, to conceive of sexual difference. See "This Sex Which Is Not One" in Irigaray 1985b.

12. See "The Hermeneutics of the Self," two 1980 lectures by Foucault, in Foucault 1999; see also Foucault 1990b.

13. See "The Hermeneutics of the Self" (Foucault 1999). I do not mean to suggest that Foucault is "wrong" about practices of confession. To the contrary, these lectures have provoked and informed my thinking here. I am merely working out a specific cultural dynamic, white guilt, that was not part of Foucault's purview in these lectures.

14. Private conversation, July 8, 2003. Marshall's work on the problem of evil suggests that this persistent future orientation also facilitates U.S. culture's projection of its own internal evil outward onto others—most often black or brown others. Just think of the string of "evil" enemies that have plagued the U.S. since World War II. See Marshall 2002.

15. M. Jacqui Alexander's essay focuses on the ways that women of color in 2002 might re-member, and reembody, the writings included in *This Bridge Called My Back*, published in 1983. But what she writes there stretches toward the kinds of memory that white guilt will always deny, and the kinds that may reinvigorate and sustain politics of resistance. I am grateful to Shireen Roshanravan for bringing this essay to my attention.

16. We can hear this fundamental narcissism at work in George W. Bush's speech at Goree Island, Senegal, on July 8, 2003. While he recognized the horrors that occurred in this place, the place where millions of Africans were deported to the North Atlantic slave trade, he nonetheless framed his speech by what that meant for America: "the stolen sons and daughters of Africa helped to awaken the conscience of America" (transcript at http://usinfo.state.gov/regional/af/potus2003/a3070815.htm). Once again, the plight of the black race is only meaningful in its relation to the white race. I also note that George W. Bush did not offer any apology for these horrors of his country's past.

6. The Freedom of Sovereignty

1. Foucault, of course, read Bataille and was influenced by him. Although he only wrote one essay on him, "Hommage à Georges Bataille" (translated into English as "A

Preface to Transgression" in Foucault 1977b), Bataille's sense of general economy, pleasure rather than desire, and non-productive expenditure thread through Foucault's thinking. More explicitly, Foucault also assisted in the publication of Bataille's *Oeuvres complètes* (1973) and was a frequent contributor to and editorial consultant for *Critique,* a journal founded by Bataille (see note 1 to "A Preface to Transgression").

2. Here we may see the critique of Hegel's infamous Master in his Master-Slave dialectic at work in Bataille's thinking. Having reduced his world to the order of utility, Hegel's Master is ultimately deluded about the order of life and thereby sublated by the Slave's eventual move into Reason. However, as I develop below, Bataille resists this move into Reason because it also inhabits a subtle valorization of utility and the order of things; it is out of this resistance that he writes of the sovereignty of non-knowing.

3. A sampling of recent such work includes Ziarek 2001, Deutscher 2002, Halperin 1995, Lorraine 1999, McWhorter 1999. Edelman 2004 was published too late for consideration here.

4. And they are sketches. Particularly with the examples of consumer practices and remembering AIDS, my work here is meant to give an outline of how these queer practices might unfold and provoke us toward further thinking; it is not a comprehensive study, I have only scratched the surface of extant scholarship in these fertile areas.

5. For one of the most comprehensive looks at the history of the institution of marriage and contemporary debates around same-sex marriage, see Warner 1999. Warner thoroughly demonstrates how this debate, which has only heightened since 1999, has effectively de-queered g/l/b/t politics. See the epilogue for further discussion of this issue.

6. This leads Lugones to conclude that resistance will lie primarily in the ability to read these multiple differences and to read them in their historical specificities: "It is of great interest for emancipatory work that we can cross-reference different realities" (2003, 15).

7. Agreeing with Lugones, bell hooks has recently suggested (in a lecture at Southwestern University on October 8, 2003) that the psychological registers of denial and disassociation may best describe the mental state of those in power in cultures of phallicized whiteness.

8. For Bataille's placement of war as an acceptable receptacle for excessive energy of market economies, see volume 1 of *The Accursed Share* (1988–91), especially 24ff.

9. Private conversation, January 23, 2004.

10. The examples of this disparity in the relation to money can become overwhelming. For a recent cultural example, see the MTV show *Pimp My Ride* (2004–) where poor people are given lavish amounts of money to fix up their broken-down cars in the most outrageous ways possible—e.g., with a home theater of six screens built into the floorboards of an old Pontiac. This is hardly a way of spending money that middle-class values of hoarding and saving can approve; and yet it likely strikes some chords of envy.

11. I am grateful to Jennifer Suchland for this example and practice, which she has developed in her own classrooms.

12. This ranking is given on the GeographyIQ.com website, at http://www.geo graphyiq.com/ranking/ranking_Televisions_top25.htm, accessed March 15, 2005.

13. These figures and rankings are taken from the CIA World Factbook (http://www.cia.gov/cia/publications/factbook/geos/th.html; http://www.odci.gov/ cia/publications/factbook/rankorder/2004rank.html) and GeographyIQ.com(http:// www.geographyiq.com/ranking/ranking_GDP_per_capita_purchasing_power_parity _dall.htm), both accessed March 15, 2005.

14. The facts regarding exports are taken from *The Economist*'s Country Briefings (http://www.economist.com/countries/Thailand/profile.cfm?folder=Profile-FactSheet), and the facts regarding television ownership are taken from the GeographyIQ.com Web page cited in note 12 (both accessed April 4, 2005).

15. For an excellent discussion of the remarkable imbalance in distribution of wealth both within the United States and globally, see Willett 2001, chapter 5. And for an analysis of the connection between this alleged scarcity and practices of pleasure and sexuality, see Singer 1993.

16. See Sontag 1989 for this argument, particularly in contrast to nineteenth-century treatments of tuberculosis and consumption, as well as medieval treatments of the bubonic plague.

17. As Douglas Crimp explains, "What is now called AIDS was first *seen* in middle-class gay men in America, in part because of our access to medical care. Retrospectively, however, it appears that IV drug users—whether gay or straight—were dying of AIDS in New York City throughout the 70's and early 80's, but a class-based and racist health care system failed to notice, and an epidemiology equally skewed by class and racial bias failed to begin to look *until 1987*" (1987, 249). See also Patton 2002 for a Foucaultian genealogy of activism prior to and in the midst of the diagnosis of AIDS as a "spectrum disease," one which has many manifestations and consequently no singular cause: it is a queer virus through and through. Patton pleads with us not to forget these histories.

18. In 1997, AIDS-related deaths in the U.S. were down 40 percent over 1996; it appeared in media reports that AIDS had been conquered. But in 1998, African American leaders declared a "state of emergency" in African American communities; and by 2002, HIV had become the leading cause of death worldwide among those 15–59 years old. As of 2004, the death toll due to AIDS is approximately 20 million. Information taken from the Kaiser Family Foundation website, http://www.kff.org/hivaids/timeline/index.cfm, accessed January 5, 2005.

19. See Patton 2002, particularly chapter 2, for an excellent analysis of how two primary models have dominated medical as well as socio-psychic discourses on AIDS: the tropical model that follows colonialist narratives of "unsafe but tantalizing" savagery and "safe and clean" home and primarily protects the masculine colonist; and the epidemiological model that reads the disease through patterns of contagion, with contamination as the primary trope, and primarily protects middle-class heterosexuals. While these two models have most often operated through overlapping and intermittent borrowing from one another, Patton concludes the text arguing that we are returning to a more purely tropical model as the pandemic sweeps into Africa and Asia. As of 2004, of the 40 million people living with AIDS, sub-Saharan Africa accounts for 64 percent (25.4 million) and South/Southeast Asia accounts for 18 percent (7.1 million); most forecasters expect a rapid explosion of infections in Russia and India, primarily due to intravenous drug use and heterosexual contact, in the coming years (Kaiser Family Foundation website, http://www.kff.org/hivaids/loader.cfm?url=/commonspot/security/getfile.cfm&pageID=49626, accessed January 5, 2005).

20. See Patton 2002, particularly chapter 1, for an excellent genealogy of these practices.

21. A visit to GMHC's website, http://www.gmhc.org, shows how this organization remains a cutting-edge effort to deal with AIDS in *all* of its manifestations, not just those limited to the identity politics of gay men. While it does maintain a focus on the

U.S., it offers services to a wide span of groups affected by AIDS/HIV: drug users, immigrants, women, sex workers, non–English speakers, and so on.

22. I draw this information from Crimp's essay; see his note 29. This sort of rapid change in behavior contrasts sharply with the lack of widespread behavioral change in response to the rhetoric of fear that drives anti-smoking campaigns in the U.S. However, as Patton cautions, the rise of the condom (to pun badly) as the symbol of safe sex is complicated, and may even have damaging effects, in transnational settings, where men who have sex with men are often already involved in safe-sex practices and the intro-duction of anal intercourse as the 'normative act' actually introduces unsafe practices where they were not being undertaken (2002: 84–86); the educational potential of this kind of eroticism seems limited to the U.S. See also Patton 2002, chapter 2, note 3, for a dis-cussion of how the condom is linked to the epidemiological model of containment and how the anti-condom practices of "bare-backing" may signify a return to the tropical model.

23. The Helms amendment, passed in 1988, forbade the use of federal funds to provide "AIDS education, information, or prevention materials and activities that pro-mote or encourage, directly or indirectly, homosexual sexual activities" (quoted in Crimp 1987, 259). See Crimp 1987 for an excellent analysis of this sex phobia that fueled the U.S. response to AIDS and threatened the care of tens of thousands of people.

24. In 2004, the Texas state legislature agreed to ban all safe-sex education materials from its textbooks; the only form of birth control, as well as of safe sex, that the youth of Texas will now be taught about is abstinence. Crimp notes that this campaign against sex itself was already a part of the fear campaign regarding AIDS launched by the federal government. Showing the general sex phobia that reigned at the time, Crimp first cites an outrageous letter from the banana industry protesting the use of a banana as a prop to educate men on how to put on a condom on PBS; he then explains how much of the federal government's advertisements regarding AIDS, particularly those targeting teen-agers, equated AIDS with sex, rendering both murderous. Thankfully, Crimp concludes his essay with the queer work of John Greyson and Isaac Julien, each of whom launched a counter-campaign against "ADS"—Acquired Dread of Sex.

25. For the information on needle-exchange programs, see information under "1998" in the concise overview of the AIDS epidemic, A Timeline of Key Milestones," on the Kaiser Family Foundation's website, at http://www.kff.org/hivaids/timeline/index.cfm. For a discussion of the World Health Organization, see Patton 2002, 28–29.

26. For an excellent discussion of the longstanding attack on pleasure that was then reinvigorated through the AIDS epidemic, see Singer 1993. Singer also connects these disciplines of pleasure (including prostitution, pornography, addiction) with economies of scarcity, particularly those constitutive of advanced capitalism.

27. The work of GMHC was never driven by identity politics: it served the needs of anyone and everyone living with AIDS. And the practices that it, along with activist groups such as ACT-UP, spawned often gave rise to powerful senses of communal selves and politics. For a graphic expression of this different sort of 'self,' see the artwork of Keith Haring, who also died of AIDS, where bodies and figures twist and turn and play with one another in such a wild conglomeration that it is never clear where one ends and another begins.

EPILOGUE

1. As cited in chapter 6, Michael Warner's analysis of the history of the institution of marriage and contemporary debates around same-sex marriage remains one of the most incisive queer critiques; see Warner 1999. For a more recent collection of progressive, if not fully queer, approaches to the intensified debates of 2004, see the articles published in the July 5, 2004, issue of *The Nation*, which was entitled *State of the Union: The Marriage Issue*. For an excellent queer analysis of the same-sex marriage movement and its implication in marriage as the site of production of properly racialized, gendered, and heterosexual citizens, see Brandzel 2005. And for a collection of articles both for and against same-sex marriage, including a few from a queer perspective, see the links listed under "Radical Queer Articles & Essays" at http://www.anarcha.org/sallydarity/radicalqueer.php, accessed April 7, 2005.

2. I have in mind particularly sex radicals' critiques of the normative function of monogamy in the same-sex marriage movement—at the expense of non-monogamous couples, people whose homes and families are not constituted by sexual relationships, polyamorous people, sex workers, s/m practitioners, etc.; for discussions of these critiques, see Warner 1999.

3. This is the number that the Human Rights Campaign circulated early in the mainstreaming of the same-sex marriage movement. See http://www.marriage equality.org/1049.pdf, accessed April 12, 2005.

4. The article also draws on the work of The National Black Justice Coalition.

5. For an enumeration of the major problems facing transgender persons, see Minter and Daley 2003. While their work admits its own limitations as a snapshot of San Francisco in 2002 and likely an overrepresentation of European Americans, it still offers a general overview of the legal challenges facing transgender people across the U.S.

6. Because such spaces are the least likely to honor gender reidentification, transgender persons are at extreme risk for violence in these spaces. As Dean Spade explained (2005), most of us—with private homes, bathrooms, sleeping quarters, and so on—do not experience the world as strictly sex-segregated; but for those living at the edges of this society, the world is completely sex-segregated. For overviews of how transgender people become both homeless and incarcerated at disproportionate rates compared to the rest of the population, see the Sylvia Rivera Law Project's Web site, http://www.srlp.org, especially the two flow charts on homelessness and incarceration.

7. For example, a "gay marriage" episode of *The Simpsons* aired in February 2005, to the great pleasure and amusement of most gay communities. An episode that received a lot of attention in the gay press, it featured the coming out of Marge Simpson's sister as she announces her plans to marry her lesbian lover. Marge rallies around the rights of gays and lesbians to marry and *The Simpsons* once more appears to be a bastion of progressive politics. But Marge discovers that the lover is actually a man posing as a woman so that she can be a competitive professional golfer. The sister is outraged and, despite the lover's pleas of adoration and commitment, she breaks off the relationship in disgust: transphobia serves up not only a platform for same-sex marriage, but a hearty laugh as well. The gay press largely loved it.

8. As Willse argues, even if the marriage laws do change, "the ability to access some of the very important material privileges of marriage would not be the same for all people. So for example: A working class gay person who has a job without health coverage will not be able to extend their nonexistent benefits to their new gay spouse. Gay people

of color in prison will still lose custody rights to their children. Queer immigrants, particularly those whose sex lives do not fit the model of marriage (for example, non-monogamous queers), will still be subjected to anti-immigrant violence, laws, and deportation. Trans parents will still have their children taken away by judges who think trans homes are inappropriate and unsafe" (2004).

REFERENCES

Abel, Elizabeth, Barbara Christian, and Helene Moglen, eds. 1997. *Female Subjects in Black and White: Race, Psychoanalysis, Feminism.* Berkeley: University of California Press.

Abelove, Henry, Michèle Aina Barale, and David M. Halperin, eds. 1993. *The Lesbian and Gay Studies Reader.* New York: Routledge.

Alexander, M. Jacqui. 1998. Imperial Desire/Sexual Utopias: White Gay Capital and Transnational Tourism. In *Talking Visions: Multicultural Feminism in a Transnational Age*, ed. Ella Shohat. Cambridge, Mass.: MIT Press.

———. 2002. Remembering *This Bridge*, Remembering Ourselves: Yearning, Memory, and Desire. In *This Bridge We Call Home: Radical Visions for Transformation*, ed. Gloria Anzaldúa and AnaLouise Keating. New York: Routledge.

American Beauty. 1999. Dir. Sam Mendes. Dreamworks.

Anzaldúa, Gloria. 1987. *Borderlands = La Frontera: The New Mestiza.* San Francisco: Aunt Lute.

Appiah, Kwame Anthony. 1992. *In My Father's House: Africa in the Philosophy of Culture.* New York: Oxford University Press.

Aristotle. 1996. *Physics.* Trans. Philip H. Wicksteed and Francis M. Cornford. Cambridge, Mass.: Harvard University Press.

Bartky, Sandra Lee. 1988. Foucault, Femininity, and the Modernization of Patriarchal Power. In *Feminism and Foucault: Reflections on Resistance*, ed. Irene Diamond and Lee Quinby. Boston, Mass.: Northeastern University Press.

Bataille, Georges. 1973. *Oeuvres complètes.* Paris: Gallimard.

———. 1985a. *Visions of Excess: Selected Writings, 1927–1939.* Ed. Allan Stoekl. Trans. Allan Stoekl, with Carl R. Lovitts and Donald M. Leslie, Jr. Minneapolis: University of Minnesota Press.

———. 1986. *Blue of Noon.* Trans. Harry Mathews. New York: Marion Boyars.

———. 1987. *The Story of the Eye.* Trans. Joachim Neugroschel. San Francisco: City Lights.

———. 1988–91. *The Accursed Share: An Essay on General Economy.* 3 vols. in 2. Trans. Robert Hurley. New York: Zone.

———. 1992. *Theory of Religion.* Trans. Robert Hurley. New York: Zone.

Belz, Herman. 1991. *Equality Transformed: A Quarter-Century of Affirmative Action.* New Brunswick, N.J.: Transaction.

Benjamin, Walter. 1969. Theses on the Philosophy of History, Thesis IX. In *Illuminations*, ed. Hannah Arendt, trans. Harry Zohn. New York: Schocken.

———. 1996. Capitalism as Religion. In *Selected Writings, Volume 1: 1913–1926*, ed.

239

Marcus Bullock and Michael W. Jennings. Cambridge, Mass.: Harvard University Press.

Bergner, Gwen. 1995. Who Is That Masked Woman? or, The Role of Gender in Fanon's *Black Skin, White Masks. Publications of the Modern Language Association* 110 (1): 75–88.

Bhabha, Homi K. 1990. Interrogating Identity: The Postcolonial Prerogative. In *Anatomy of Racism,* ed. David Theo Goldberg. Minneapolis: University of Minnesota Press.

Bledsoe, Casey. 1997. Becoming-Embodied through Deleuze, Irigaray, and Grosz: A Feminist, Anti-fascist Corporeality. Honors thesis, Southwestern University.

Borges, Jorge Luis. 1968. *Other Inquisitions, 1937–1952.* Trans. Ruth L. C. Simms. New York: Simon and Schuster.

Bornstein, Kate. 1994. *Gender Outlaw: On Men, Women, and the Rest of Us.* New York: Routledge.

Boswell, Maia. 1999. "Ladies," "Gentlemen," and "Colored": "The Agency of (Lacan's Black) Letter" in the Outhouse. *Cultural Critique* 41 (Winter): 108–38.

Braidotti, Rosi. 1991. *Patterns of Dissonance: A Study of Women in Contemporary Philosophy.* Trans. Elizabeth Guild. New York: Columbia University Press.

———. 1994. *Nomadic Subjects: Embodiment and Sexual Difference in Contemporary Feminist Theory.* New York: Columbia University Press.

Brandzel, Amy L. 2005. Queering Citizenship? Same-Sex Marriage and the State. *glq: A Journal of Lesbian and Gay Studies* 11 (5): 171–204.

Brennan, Teresa. 1993. *History after Lacan.* New York: Routledge.

Brown, Wendy. 1995. *States of Injury: Power and Freedom in Late Modernity.* Princeton, N.J.: Princeton University Press.

———. 2002. Tolerance and the Legitimation of State Violence. Public lecture delivered at the University of Texas at Austin, February 28.

Burke, Carolyn. 1994. Translation Modified: Irigaray in English. In *Engaging with Irigaray: Feminist Philosophy and Modern European Thought,* ed. Carolyn L. Burke, Naomi Schor, and Margaret Whitford. New York: Columbia University Press.

Butler, Judith. 1989. *Gender Trouble: Feminism and the Subversion of Identity.* New York: Routledge.

———. 1992. The Body You Want: An Interview with Judith Butler. *Artforum* 31 (3): 82–89.

———. 1993. *Bodies That Matter: On the Discursive Limits of "Sex."* New York: Routledge.

———. 2004. *Precarious Life: The Powers of Mourning and Violence.* New York: Verso.

Califia, Pat. 2000. *Public Sex: The Culture of Radical Sex.* San Francisco: Cleis.

Chanter, Tina. 1995. *Ethics of Eros: Irigaray's Rewriting of the Philosophers.* New York: Routledge.

Chasin, Alexandra. 2000. *Selling Out: The Gay and Lesbian Movement Goes to Market.* New York: St. Martin's.

Clifford, James. 1989. Notes on Theory and Travel. *Inscriptions* 5: 177–88.

Copjec, Joan. 1994. *Read My Desire: Lacan against the Historicists.* Cambridge, Mass.: MIT Press.

Cornell, Drucilla. 1992. *The Philosophy of the Limit.* New York: Routledge.

Crimp, Douglas, 1987. How to Have Promiscuity in an Epidemic. In *AIDS: Cultural Analysis, Cultural Activism,* ed. Douglas Crimp. Cambridge, Mass.: MIT Press.

Cuomo, Chris J., and Kim Q. Hall, eds. 1999. *Whiteness: Feminist Philosophical Reflections.* Lanham, Md.: Rowman & Littlefield.

Davis, Angela. 1981. *Women, Race, and Class.* New York: Random House.

Davis, Mike. 1994. *City of Quartz: Excavating the Future in Los Angeles.* New York: Verso.

Delphy, Christine. 1993. Rethinking Sex and Gender. Trans. Diana Leonard. *Women's Studies International Forum* 16 (1): 1–9.

Derrida, Jacques. 1978. From Restricted to General Economy: A Hegelianism without Reserve. In *Writing and Difference,* trans. Alan Bass. Chicago: University of Chicago Press.

Descartes, René. 1964. *The Meditations Concerning First Philosophy.* In *Philosophical Essays,* trans. Laurence LaFleur. New York: Macmillan.

Deutscher, Penelope. 2002. *A Politics of Impossible Difference: The Later Work of Luce Irigaray.* Ithaca, N.Y.: Cornell University Press.

Duggan, Lisa. 2004. *The Twilight of Equality? Neoliberalism, Cultural Politics, and the Attack on Democracy.* Boston, Mass.: Beacon.

Duggan, Lisa, and Nan D. Hunter, eds. 1995. *Sex Wars: Sexual Dissent and Political Culture.* New York: Routledge.

Dyer, Richard. 1997. *White.* New York: Routledge.

Echols, Alice. 1989. *Daring to Be Bad: Radical Feminism in America, 1967–1975.* Minneapolis: University of Minnesota Press.

Edelman, Lee. 2004. *No Future: Queer Theory and the Death Drive.* Durham, N.C.: Duke University Press.

Ellison, Ralph. 1952. *Invisible Man.* New York: Modern Library.

Eze, Emmanuel Chukwudi. 2001. *Achieving Our Humanity: The Idea of the Postracial Future.* New York: Routledge.

Fanon, Frantz. 1967. *Black Skin, White Masks.* Trans. Charles Lam Markmann. New York: Grove.

Farrow, Kenyon. 2004. Is Gay Marriage Anti-Black? http://www.illegalvoices.org/knowledge/general_articles/is_gay_marriage_anti-black_.html, accessed April 7, 2005.

Ferrell, Robyn. 1996. *Passion in Theory: Conceptions of Freud and Lacan.* New York: Routledge.

Foucault, Michel. 1970. *The Order of Things: An Archaeology of the Human Sciences.* New York: Vintage.

———. 1972. *The Archaeology of Knowledge and the Discourse on Language.* Trans. A. M. Sheridan Smith. New York: Pantheon.

———. 1977a. *Discipline and Punish: The Birth of the Prison.* Trans. Alan Sheridan. New York: Vintage.

———. 1977b. *Language, Counter-Memory, Practice: Selected Essays and Interviews by Michel Foucault.* Ed. Donald F. Bouchard. Ithaca, N.Y.: Cornell University Press.

———. 1978. *The History of Sexuality.* Vol. 1, *An Introduction.* Trans. Robert Hurley. New York: Vintage.

———. 1990a. *The History of Sexuality.* Vol. 2, *The Use of Pleasure.* Trans. Robert Hurley. New York: Vintage.

———. 1990b. *The History of Sexuality.* Vol. 3, *Care of the Self.* Trans. Robert Hurley. New York: Vintage.

———. 1997. *Ethics: Subjectivity and Truth.* Ed. Paul Rabinow. Trans. Robert Hurley and others. Vol. 1 of *The Essential Works of Michel Foucault.* New York: New Press.

———. 1999. *Religion and Culture: Michael Foucault*. Ed. Jeremy R. Carrette. New York: Routledge.

Frankenberg, Ruth. 1997a. *Displacing Whiteness: Essays in Social and Cultural Criticism.* Durham, N.C.: Duke University Press.

———. 1997b. White Women, Race Matters: The Social Construction of Racism. In *Critical White Studies: Looking behind the Mirror,* ed. Richard Delgado and Jean Stefancic. Philadelphia: Temple University Press.

Fuss, Diana. 1989. *Essentially Speaking: Feminism, Nature, and Difference.* New York: Routledge.

———. 1995. *Identification Papers.* New York: Routledge.

Gadamer, Hans-Georg. 1986. *The Idea of the Good in Platonic-Aristotelian Philosophy.* Trans. P. Christopher Smith. New Haven, Conn.: Yale University Press.

Gatens, Moira. 1996. *Imaginary Bodies: Ethics, Power, and Corporeality.* New York: Routledge.

Giddings, Paula. 1984. *When and Where I Enter: The Impact of Black Women on Race and Sex in America.* New York: William Morrow.

Gilman, Sander. 1993. *Freud, Race, Gender.* Princeton, N.J.: Princeton University Press.

Gilroy, Paul. 1993a. *The Black Atlantic: Modernity and Double Consciousness.* Cambridge, Mass.: Harvard University Press.

———. 1993b. *Small Acts: Thoughts on the Politics of Black Cultures.* London: Serpent's Tail.

———. 2000. *Against Race: Imagining Political Culture beyond the Color Line.* Cambridge, Mass.: Harvard University Press.

Gleick, James. 1999. *Faster: The Acceleration of Just About Everything.* New York: Pantheon.

Goldberg, David Theo. 1993. *Racist Culture: Philosophy and the Politics of Meaning.* Cambridge: Blackwell.

Goodman, Mary Ellen. 1952. *Race Awareness in Young Children.* New York: Collier.

Gordon, Lewis. 1997. *Her Majesty's Other Children: Sketches of Racism from a Neocolonial Age.* New York: Rowman & Littlefield.

Gratz v. Bollinger. 2003. 539 U.S. 244.

Grewal, Inderpal, and Caren Kaplan, eds. 1994. *Scattered Hegemonies: Postmodernity and Transnational Feminist Practices.* Minneapolis: University of Minnesota Press.

Grosz, Elizabeth. 1989a. *Sexual Subversions: Three French Feminists.* Boston, Mass.: Allen and Unwin.

———. 1989b. *Volatile Bodies: Toward a Corporeal Feminism.* Bloomington: Indiana University Press.

———. 1990. *Jacques Lacan: A Feminist Introduction.* New York: Routledge.

———. 1994. The Hetero and the Homo: The Sexual Ethics of Luce Irigaray. In *Engaging with Irigaray: Feminist Philosophy and Modern European Thought,* ed. Carolyn L. Burke, Naomi Schor, and Margaret Whitford. New York: Columbia University Press.

Grutter v. Bollinger. 2003. 539 U.S. 306.

Guha, Ranajit, and Gayatri Chakravorty Spivak, eds. 1988. *Selected Subaltern Studies.* New York: Oxford University Press.

Hall, Stuart. 1996a. The After-Life of Frantz Fanon: Why Fanon? Why Now? Why *Black Skin, White Masks*? In *The Fact of Blackness: Frantz Fanon and Visual Representation,* ed. Alan Read. Seattle, Wash.: Bay.

———. 1996b. *Race, the Floating Signifier.* Northampton, Mass.: Media Education Foundation.

Halperin, David M. 1990. *One Hundred Years of Homosexuality, and Other Essays on Greek Love.* New York: Routledge.

———. 1995. *Saint Foucault: Towards a Gay Hagiography.* New York: Oxford University Press.

Haraway, Donna. 1997. *Modest_Witness@Second_Millennium.FemaleMan_Meets_Onco Mouse: Feminism and Technoscience.* New York: Routledge.

Hartsock, Nancy C. M. 1983. *Money, Sex, and Power: Toward a Feminist Historical Materialism.* Boston, Mass.: Northeastern University Press.

Hayden, Casey, and Mary King, 1966. Sex and Caste: A Kind of Memo. *Liberation,* no. 10 (April).

Hegel, G. W. F. 1969. *Hegel's Science of Logic.* Trans. A. V. Miller. Atlantic Highlands, N.J.: Humanities Press International.

———. 1975. *Hegel's Logic: Being Part One of the Encyclopaedia of the Philosophical Sciences (1830).* Trans. William Wallace. Oxford: Clarendon.

———. 1977. *Phenomenology of Spirit.* Trans. A. V. Miller. Oxford: Oxford University Press.

Hill, Christopher. 1980. *The Century of Revolution: 1603–1714.* New York: Norton.

Hirschmann, Nancy J. 1992. *Rethinking Obligation: A Feminist Method for Political Theory.* Ithaca, N.Y.: Cornell University Press.

Holstun, James. 2000. *Ehud's Dagger: Class Struggle in the English Revolution.* London: Verso.

hooks, bell. 1981. *Ain't I a Woman: Black Women and Feminism.* Boston, Mass.: South End.

———. 1984. *Feminist Theory from Margin to Center.* Boston, Mass.: South End.

———. 1990. *Yearning: Race, Gender, and Cultural Politics.* Boston, Mass.: South End.

———. 1992. *Black Looks: Race and Representation.* Boston, Mass.: South End.

———. 1995. *Killing Rage: Ending Racism.* New York: Henry Holt.

Husserl, Edmond. 1977. *Cartesian Meditations: An Introduction to Phenomenology.* Trans. Dorion Cairns. The Hague: Martin Nijhoff.

Irigaray, Luce. 1985a. *Speculum of the Other Woman.* Trans. Gillian C. Gill. Ithaca, N.Y.: Cornell University Press.

———. 1985b. *This Sex Which Is Not One.* Trans. Catherine Porter with Carolyn Burke. Ithaca, N.Y.: Cornell University Press.

———. 1993a. *An Ethics of Sexual Difference.* Trans. Carolyn Burke and Gillian C. Gill. Ithaca, N.Y.: Cornell University Press.

———. 1993b. *Je, tu, nous: Toward a Culture of Difference.* Trans. Alison Martin. New York: Routledge.

———. 1993c. *Sexes and Genealogies.* Trans. Gillian C. Gill. New York: Columbia University Press.

———. 1994. *Thinking the Difference: For a Peaceful Revolution.* Trans. Karin Montin. New York: Routledge.

Jagose, Annamarie. 1996. *Queer Theory: An Introduction.* New York: New York University Press.

Johnson, Barbara. 1998. *The Feminist Difference: Literature, Psychoanalysis, Race, Gender.* Cambridge, Mass.: Harvard University Press.

References

Kaplan, Caren. 1996. *Questions of Travel: Postmodern Discourses of Displacement.* Durham, N.C.: Duke University Press.

Katz, Jonathan Ned. 1990. The Invention of Heterosexuality. *Socialist Review* 21 (1): 7–34.

Kincaid, Jamaica. 1988. *A Small Place.* New York: Penguin.

Lacan, Jacques. 1977. *Écrits: A Selection.* Trans. Alan Sheridan. New York: Norton.

———. 1988. *Freud's Papers on Technique, 1953–1954.* The Seminar of Jacques Lacan 1. Ed. Jacques-Alain Miller. Trans. John Forrester. New York: Norton.

Lane, Christopher, ed. 1998. *The Psychoanalysis of Race.* New York: Columbia University Press.

Lee, Richard A. 2002. Ethics beyond Tragedy: Bataille's "Copernican Turn." Paper presented at the meeting of the Society of Phenomenology and Existential Philosophy.

Lingis, Alphonso. 1994. *Foreign Bodies.* New York: Routledge.

———. 2000. *Dangerous Emotions.* Berkeley: University of California Press.

Locke, John. 1960. *Two Treatises of Government.* Ed. Peter Laslett. Cambridge: Cambridge University Press.

Lorraine, Tamsin E. 1999. *Irigaray and Deleuze: Experiments in Visceral Philosophy.* Ithaca, N.Y.: Cornell University Press.

Loy, David R. 1997. The Religion of the Market. *Journal of the American Academy of Religion* 65 (2): 275–90.

Lugones, María. 2003. *Pilgrimages/Peregrinajes: Theorizing Coalition against Multiple Oppressions.* New York: Rowman & Littlefield.

MacKinnon, Catharine A. 1989. *Toward a Feminist Theory of the State.* Cambridge, Mass.: Harvard University Press.

MacPherson, C. B. (Crawford Brough). 1962. *The Political Theory of Possessive Individualism: Hobbes to Locke.* Oxford: Clarendon.

Marshall, Stephen. 2002. Evil and the Problem of Politics. Ph.D. diss., Harvard University.

McClintock, Anne. 1995. *Imperial Leather: Race, Gender, and Sexuality in the Colonial Conquest.* New York: Routledge.

McWhorter, Ladelle. 1999. *Bodies and Pleasures: Foucault and the Politics of Sexual Normalization.* Bloomington: Indiana University Press.

Miller, Tim. 2002. *Body Blows: Six Performances.* Madison: University of Wisconsin Press.

Mills, Charles. 1997. *The Racial Contract.* Ithaca, N.Y.: Cornell University Press.

Mills, Nicolaus. 1994. To Look like America. Introduction to *Debating Affirmative Action: Race, Gender, Ethnicity, and the Politics of Inclusion,* ed. Nicolaus Mills. New York: Delta.

Minter, Shannon, and Christopher Daley. 2003. Trans Realities: A Legal Needs Assessment of San Francisco's Transgender Communities, Executive Summary. http://www.transgenderlawcenter.org/tranny/pdfs/Exec%20Summary.pdf, accessed April 12, 2005.

Moraga, Cherríe, and Gloria Anzaldúa, eds. 1983. *This Bridge Called My Back: Writings by Radical Women of Color.* 2nd ed. New York: Kitchen Table, Women of Color Press.

NGLTF (National Gay and Lesbian Task Force). 2004. Black Couples Have Most at Stake in the Same Sex Marriage Debate, Census Analysis Shows. Press release, October 6. http://www.thetaskforce.org/media/release.cfm?releaseID=743, accessed April 12, 2005.

Nietzsche, Friedrich Wilhelm. 1967. *On the Genealogy of Morals.* Trans. Walter Kaufmann and R. J. Hollingdale. New York: Vintage.

———. 1989. *Friedrich Nietzsche on Rhetoric and Language.* Trans. Sander L. Gilman, Carole Blair, and David J. Parent. New York: Oxford University Press.

Okin, Susan Moller. 1989. *Justice, Gender, and the Family.* New York: Basic Books.

Oliver, Kelly. 1993. *Reading Kristeva: Unraveling the Double-Bind.* Bloomington: Indiana University Press.

———. 2001. *Witnessing: Beyond Recognition.* Minneapolis: University of Minnesota Press.

Pateman, Carole. 1988. *The Sexual Contract.* Cambridge: Polity.

Patterson, Orlando. 1982. *Slavery and Social Death: A Comparative Study.* Cambridge, Mass.: Harvard University Press.

Patton, Cindy. 2002. *Globalizing AIDS.* Minneapolis: University of Minnesota Press.

Pellegrini, Ann. 1997. *Performing Anxieties: Staging Psychoanalysis, Staging Race.* New York: Routledge.

Puar, Jasbir Kaur. 2002. Circuits of Queer Mobility: Tourism, Travel, and Globalization. *glq: A Journal of Lesbian and Gay Studies* 8 (1–2): 101–37.

Roudinesco, Elisabeth. 1997. *Jacques Lacan.* New York: Columbia University Press.

Rubin, Gayle S. 1993. Thinking Sex: Notes for a Radical Theory of the Politics of Sexuality. In *The Lesbian and Gay Studies Reader,* ed. Henry Abelove, Michèle Aina Barale, and David M. Halperin. New York: Routledge.

Saramago, José. 1998. *Blindness.* Trans. Giovanni Pontiero. New York: Harcourt Brace.

Schwab, Gail M. 1994. Mother's Body, Father's Tongue: Mediation in the Symbolic Order. In *Engaging with Irigaray: Feminist Philosophy and Modern European Thought,* ed. Carolyn L. Burke, Naomi Schor, and Margaret Whitford. New York: Columbia University Press.

Scott, Joan W. 1993. The Evidence of Experience. In *The Lesbian and Gay Studies Reader,* ed. Henry Abelove, Michèle Aina Barale, and David M. Halperin. New York: Routledge.

Sedgwick, Eve Kosofsky. 1993. *Tendencies.* Durham, N.C.: Duke University Press.

Seshadri-Crooks, Kalpana. 1998. The Comedy of Domination: Psychoanalysis and the Conceit of Whiteness. In *The Psychoanalysis of Race,* ed. Christopher Lane. New York: Columbia University Press.

———. 2000. *Desiring Whiteness: A Lacanian Analysis of Race.* New York: Routledge.

Sheperdson, Charles. 2000. *Vital Signs: Nature, Culture, Psychoanalysis.* New York: Routledge.

Singer, Linda. 1993. *Erotic Welfare: Sexual Theory and Politics in the Age of Epidemic.* Ed. Judith Butler and Maureen MacGrogan. New York: Routledge.

Sontag, Susan. 1989. *AIDS and Its Metaphors.* New York: Doubleday.

Spade, Dean. 2005. Public lecture given at ALLGO's Tillery Street Theater, Austin, Texas, March 11.

Spillers, Hortense. 1996. "All the Things You Could Be by Now, If Sigmund Freud's Wife Was Your Mother": Psychoanalysis and Race. *Boundary 2* 23 (3): 75–141.

Sprinkle, Annie. 2001. *Hard Core from the Heart: The Pleasure, Profits, and Politics of Sex Performance.* New York: Continuum.

SRLP (Silvia Rivera Law Project). 2005. http://www.srlp.org, accessed April 12, 2005.

Straayer, Chris, and Tom Waugh, eds. 2005. Moving Image Review: Queer TV Style. *glq: A Journal of Lesbian and Gay Studies* 11 (1): 95–117.

245

References

Turner, William B. 2000. *A Genealogy of Queer Theory*. Philadelphia: Temple University Press.

Vergès, Francoise. 1997. Creole Skin, Black Mask: Fanon and Disavowal. *Critical Inquiry* 23 (1): 578–95.

Walton, Jean. 1995. Re-placing Race in (White) Psychoanalytic Discourse: Founding Narratives of Feminism. *Critical Inquiry* 21 (2): 776–804.

Warner, Michael. 1993. *Fear of a Queer Planet: Queer Politics and Social Theory*. Minneapolis: University of Minnesota Press.

———. 1999. *The Trouble with Normal: Sex, Politics, and the Ethics of Queer Life*. New York: Free Press.

Welch, Todd S. 1996. The Supreme Court Ruled Correctly in *Adarand*. In *The Affirmative Action Debate,* ed. George E. Curry. Reading, Mass.: Perseus.

Wendling, Amy E. 2002. Consumption, Sovereignty, Revolution: Bataille's Marxism. Paper presented at the meeting of the Society of Phenomenology and Existential Philosophy.

Whitford, Margaret. 1991. *Luce Irigaray: Philosophy in the Feminine*. New York: Routledge.

Willett, Cynthia. 1995. *Maternal Ethics and Other Slave Moralities*. New York: Routledge.

———. 2001. *The Soul of Justice: Social Bonds and Racial Hubris*. Ithaca, N.Y.: Cornell University Press.

Williams, Eric Eustace. 1944. *Capitalism and Slavery*. London: Andre Deutsch.

Williams, Patricia J. 1991. *The Alchemy of Race and Rights*. Cambridge, Mass.: Harvard University Press.

Willse, Craig. 2004. Ban Marriage! Lecture delivered at Sarah Lawrence College, March 6. http://www.makezine.org/banmarriage.html, accessed April 7, 2005.

Winnubst, Shannon. 1999. Exceeding Hegel and Lacan: Different Fields of Pleasure within Foucault and Irigaray. *Hypatia: A Journal of Feminist Philosophy* 14 (1): 13–37.

———. 2003. Vampires, Anxieties, and Dreams: Race and Sex in the Contemporary U.S. *Hypatia: A Journal of Feminist Philosophy* 18 (3): 1–20.

Wittig, Monique. 1981. One Is Not a Woman Born. *Feminist Issues* 1 (4): 47–54.

Wojnarowicz, David. 1991. *Close to the Knives: A Memoir of Disintegration*. New York: Vintage.

Wright, Richard. 1966. *Native Son*. New York: Harper & Row.

Young, Iris Marion. 1990. *Justice and the Politics of Difference*. Princeton, N.J.: Princeton University Press.

Zack, Naomi. 1996. *Bachelors of Science: Seventeenth-Century Identity, Then and Now*. Philadelphia: Temple University Press.

———. 1997. The American Sexualization of Race. In *Race/Sex: Their Sameness, Difference, and Interplay,* ed. Naomi Zack. New York: Routledge.

Ziarek, Ewa Plonowska. 2001. *An Ethics of Dissensus: Postmodernity, Feminism, and the Politics of Radical Democracy*. Stanford, Calif.: Stanford University Press.

Žižek, Slavoj. 1989. *The Sublime Object of Ideology*. London: Verso.

———. 1998. Love Thy Neighbor? No, Thanks! In *The Psychoanalysis of Race,* ed. Christopher Lane. New York: Columbia University Press.

Index

abundance, 56; and affirmative action, 56–57; economies of, 27, 32–38, 56–57; nature's, 28, 31–38
The Accursed Share, 3, 140–45, 150, 176, 179–85, 199–200
affirmative action, 42, 43, 49–57
AIDS, 195–99; and colonialism, 197, 234n19; and temporality, 152, 231n2
Alexander, M. Jacqui, 172–73, 190, 232n15
alterity. *See* Other
American Beauty, 215n25
Angelus Novus, 169–70
anxiety, 120–21; and Bataille, 200; and capitalism, 182; and desire, 120–21; and Foucault, 121, 136; and heterosexuality, 128–31; and queering, 139, 230n43; and reason, 136, 139; and transgression, 121; and whiteness, 128–31
Anzaldúa, Gloria, 12, 134, 228–29n33
The Archaeology of Knowledge, 4, 136
Aristotle, 81–91; and Hegel, 230n42; *Physics,* 81–91
Augustine, 155, 171

Bartky, Sandra, 68
Bataille, Georges, 1–6, 30, 50, 107, 150, 176, 221n18; on animality, 141–43, 145, 184; on anticipation, 183–85; on anxiety, 200; on death, 183–85; economies of abundance, 183–85; erotic fiction, 146–48; on eroticism, 140–48, 181; on expenditure, 3, 37, 145, 179–85, 190–91; and Foucault, 4–6, 144–47, 179, 230n46, 232–33n1; on freedom, 200; on the future, 183–85; on general economy, 3, 5–6, 143–46, 182–83; and Hegel, 233n2; and instrumental reason, 179–85; on joy, 3, 20, 181, 200; on limits, 122, 140–41; with Locke, 145; on luxury, 3, 180–85, 191–92; on prohibitions, 140, 142–44; and psychoanalysis, 142–43; and queering, 135, 140–49, 179, 182–83; on reason, 3, 144; on

scarcity, 30, 179–85, 190–91; on sexuality, 140–48; on sovereignty, 141–46, 183–85; on transgression, 140–44, 179–85; on utility, 3 140, 144–46, 179–83
Benjamin, Walter, 169–70
Bergner, Gwen, 71, 72
Bledsoe, Casey, 218n19
Borges, Jorge, 7–9, 135–56
Bornstein, Kate, 146
Boswell, Maia, 61–62, 217n9
Bray, Michael, 212n28
Brown, Wendy, 118, 215n27
Burke, Carolyn, 79, 80, 220n2
Bush, George W., 23, 48, 194, 232n16
Butler, Judith, 12, 219n33, 220n36, 221n16; on Hegel, 111; on Irigaray, 78, 79, 96, 102–104, 107, 223n31

Califia, Pat, 146
capitalism: and anxiety, 182; and death, 183–85; and Locke, 25, 32, 37, 38, 56; as miserly, 181–82; and modernity, 43–44; and pleasure, 156–57; and power, 176–78; and scarcity, 55–56, 179–83, 190–91; and utility, 180–83
Chanter, Tina, 13, 94, 210n10, 220n8, 222n24, 223n32, 224–25n45
Chasin, Alexandra, 212n27, 212–13n4
Christianity: and liberalism, 27–28, 31; and whiteness, 47–48, 75, 129–30
Civil Rights Act, 50
Civil Rights Movement, 5, 10, 209n9
class: and affirmative action, 50–51, 52; category of identity, 2, 12, 17; in Locke, 31–32, 38; and same-sex marriage, 206–207; with sexuality, 18–19
Clinton, Bill, 166, 170, 198, 215n25
Close to the Knives: A Memoir of Disintegration, 195–96
colonialism, 1–2, 44, 117, 122–23; and AIDS, 197, 234n19; and modernity, 43; and temporality, 152, 197; and traveling, 157–58

Index

Index

Index